The Retrospective Raj

The Retrospective Raj

Medicine, Literature and History after Empire

Sam Goodman

EDINBURGH
University Press

Edinburgh University Press is one of the leading university presses in the UK. We publish academic books and journals in our selected subject areas across the humanities and social sciences, combining cutting-edge scholarship with high editorial and production values to produce academic works of lasting importance. For more information visit our website: edinburghuniversitypress.com

© Sam Goodman, 2022

Edinburgh University Press Ltd
The Tun – Holyrood Road, 12(2f) Jackson's Entry, Edinburgh EH8 8PJ

Typeset in 11/13 Adobe Sabon by
IDSUK (DataConnection) Ltd

A CIP record for this book is available from the British Library

ISBN 978 1 4744 4874 1 (hardback)
ISBN 978 1 4744 4876 5 (webready PDF)
ISBN 978 1 4744 4877 2 (epub)

The right of Sam Goodman to be identified as the author of this work has been asserted in accordance with the Copyright, Designs and Patents Act 1988, and the Copyright and Related Rights Regulations 2003 (SI No. 2498).

Chapters 2 and 3: Wellcome Trust Research Bursary award, Grant Reference Number: 208333/Z/17/Z, 'Colonial Consumption: Alcohol, Medicine and Society in British India' (2018–19).

Contents

Acknowledgements

This book has been a long time in the making, and the list of people who deserve my thanks is a lengthy one. It seems only right to start with John McLeod, who asked, about a decade ago now, whether I'd read anything by a writer called J. G. Farrell, just in case it might be a useful addition to my thinking. It turns out it was pretty useful, John, and I am forever grateful for the suggestion, as well as your ongoing interest in my work. Over the years of planning and development, research and writing that have gone into this book I have benefited from the generosity of time, support and interest from numerous other people too, and especially from conversations with Mariadele Boccardi, Nadine Muller, Jane MacNaughton, Mary Robson and the Durham New Generations in Medical Humanities cohort, Pam Lock, James Kneale and the Drinking Studies Network, Kelly and Bob at Good Chemistry Brewing, the Indian Civil Service Association, Tom Sperlinger, Sarah Arens, Aggelis Zarakostas, Matt Hayler, Florian Stadtler and my colleagues at Bournemouth University, particularly Alexandra Alberda, Hywel Dix, Simon Frost, Rebecca Mills, Julia Round, Yugin Teo and Bronwen Thomas. My thanks too to my reviewers and those people who read this book in draft, and were so conscientious and thoughtful with their feedback; it is an immeasurably better book as a result. My most heartfelt thanks are to Victoria Bates, whose thinking is always streets ahead of mine, but who always waits for me to catch up; I owe her so very much, and can never tell her often enough how grateful I am.

I would like to acknowledge Bournemouth University's Narrative, Culture and Community Research Centre and Department of Humanities and Law, and the Wellcome Trust, whose support enabled this research. I acknowledge with thanks the Stuart A. Rose Manuscript, Archives, and Rare Book Library at Emory University, and the Board of Trinity College, University of Dublin, for access to their archives. Moreover, I am grateful to the archivists at Trinity, MARBL, and to Antonia Moon and the staff of the Asian and African Studies reading room at the British Library especially (particularly Arlene, Marie, Victoria and Mr Huq) for their patience, good humour and occasional forbearance. I acknowledge with gratitude David Higham Associates, Rogers, Coleridge & White, Peters Fraser and Dunlop, Wylie and John Murray for permission to reproduce original material from the novels of Scott, Farrell, Rushdie, Masters and Jhabvala.

In the same way as these Raj Revival texts are a result of their circumstances of production, so is this volume, and, by extension, so too am I. This book has been composed over the last half-decade, during which time the sound and fury of Britain's post-imperial nostalgia has become harder and harder to ignore. It was written in snatched moments in libraries, on trains and in cafés with Brexit rumbling away on a separate tab, and latterly, in the detachment of my home against the background of the global pandemic and the martial medical metaphor of an increasingly jingoistic British state. Its pages reflect the tenor of these years, those of fractious disputes over statues, balance sheets, bronzes, marbles, stately homes and more, alongside an unabated growth in the popularity of historical fictions of Empire. Although chronologically far from us and our circumstances, it seems that the same disputes over the real and imagined of British history that produced the Raj Revival are still very much close at hand.

I grew up surrounded by the discourses of nationhood, Britishness and the modern relationship to the history of Empire that have taken place over the last forty years, and this book exists as my response to fathoming less how such ideals came to exist, but more why they have never seemingly come to an end. My parents are 'Children of Empire' (born 1937 and 1944), and despite living through the period of its most precipitous decline had imbibed enough of its values by the time of its demise to believe in it forever. Those values, their memories, their *love* for a Britain of Empire (despite never having lived in any of its territories other than the British Isles) has stayed with them their entire lives, expressing itself in their unstinting support of the Conservative Party, pride at British action in the Falklands, near-religious observance of the Last Night of the Proms or the first day of the Test, and a constant, pervasive nostalgia for the way things once were (or how they might be again). Questions of Britishness were likewise always at hand: multiculturalism was suspect, blue passports were talismans lost lamentably to the past, 'Other: English' was an option ticked repeatedly on forms. Tebbit was my Nan's MP. So the world and the themes that these novels describe was also partly the world of my childhood; one littered with the after-images and echoes of Empire, from Kipling's *The Jungle Book* and 'Gunga Din', the phrases ('doolally tap' a particular favourite), *Zulu* on at every Christmas, a set of ivory dominoes belonging to a great-grandad acquired somewhere east of Suez, and the stuffed elephant's foot stored for many years in our various lofts and garages, until it was finally, thankfully, disposed of.[1] It is, in part, for them, because of them even, that this book has been written. It is an effort of affection as much as it is criticism, and an attempt to understand the motivations behind these continued allegiances and how they replicate, repeat and refract across generations; it is no accident that my brothers have gravitated towards the military and the civil service, towards flags and ideals of duty, and the belonging they might afford. At the risk of a little navel-gazing solipsism, as well as understanding them, it is a way of understanding a little more of myself too and fathoming to what extent these prejudices might remain in my own psyche, habits and behaviours.

Grateful acknowledgement is made to the following sources for permission to reproduce material previously published elsewhere. Every effort has been made to trace the copyright holders, but if any have been inadvertently overlooked, the publisher will be pleased to make the necessary arrangements at the first opportunity.

The Hill Station and *The Siege of Krishnapur* by J. G. Farrell. Copyright © The Estate of J. G. Farrell. Reproduced by permission of the Estate c/o Rogers, Coleridge & White Ltd, 20 Powis Mews, London W11 1JN.

Midnight's Children by Salman Rushdie. Copyright © 1981, Salman Rushdie, used by permission of The Wylie Agency (UK) Limited.

Note

1. Its provenance was a mystery; handed to us 'temporarily' by a relative, we had no idea whether it had once belonged to an African or Indian elephant, and there was no Google then that might have helped us check.

Abbreviations

Novels

J. G. Farrell

The Siege of Krishnapur (1973): SoK
The Hill Station (1981): THS

Ruth Prawer Jhabvala

Heat and Dust (1975): HaD

John Masters

Bhowani Junction (1954): BJ
To the Coral Strand (1962): TtCS

Salman Rushdie

Midnight's Children (1981): MC

Paul Scott

The Jewel in the Crown (1966): JiTC
The Day of the Scorpion (1968): TDotS
The Towers of Silence (1971): TToS
A Division of the Spoils (1975): ADotS
Staying On (1977): SO

Archives

British Library: BL
J. G. Farrell, Personal Papers and Manuscripts, Trinity College
Dublin: Trinity
Salman Rushdie Papers, Stuart A. Rose Manuscript, Archives, and
Rare Book Library (MARBL), Emory University: MARBL

Introduction: Retrospective Diagnosis: Medicine and Post-Imperial Literature

'A moment comes, which comes but rarely in history, when we step out from the old to the new, when an age ends, and when the soul of a nation, long suppressed, finds utterance.'

Jawaharlal Nehru, 15 August 1947

Monday, 15 August 2022 marks seventy-five years since the declaration of Indian independence and the beginning of the end of the British Empire. Independence inaugurated a new age for India, as Nehru acknowledged, but also for Britain, precipitating a long process of decolonisation from British rule across the globe that was to last the rest of the century. Though many other colonial possessions would claim their independence with increasing rapidity and alacrity within the two decades that followed, the sun finally set on the Empire with the handing back of Hong Kong in 1997, a full fifty years after that first stroke of midnight on the subcontinent.[1] That new age of decolonisation began over a lifetime ago, and although there might now be relatively few people who remember life in India under British rule, this does not mean that interest in colonial history has likewise diminished. Instead, interest in the world of Empire remains as prevalent as ever, visible across the worlds of fiction, popular history, politics and the public sphere.[2]

India, in particular, has always been a national obsession for the British. Ralph J. Crane argues that there is no 'simple explanation for the hold India has had on the British mind'.[3] The fixation with India within the collective British imagination, as well as those of individual writers, artists, philosophers and others, has indeed been varied and long-lasting, bound up in repeated and self-reinforcing narratives of exoticism and otherness, of adventure and of efforts at reconciliation and atonement. Crane's observation is astute in identifying the multiple ways British artists have turned to India for inspiration in the past and also implicitly acknowledges the lack of closure at the heart of Britain's relationship with the world of India, Empire and the Raj. The ending of British dominion in India did not call to a close the cultural fascination with this world, but rather intensified it by presenting new and complex questions for cultural works to consider. No longer was the enquiry limited to that of E. M. Forster's question, namely whether or not Indians and Britons could ever exist on equal footing as friends given the structural inequalities of Empire; instead, and in response to the seismic shift in British standing, these texts now sought to ask more searching questions of the colonial relationship in order to fathom how this state had come to pass, and what had happened for Britain to have reached this point of international impoverishment. India's independence urged Britain to examine its imperial past with new scrutiny, to engage in a veritable post-mortem of Empire in aid of determining its errors and shedding light on its malpractices, certainly; but also, and perhaps more vitally to those who sought to come to terms with the swiftness of its ending, to consider the legacies (or try to argue the benefits) that the Empire had supposedly left in its wake.[4]

This retrospective take on the Raj was the work of decades. In response to the long shadow that the loss of Empire cast over Britain, it seems that the more time that has elapsed since the declaration of Indian independence, the greater the pull of the Raj on the collective national imagination, with a steady accumulation of films, novels, television series and other media all fixated with the British colonial presence in India appearing over the ensuing years. This resurgent interest in colonial India across a range of media in the 1970s and 1980s became known as the 'Raj Revival'.[5] Coined by Salman Rushdie and a testament to his flair as an advertising executive, the 'Raj Revival' seemed an ideally apposite phrase for a process of cultural production that returned to the heyday of Empire and thus as much breathed new life into the imperial myth as it did consider its passing into history. It suited especially those lavish productions that sought once more to associate colonial India with the pomp and circumstance with which it had once been regarded, like the HBO/Goldcrest adaptation of M. M. Kaye's expansive, romantic epic *The Far Pavilions* (1978), first shown in Britain in 1984.[6] *The Far Pavilions* joined a wealth of other texts of the period, including Richard Attenborough's *Gandhi* (1982), the Merchant Ivory production of Ruth Prawer Jhabvala's *Heat and Dust* (1983), David Lean's take on

Forster's *A Passage to India* (1984) and ITV's dramatisation of Paul Scott's *Jewel in the Crown* (1984), all of which affirmed the British interest in its colonial past at this time.[7]

It is of course no coincidence that this was the period in which the last generations of adult Britons who had lived and worked in colonial India, and had been witness to its ending, were reaching retirement or advanced old age. Similarly, their children, those Britons born at the twilight of the Raj, were by now adults who responded enthusiastically to these works offering a nostalgic view of the world of their childhood. This moment of acute contextual importance was recognised by the India Office Archive, part of the newly instituted British Library under the directorship of Sir Harry Hookway. The India Office Archive – perhaps inspired by the efforts of historian Noble Frankland at the Imperial War Museum, advisor on the ITV series *The World At War* (1973), to record the gamut of experiences of the Second World War – sought out and encouraged former colonial administrators and residents to commit their experiences and memories to record before it was too late.[8] Though these narratives were recorded largely for posterity (the majority of the manuscripts remain unpublished, at least in full), they demonstrate not just a recognition that the experiences of these respondents might, if unrecorded, be lost to history, but that their insights and perspectives into the vanished world of the Raj were possessed of a particular currency and import relevant to the time and age.[9] The British Library's recognition was no doubt also driven by the context of a major documentary entitled *The British Empire*, broadcast on the BBC in 1972. Adopting a critical approach to the actions of colonial administrations and individual Britons over the past 300 years, the series was responsible for sparking a public debate over the legacy of Empire, and how it should be remembered within British social and cultural life, that continues to our present moment.[10]

As a result of these contributing factors, there existed at this point an atmosphere of textual production and consumption around the British Raj where these various strands of interest and experience intersected, from those memoirists and novelists drawing on their experience for the purposes of narrative, alongside an eager and receptive public waiting to receive them. Additionally, the state of the 1970s as a moment of crisis and fracture for Britishness and national identity likewise drove this pursuit of Empire and its connotations of security, safety and global pre-eminence in fiction. The 1970s was a time of acute national awareness of the significance of Empire in connection to post-war immigration, events in former British colonial states such as Uganda, and growing neo-nationalism.[11] Empire thusly adopts the position of cause and solution with regard to these various difficulties. Against the continual declining direction of post-imperial Britain on the geopolitical stage and diminished prosperity at home, a desire to return to the pre-eminence of Empire, as well as the splendour and the glamour of the Raj, was tempting to some.[12] As Hilary Spurling argues, the Empire was too recent for objective consideration of its legacy to be possible, and a general ethos of 'looking back' became commonplace instead.[13] Even those writers like J. G. Farrell, who were more inclined to view imperial nostalgia with cynicism and irony, nonetheless gravitated into the Revival's orbit. Their approach was far less celebratory or spurred by fond reminiscence, however, than it was motivated by a desire to fathom the exigencies of their contemporary moment and to try and make sense of the national narrative after Empire through the lens of fictional ones.

Although he provided it with its memorable name, Rushdie would seek to distance himself from the genre, viewing it as the embodiment of 'the fantasy that the British Empire represented something "noble" or "great" about Britain; that it was, in spite of all its flaws and meannesses and bigotries, fundamentally glamorous'.[14] However, despite Rushdie's intentions to the contrary, the glamour associated with the colonial Empire remained largely intact, and when considering the British cultural obsession with its recent past, we might observe a second period of Raj Revivalism likewise driven by various competing and complementary contextual factors as well as a pervasive personal and collective nostalgia. In a similar fashion to the combination of the British Library's efforts, context, and a turn towards Empire in popular history and revisionist historiography, there was again a resurgent interest in Empire and its legacies around the turn of the millennium prompted by the handover of Hong Kong in 1997, and expressed in various documentary efforts including Simon Schama's *A History of Britain* (2000–2), *The British Empire in Colour* (2002) and Niall Ferguson's *Empire* (2003).[15]

The result is that the Raj Revival's other main era of popularity is therefore arguably our own, and the genre has once again come to the fore of British culture in the last two decades. Raj Revivalist productions still appear frequently, with seemingly little change in their character, preserving approaches to reading and representing the British Raj similar to those texts of the previous era. For example, *Victoria and Abdul* (2017), set firmly at the zenith of Britain's imperial power, depicts a deep and abiding friendship between Queen Victoria and her Indian servant Abdul Karim, intended presumably in allegory for the relationship between Britain and India, and offering an uncomfortable suggestion of continued subservience in return.[16] Similarly, *The Best Exotic Marigold Hotel* (2011), based on Deborah Moggach's novel *These Foolish Things* (2004), is arguably a post-imperial fantasy, emphasising an orientalist image of India's otherness replete with various tropes of colonial fiction, from the xenophobe who learns to love India and Indians to the multiple characters who come either to find themselves, or a fresh start far from home.[17]

Alternately, Channel 4's *Indian Summers* (2015–16) and Gurinder Chadha's *Viceroy's House* (2017) have, like Scott, Jhabvala and John Masters, charted the decline and end of British India. Rather than the height of British colonial dominance, these productions instead focus on the Raj's attenuation, with the civil servants of *Indian Summers*' Shimla coming to terms with the steadily shifting balance of power in the 1930s, and *Viceroy's House* depicting a troubled Lord Mountbatten gravely determined 'not to let the side down' in the final days before Partition. Elsewhere in fiction, novels and novelists have returned to the frontiers of the former Empire for inspiration, with Philip Hensher's *The Mulberry Empire* (2002) exploring the then-contemporary resonances of the Great Game in Afghanistan; Grant Sutherland's *The Cobras of Calcutta* (2010) choosing to focus on the Battle of Plassey and the consolidation of Britain's Indian empire; M. J. Carter's *The Strangler Vine* (2014) following the detective efforts of East India Company officer William Avery in the 1830s; Ian McGuire's *The North Water* (2016) contrasting the frigid extremes of polar exploration with its protagonist's recollections of the stifling heat and intensity of his colonial service in that most familiar of Anglo-Indian literary settings, the Indian Rebellion of 1857; and Natasha Pulley's *The Bedlam Stacks* (2017) sending the evocatively named former East India Company smuggler Merrick Tremayne into Peru in search of quinine.[18] More recently still, and in contrast to her previous work, Gurinder Chadha has gone further back in time to consider the Empire in ascendency for her series *Beecham House* (2019), set in 1795.[19]

Beyond the specificities of each of these texts, this consistent return to Empire and India is revealing in itself. As has been noted of another recent Anglo-Indian adaptation, Vikram Seth's *A Suitable Boy*, produced for the BBC in 2020, 'great period drama speaks to [its] times', saying as much about the circumstances of its production as its subject.[20] The recent wealth of Raj Revivalist texts are notable for their appearance at another point of crisis for British identity, with their relevance intensified in part by public debates on Britain's 'global' role after Brexit and the referendum on the European Union in 2016. Rather than indulging the memories of an adult generation that proved so receptive to the productions of the early 1980s with a dose of imperial nostalgia, the return to colonial themes in the twenty-first century is to reassess the imperial past as a means of making sense of the postcolonial present. It is to focus on the terminus of British colonial dominance in order to understand how the nation has arrived at its current position; these fictions revisit the point of departure from a position of perceived security and power to explore the journey towards the current divisions that pervade British society, as well as the decades-long uncertainty of British geopolitical standing.[21]

Such texts appear at a time of renewed focus on Empire in public and political discourses, and one as febrile, and often hostile, as that of the 1970s. On one side of the divide, surveys and polls such as those conducted by YouGov in 2014 and 2016 find broad support for the idea of Empire, with 59 per cent of respondents claiming to believe that the British Empire was 'something to be proud of' in 2014, and 43 per cent supporting the statement that Empire and colonialism was 'a good thing' in 2016 – more than double the percentage who disagreed with the statement.[22] A more recent follow-up in 2020 found that 33 per cent of Britons felt that formerly colonised nations were better off as a result of the British presence.[23] However, at the same time there was also growing support for the further decolonisation of the British national school curriculum and a more rigorous engagement with the history of the British Empire, similar to that of German state educational approaches to the Holocaust.[24] Whilst in literature and culture, high-profile publications of the last half-decade such as Nikesh Shukla's *The Good Immigrant* (2016), Reni Eddo-Lodge's *Why I'm No Longer Talking to White People About Race* (2017), Afua Hirsch's *Brit(ish)* (2018), Akala's *Natives: Race and Class in the Ruins of Empire* (2018) and Johny Pitts' *Afropean: Notes from Black Europe* (2019) represent significant and incisive advances in popular discussions around the diasporas that constitute British society as a result of colonialism, they jostle uncomfortably against attempts to deny the existence of such voices and their prevalence within the fabric of British life.

For instance, the Windrush scandal of 2018, in which British citizens of Caribbean descent were deported to 'home' countries that they had barely, if ever, known, is just one example of the cognitive dissonance with which modern Britain considers its colonial history. The Windrush generation, stripped of their rights as a result of 'hostile' legislation introduced in 2014, were featured just a few years earlier as part of the 'Isles of Wonder', the opening ceremony for the 2012 Olympic Games in London, alongside representations of the Industrial Revolution, the Beatles, the Jarrow Marchers and other such signifiers of Britishness and British history, acknowledging the intrinsic relationship between Empire and modern Britain that the later deportations and denial of status sought to deny. David Lammy, MP for Tottenham and a descendent of Caribbean Britons, pushed further into this contradiction in response to the situation, noting: 'There is no British history without the history of Empire. I am here because you were there. My ancestors were not British subjects because they came to Britain. They were British subjects because Britain came to them and sold them into slavery.'[25] Whilst such an overt system of slavery as the Atlantic triangular trade was not the primary British intention in India, slavery was practised in India under British rule until the 1840s, and thus the connection between the nations, imbalanced disproportionately in favour of white Britons, bears similar hallmarks.[26] As such, the British relationship with the history of Empire in India is a comparable mixture of self-congratulatory pride and concerted denial, asserting the Raj's status as a worthy British achievement whilst simultaneously minimising its violence and seeking to keep at arm's length its contemporary repercussions.

Such attitudes have been entrenched in national discourse by the prevailing rhetoric of the right-wing press and electorate in their alleged support of 'indigenous' British communities.[27] Such efforts may be viewed as a metaphorical attempt to reset the board and return all the pieces to their starting positions, however, without any recognition of the fundamental absurdity and impossibility of such notions. As A. A. Gill for *The Times* and others have suggested, demands such as 'I want my country back' are informed by nostalgia for a supposedly secure Britain of years past, itself never truly real, and representative of what Paul Gilroy has labelled 'postimperial melancholia', the feeling engendered by recognition of this lost status.[28] Combined with the support of cultural output in the Raj revivalist vein, such positions have amounted to support amongst some generations of Britons for a renewed 'Anglosphere' of British influence, dubbed, at first satirically but later taken up by supporters without such self-reflexivity or awareness of its ironic intent, as 'Empire 2.0'.[29]

Whilst these two periods represent a British fascination with Empire at its most intense, it is important to emphasise the continuous and ongoing nature of the connections between culture and the 'lost world' of colonial India. Rather than two isolated, freak waves of Raj Revivalism, we might think of these points as high-water marks of a continuous tidal flow. For the fact of the matter is that there has always been an undercurrent of fiction that has sought a return to such colonial imaginings. From the very beginning of the end of British power in India in the 1940s, authors, screenwriters, historians and memoirists have sought to represent the swift and startling reversal in British fortunes; namely the contradiction and irony that having emerged victorious from the Second World War, in which the connections and bonds of Empire were the vital lifeblood of its war effort, Britain found itself so quickly impoverished and seemingly devoid of a role on the global stage.

Such an awareness of Britain's diminished status is acknowledged throughout the novels that constitute this study, and even, despite Rushdie's assertions to the contrary, the broader canvas of the genre. Even though they often draw inspiration from a time when the power and prestige of Empire was at its height, the texts of the Raj Revival are as much works of criticism, or elegy, as they might be thought of as celebration. Indeed, their success is arguably found in the bittersweet nature of their composition, allowing authors and readers to indulge in the supposed glamour of Empire or thrill to the 'heroic' events of the Indian Rebellion, itself a staple sub-genre of Anglo-Indian publishing culture from its own contemporary moment onwards, whilst simultaneously aware of the Empire's historical terminus. Indeed, no Anglo-Indian work of the last seventy-five years, not even the most indulgent, can ignore the Raj's demise; its ending is always bound up in the telling.[30]

By the book: reading the Raj Revival

In response to the cultural and literary turn towards historical fictions of Empire, this book assesses the novels of a range of authors writing about, in, or relating to India published between 1950 and 1990. At the forefront of the various writers it analyses are Salman Rushdie, J. G. Farrell, Ruth Prawer Jhabvala and Paul Scott. Although all the writers acknowledged in this volume achieved success with their writing, it is these authors in particular who most skilfully captured, reflected and channelled the mood of their contemporary moment, and whose contribution to literature and our critical understanding of the postcolonial novel represents a legacy of its own.

Despite the widespread cultural evidence of the turn towards the Raj after the Second World War and the end of Empire outlined above, it is important that the 'flowering of the historical novel' in this period is not read as indicative of a collective and unified literary project.[31] The authors considered within this volume were never part of an organised or cohesive literary group. They did not, as many of the modernists did, generally play a direct role in the development of each other's work; they did not gather around a bar, at a salon or in the same city, and they were not intimates with one another socially; they did not write under an agreed-upon set of artistic or aesthetic principles, nor were they, like The Movement, brought together by their university studies and linked by the intellectual circles that rippled out from that formative educational centre. They include variously amongst them war veterans, refugees, expats, atheists, prize-winners, ad men, accountants, schoolteachers, broadcasters and scriptwriters. From the various biographies available, one surmises that if they had ever come together they would have been unlikely to agree on much.

Despite the pluralism of their backgrounds, these authors were united by their shared sensitivity to the rapidity of British decline on the global stage and a recognition of how the currents of the history and legacy of Empire, especially in relation to British India, are bound up in the shifting sense of nationhood that characterises the period in which they wrote. Though they would do so at different times and in differing personal and professional contexts, Rushdie, Scott, Jhabvala, Farrell and many others in this period all turned to literature to explore the interrelation of the past and present, both real and imagined, of Britain's relationship with Empire. Furthermore, as this volume will outline, one of the key themes of their literary exploration of colonialism would be the significance of medicine and health in relaying the human experience of the Raj. Given the common means of their approaches and their lack of formal association notwithstanding, as the pre-eminent writers on Anglo-Indian responses to Empire in this period it is logical to suppose that they themselves perceived a shared literary association or endeavour, even if they were not directly connected to one another nor such a project explicitly defined.[32]

For all their surface differences, then, there is much to unite the writers and novels that comprise this book, not least their shared historical and medical focus on the subcontinent. For instance, other than John Masters, the primary authors that constitute this volume are linked by their receipt of the Booker Prize for Literature. Established and first awarded in 1969, a year that Mariadele Boccardi argues was a watershed for historical fiction in post-war Britain, the Booker itself is steeped in the history of postcolonialism and the representation of Empire, arising in the midst of Britain's late twentieth-century decline and with an explicit focus on novels written in English by Commonwealth writers.[33] Of the authors included here, winners of the prize include J. G. Farrell, for *Troubles* (1970, though awarded retrospectively in 2010) and *The Siege of Krishnapur* (1973); Ruth Prawer Jhabvala, for *Heat and Dust* (1975); Paul Scott, for *Staying On* (1977); and Salman Rushdie, for *Midnight's Children* (first in 1981, as 'Booker of Bookers' in 1993, and again as 'Best of the Booker' in 2009).[34]

Aside from acting as a means of evidencing a certain continuity of thought amongst writers of this period, the Booker Prize is also contextually relevant and acts as a means of further reading the relationship between British society and the history of Empire after the Second World War. In part as a result of the Booker Group's dominance of the sugar trade in colonial Guyana throughout the nineteenth century, Graham Huggan and Luke Strongman have argued that the Booker Prize cannot be read as politically or ideologically neutral. Strongman observes that despite differences in extent, '[a]ll of the Booker Prize winning novels have an implied relationship with Empire, whether this be writing in the form of counter-discourse, subscription to imperial rhetoric, nostalgia for Empire or of an articulation of identity in the fluid internationalisms which emerge after Empire.'[35] Huggan also questions the status and effects of prize culture itself, and what distinction and elevation above other literature of the period may mean to public perception of such works. Rather than solely reflecting accomplished literary work, Huggan argues, the Booker has instead conferred a sense of literary respectability to what are essentially middlebrow works of fiction reflective of the particular thematic concerns and interests of the panel at a given point in the award's history.[36] In the early years of the Booker, these concerns were primarily those of decolonisation and the British experience of Empire. It is logical then to read the Booker contextually as another driver of the burgeoning culture of publication that arose around post-imperial or postcolonial works of fact and fiction throughout this period. Thus, in another example of the interplay between historical and literary writing, such works share a degree of formal as well as political sensibility. Indeed, Huggan goes as far as to label a number of the Booker-winning novels from the 1970s and 1980s as revisionist histories.[37]

The decisions made by the Booker judging committee, whilst themselves not necessarily representative of the reading habits of the nation (then as now), nonetheless provide a revealing glimpse into the thoughts and feelings of those assembled to decide upon the very best in contemporary literature in English; given their choices and repeated return to the fiction of Empire, it seems justified to conclude that the effects of decolonisation, and their narrative mediation, were integral to the zeitgeist at this point in time. To focus on these authors, then, is to seek to engage with this process of reciprocity between literature and the reading public of the post-war period, and to explore how literary visions of the Raj, along with other imagined colonial spaces of the former Empire, became so deeply ingrained within the national cultural landscape and consciousness.

Of this group, Salman Rushdie is the most well-known, if not notorious, among them, both for the complexity and bravura of his writing and for the events that would affect his professional and personal life after the publication of *The Satanic Verses* (1988). His breakthrough novel, *Midnight's Children* (1981), has long been considered a landmark text in the development of postcolonial literature and the Anglo-Indian response to Empire, receiving extensive and justifiable attention as a result. Rushdie is the most securely canonical author included in this study, and as such, his work has been the subject of extensive literary criticism in general and has been assessed in relation to a wide variety of topics and themes.[38] It is of course understandable that critical approaches to Rushdie's fiction have focused largely on the postcolonial and political aspects of his work, especially when it comes to understanding the relationship between the past and present in novels such as *Midnight's Children* or the more sharply satirical *Shame* (1983). Such approaches were driven by their historical and literary context and remain instructive to subsequent engagement with the novel and interpretations of its multifaceted critique of Empire.[39]

Rushdie's inclusion in this volume adds much to the plurality of perspectives dealing with the colonial past and legacy of British India. However, in his focus on essentially middle-class Indian voices, Rushdie's view is not one necessarily of an authentic postcolonial selfhood, and instead covers a class of society whose identity, actions and relationship with the past is deeply indebted to Empire. As Richard Cronin argues, 'Rushdie has more in common with Rudyard Kipling than Premchand or Bankim Chandra Chatterji.'[40] As such, V. G. Julie Rajan suggests that Rushdie's prominence within postcolonial studies should be treated critically, stating that (along with Gayatri Chakravorty Spivak) 'the visibility these authors have gained in the west is also affected by the degree to which their writing answers to Western imaginaries of India'.[41] Given Rushdie's background, such implication within the structures of imperial writing

is hardly surprising, and is precisely what makes his work so pertinent to this study. Rushdie's position as an Indian novelist, educated
and residing in Britain and writing in English, adds a further dimension and depth to the analysis here; although his focus in *Midnight's
Children*, and in *Shame*, is primarily on the experiences of Indians
or Pakistanis and the decolonised subject, his own position, with his
British schooling and long-term residence in Britain and America,
offers him an altered perspective as a member of the Indian (specifically Kashmiri via Bombay) diaspora. Similarly, it was his focus in on
the advantages of his own perspective that transformed his writing
career. *Grimus* (1975), a science fiction parable, was largely ignored.
The scope of Rushdie's writing grew when he began to transpose
elements of his personal history alongside that of India's. To paraphrase Nehru, Rushdie's textualisation of his own life alongside that
of the life of a nation gave both a means of utterance.[42]

In contrast to the spotlight on Rushdie, the work of James Gordon
Farrell has seemingly always existed as if in partial shadow. Despite
a successful writing career that spanned the 1960s and 1970s, supported by the Booker in 1973, Farrell was never, in the manner of
his other contemporaries, wholly part of a literary movement such as
magical realism or postmodernism. The lack of critical coordinates
within which to locate either him or his work after his death in 1979
meant that Farrell's novels became largely the preserve of dedicated
admirers, despite receiving critical praise from writers and reviewers
such as Margaret Drabble and Malcolm Dean. Farrell attracted occasional scholarly attention as a result of his inclusion at the fringes of
postcolonial and postmodern literature, but, in another indication
of the resurgent national interest in literary and cultural responses
to Empire, it has only been in the last decade that his work has once
again begun to be widely read or known. The posthumous award of
the Lost Booker prize for *Troubles* (1970) served to rekindle popular
interest in him and his writing.[43] Farrell became one of only three
authors to win the Booker on more than one occasion at that time,
which has led to a reassessment of his place within contemporary literary history.[44] This interest has focused mainly on the loosely structured sequence of 1970s novels comprising *Troubles*, *The Siege of
Krishnapur* and *The Singapore Grip* (1978) that have come to be
known as the 'Empire Trilogy'. However, consideration of Farrell's
later work should include the unfinished, posthumously published
novella *The Hill Station* (1981), which suggests Farrell's continued
interest in Empire beyond his completed books, as well as a return to
the society and themes of colonial India.[45]

Farrell's Empire series consists of novels based around key episodes from the history of the British Empire, all of which share a characteristic emphasis on decline. Representative of the embattled after-Empire context in which he and the other authors that make up this book were writing, Farrell portrays the Empire at key points of historical crisis or conflict: Anglo-Protestant society in Ireland on the cusp of the Irish War of Independence of 1919 in *Troubles*; an East India Company station during the Rebellion of 1857 in *The Siege of Krishnapur*; and the last months of British rule in Singapore before the Japanese invasion and occupation in 1942 in *The Singapore Grip*. *The Hill Station* meanwhile explores themes of spiritual conflict, set in the context of doctrinal disputes within the Anglican church in 1871, and juxtaposing these with the professional and social introspection of its protagonist Dr McNab, a survivor of Krishnapur, making his way to the summer retreat of Shimla. As Rushdie would do not long after him, Farrell sought to strip away the veneer of nostalgia already extant in literature and culture dealing with Empire; his fictionalised re-engagements with history and received imperial mythology are neither nostalgic nor celebratory of the British past, but are instead written with an instructive contemporary relevance as Farrell seeks to fathom the circumstances of the British present through the re-examination of its history. The subtlety of Farrell's style has occasionally been overlooked, however, and his whimsy and humour has sometimes been mistaken as a degree of tacit support or identification with the world of Empire that his novels recreate.[46] Whilst it is true his novels lack the overt criticism present in those produced by some of his contemporaries, Farrell's satire of Empire is nonetheless evident on even a cursory reading and, as this book will illustrate, readily apparent in his archive and the research materials that informed his writing.

If Farrell, even with two Booker prizes to his name, might be thought of as being overlooked within the contemporary public consciousness, then Ruth Prawer Jhabvala is likely an even harder novelist for many to place.[47] Although again she may not be familiar to contemporary readers in the same way as Rushdie, such a lack of recognition should not obscure Jhabvala's enormous contribution to Anglo-Indian literature, film and screenwriting in a career spanning over half a century. As Crane asserts, Jhabvala and her writing must be understood in light of the repeated cultural and geographic displacement she experienced throughout her life, and how this feeling of being a perennial outsider affected her approach to writing and to India more generally.[48] As Crane, Peter Morey and others have noted, Jhabvala's life was marked by several significant migrations: first from Germany to Britain in 1939 to escape the persecutions of National Socialism, then from Britain to Delhi in 1951 with her new husband Cyrus S. H. Jhabvala, and then again from Delhi to New York in 1975.[49] These journeys, especially to a newly independent India in the early 1950s, gave Jhabvala the impetus, opportunity and subject matter for the beginning of her work as a novelist, as well as a keen appreciation of how national character is expressed by people when in foreign lands.

Though her focus on the Raj is not as direct as that of Rushdie, Farrell or Scott in that she did not set out to write the kind of serial narratives that her contemporaries did, her interest in the history and legacy of British India, as well as how it affects the actions and identities of individuals, is clear. Although Crane argues that the Raj does not become an active force or setting in her fiction until *Heat and Dust*, memories of the British Empire are never far beneath the surface of her earlier work, affecting the behaviour, beliefs and prejudices of her characters.[50] Alongside the popularity and public recognition she achieved through *Heat and Dust* and its Booker Prize in 1975, Jhabvala also became well known through her collaboration with Merchant Ivory Productions. Her long-standing involvement as a screenwriter for Merchant Ivory, which included the adaptations of her own works *The Householder* in 1963 and *Heat and Dust* in 1983 as well as various other literary texts, meant that her role in helping to establish the character of the Raj Revival, as well as her contribution to the general historical turn within post-war culture that Boccardi identifies, was not a limited one but rather the work of decades.

Jhabvala's work and its underpinning concerns of dislocation are thus representative not just of her own biography, but also that of the postcolonial period of British decolonisation more generally. The process of introspection inherent to her characterisation of the European in India, and again drawn from her own experience in Delhi, is representative of the much broader move towards reflection and retrospection in British culture throughout the post-war decades, as Britons and other Europeans sought to fathom the change in their circumstances and rethink their former colonial connections to India and other newly independent states either at a distance or first-hand. Jhabvala writes in *An Experience of India* (1971) that all Europeans undergo three stages of response to India during their time there: 'first stage, tremendous enthusiasm – everything Indian is marvellous; second stage, everything Indian not so marvellous; third stage, everything Indian abominable. For some people it ends there, for others, the cycle renews itself and goes on.'[51] Jhabvala would use this process, one that she likened to being 'strapped to a wheel', not only to inform the characterisation of Olivia and her modern narrator in *Heat and Dust* and their experiences within the narrative, but as an overarching theme of the novel, illustrating the inherent circularity to colonial history and the idea of Empire more generally. Indeed, it is possible to use Jhabvala's process to reflect on the advent of the Raj Revival itself, with its resurgence after a period of British disinterest in the colonial experience indicative of the process beginning again and the wheel rolling round once more.

Paul Scott's work has likewise had a changeable public life over the last forty years. Successful, if not truly popular, in the 1970s, his work is often now overlooked or, as Farrell's once was, critically ignored, having largely fallen out of fashion.[52] In part, this may be related to the scale of Scott's central work, *The Raj Quartet* (1966–75). Running to over 2,000 pages (even more if its coda novel *Staying On* is included also), this succession of meticulously detailed novels is testament to how Scott's writing became first interested in, and later subsumed by, the desire to fathom the life and death of British India. Scott believed that his experiences in India were what made him, and transformed his writing; although he had been writing for much of his life, his success did not occur until the 1960s, when his skill as a writer had reached a point whereby he could do justice to his Indian experiences and when the British reading public were disposed to receive them.

Considering his background, it is easy to see how India was transformative for Scott. His early life was largely unremarkable. Born in 1920 in suburban North London, Scott's childhood was one of genteel lower-middle-class poverty on the fringes of respectability. Despite an artistic temperament, Scott was apprenticed as an accountant out of financial necessity and worked in central London throughout the late 1930s.[53] Finding kindred spirits in his suburban sphere encouraged him to write, however, and he published his first (unsuccessful) collection of poetry in 1941. Like millions of others in this period, though, Scott's life was to be altered radically by the events of the war. He enlisted and, after a period with Military Intelligence, was posted initially to Belgaum in India in 1943 for officer training, then spent the remainder of the war supporting the advance against the Japanese forces in Burma. He was finally demobilised in 1946 when he tried, again unsuccessfully, to fashion himself as a playwright whilst also working in the publishing industry. After a number of further false starts (Scott published eight novels before *The Jewel in the Crown*), his turn towards exploration of the intense hierarchical social structure of British India provided him with the focus and clarity his other novels had lacked.

It is important to note that Scott is the only English writer of the four main authors that comprise the central focus of this volume. Scott's origins, however, do not mean that his loyalties or those of his characters lie with the British in India, nor does it follow that the ethos of his novels is to present an apologia for Empire; quite the opposite. Scott's work is instead suffused with conflict and frustration. On the one hand, and following the tradition of Anglo-Indian writing since the eighteenth century, his novels burst with an evident orientalist love for India, Indians and the sensory spectacle of the subcontinent. On the other, Scott's novels also go to great pains to capture the dullness, snobbery and smallness of mind that characterised the British community during the Raj. Life in Mayapore or Pankot, the fictional cities of *The Raj Quartet*, is suffocating in its adherence to rank and precedence and exhausting in its pettiness, as characters inflict a myriad of slights both deliberate and inadvertent upon each other. Moreover, Scott's novels reveal his awareness of the central tragedy that exists within British and Indian relations; namely that the systems of prejudice and exclusion in place in British India are self-reinforcing and self-replicating, and that despite recognition of their falsehood, individuals nonetheless fall into their expected behaviours because the rigidity of colonial society offers them no alternative. From the brutality of the District Superintendent of Police, Ronald Merrick, imposed because he can and because he believes he must, through to the mollifying nature of the *mali*, Scott's characters must fill the roles that have been cast for them in this elaborate social theatre, as failure to do so invites the same fate as his protagonist Hari Kumar, the Indian raised as an Englishman: an existence without fulfilment, or fit.

In scanning the selection of authors and texts in this book, it will be apparent that there is both a gendered imbalance as well as one of ethnic or national perspective. This selection of authors has not been arrived at without deliberation, but is rather by design; this book does not offer an exhaustive account of literature dealing with Empire and India since the Second World War, but instead draws focus on those writers and voices that sought to combine the various currents of history, legacy and medicine within their work. Given the nature of these concerns, it is perhaps no great surprise that these writers would predominantly be white and British in their origin.

Likewise, as particular chapters will illustrate and argue, colonial India was a predominantly masculine environment, with its demographics dictated by military or civil service, or by business. Of course, the mythology of the redoubtable Memsahib is a counterpoint to this assertion, and the social composition of British India changed greatly over the course of its last century, with more and more women living and working there; however, those authors who turned to India for inspiration in the late twentieth century remained male, and would often focus their narratives similarly on men.

This is not to say that the writers that constitute the focus of this book were singular or homogeneous in their perspectives, or indeed their own identities. It is likewise apparent that Rushdie, Farrell and Jhabvala in particular offer a far more mixed perspective than typically assumed. Rather than considering them representative of a monocultural British view, much might be read instead into their outsider status, and thus their motivation behind engaging with the Empire throughout their work. For Rushdie and Farrell, their respective Indian and Irish descent confers on them a national and cultural hybridity that brings with it the potential, and expectation, for more critical intentions when addressing the history and aftermath of Empire. Jhabvala's background likewise offers her the perspective of someone outside the realm of typical Britishness, a position potentially crucial to her success with Merchant Ivory in helping to realise the imperial world on screen. Whilst Scott might be solidly English in terms of his origins, he nonetheless spent the majority of his life acutely aware of divisions of class, education and status within British and Anglo-Indian life; as Spurling notes, his life in suburban Surrey was at odds with his artistic ambitions, lack of university education and oblique allusions to a homosexual love affair in his youth (a subject he refused to discuss openly), suggesting a familiarity with the experience of the outsider counter to the security implied by his background.[54] Crane alleges that, traditionally, the literature of Empire falls into two categories: British authors only write about the British experience, whilst Indian novelists confine themselves to the Indian experience in response. Therefore, Crane argues, the critic must explore them both for the full picture.[55] However, there is as much to be made of the middle ground in Anglo-Indian fiction as there is these two extremes, especially in the split perspectives of writers such as Rushdie, Jhabvala and Farrell, and the efforts of Scott's novels to explore the interrelation of coloniser and colonised.

In my prior work on the period, I have previously argued that literature after the Second World War splits into two distinct, yet connected, branches in relation to understandings of postcoloniality.[56] Firstly, the post-imperial or post-colonial in a literal sense, encompassing those works or authors that focused on the process of decolonisation and the period immediately after that of colonial rule, and that sought to explore continued British engagement with India in the historical present. Secondly, those writers that chose to re-engage directly with the history of the British Empire through historical fiction or historiographic metafiction. These texts adopted a more recognisably postcolonial approach in that they sought to deconstruct critically the power relations and structures that sustained the system of Empire, and drew focus on their effects.[57] Often, however, the authors under discussion in this monograph do not adequately fit into such neat categorisation. Many of them, such as Scott, Farrell, Masters and Jhabvala, appear to do both in simultaneity, producing historical novels that speak to the concerns of Britain after Empire as its power continues to wane and its taste for the fictions of the past grow in correlation. Rushdie, too, has been consistently argued to fit the latter category in terms of his representation of postcolonial consciousness in the form of Saleem's narrative and, indeed, the use of his own biographical experiences in a novel like *Midnight's Children*.[58] However, at the same time, he is writing about the immediate aftermath of Empire and how such identities are formed by an era of decolonisation, so shares some similarity to Masters and Scott.

Another point of slippage is in those novels and fictions that return to the high-water mark of Empire long before 1947, such as those of Farrell, Fraser, Masters or M. M. Kaye. Critics such as Gautam Chakravarty have tended to give such works short shrift when it comes to their significance, artistry and literary skill, writing off the work of Farrell, Fraser, Norman Partington and others as chronologically out of its time and representing 'little more than ironic coda or naive nostalgia' in the post-imperial world.[59] Deeper consideration of these novels suggests the opposite, however, and their works offer instead, as Hywel Dix argues of Farrell in particular, a parodic and cynical critique of the past as a means of coming to terms with the realities of the British present.[60] Although less openly critical and less aesthetically significant, Partington and Kaye's novels are nonetheless important to acknowledge within the debate around historical fiction after Empire. Such texts are again post-imperial in so much as they appear chronologically after the end of Empire but complicate this categorisation as it is decolonisation that drives their production and their popularity. As such, they can be considered more akin to pastiche rather than parody, written to meet the desires of the former coloniser in an era of decolonisation. As part of this pastiche they too often seek accuracy in their representation of the past; such efforts at verisimilitude extend to the representation of medicine and the inclusion of health, disease and sickness as part of their narratives, and thus warrant their inclusion within analysis of the period and its tropes. Moreover, such texts can be considered as part of the established relationship between textual production and British imperialism. Elleke Boehmer argues that the Empire was profoundly literary in nature, a 'textual exercise' created by multiple overlapping formats, from colonial reports to British readers of newspapers, through to administrators who consulted religious texts as a means of writing British Indian law, through to fiction.[61] The variable literary status and skill of such texts might be debatable; however, their validity within the culture of publication that created and sustained Empire is evident.

In this book's approach to the Anglo-Indian novel, it does not aim to settle the dispute over the terms used to assess these works, if indeed such a thing would be possible, or even desirable. Instead, the analysis that follows seeks to remain cognisant of these competing and complementary currents of criticism that exist around the return to the British Empire in fiction, or that explore the circumstances and effects of its demise and reflect on post-imperial and postcolonial approaches alike.

Long-term sickness: medicine and the legacies of Empire

As well as considering the character of the return to the past of the British Empire through historical fiction, we must also consider how notions of the Empire's legacy inform works produced in this period and indeed the wider genre of Anglo-Indian fiction. Like the approaches to the history and culture of British India adopted by these authors, their notion of what is meant by the term 'legacy' is similarly pluralistic, varied and evocative of the metaphorical associations of decolonisation and the end of Empire. By way of definition, a legacy can be thought of as the consequence of a deliberate or inadvertent phenomenon with a long-lasting effect: an event, (in)action or (in)decision, the implications of which can be felt or observed beyond the temporal confines of its enactment.[62] This notion of temporality is significant within a genre preoccupied with the events of the past viewed from a contemporary perspective, either within the narrative or in the mind of the author. Legacies are the left-behind: what remains as wake or aftermath, and how these phenomena are encountered in the immediate present, or at some point to come. Legacies can thus also be mutable, open to negotiation or interpretation using the values of a particular social or political perspective. Alternately, a legacy can be an active bequest and exist intangibly in a future temporality. Indeed, the notion of the legacy of Empire was often at the forefront of colonial administration and activity. It is visible in Thomas Babington Macaulay's 'Minute on Indian Education' (1835), designed to create an Indian governing class steeped in British sensibility; in the activities of the Anglo-Indian Temperance League; and in the favourite subjects of those wishing to retrospectively ascribe benevolent intent to Empire: the building of the railways and the continued Indian propensity for cricket.

Legacies must therefore be understood as multiple and varied in both form and function. Some are less obvious than those listed above, or less tangible, like an established custom, a linguistic turn of phrase or a vague understanding of a way of doing things particular to a space or place; yet they are no less meaningful as a result. Alternately, legacies can be expressed in space itself, from the architectural legacy of the British presence in colonial spaces across the globe left in buildings, monuments, battlefields and cemeteries, through to the self-perpetuating characters of neighbourhoods and locales both exclusive and impoverished. The streets of Britain and its former colonies remain littered with such material traces, from the effigies of exceptional imperial soldiers or statesmen set in stone or cast in bronze, to the involvement of those anonymous participants collectively recalled in plaques, memorials or street names. Such legacies are likewise subject to change, the projection of their power or the very fabric of their existence altered, weathered or demolished as sensibilities and opinions shift.[63] The novels that comprise this volume are as much the Empire's monuments as any example of architecture or statuary, and they too revive and sustain it beyond the point of its demise. Within the frame of postmodernism, the work of Scott, Rushdie, Jhabvala, Farrell and others acknowledges a legacy of imperial writing, inheriting and reworking the concerns of Kipling or Forster alongside the history of Empire itself.[64] Their novels stand as testament to an acute temporal fixation with Empire in the post-war period, but one with its own far-reaching implications: rather than simply acknowledging or commemorating its passing, their existence drives the political and cultural return to Empire that continues to this day.

This temporal mutability of a legacy means that it can also be thought of as a dialogue. As Ambalavaner Sivanandan's words on the history of the Empire suggest, legacies are not monodirectional, and instead effect a change on all parties involved. In relation to the Empire, the legacy of colonialism is exerted on the coloniser as well as the colonised. Beyond the rather limited means through which critics such as Bernard Porter believe this influence is manifest (the 'visible detritus' of tokens left in the British social vernacular), and beyond even the continued life of a memory or way of thinking into the present, the legacy of Empire within the British national consciousness or psyche is encapsulated in the somewhat paradoxical state of contradictory feeling about the British past. It is again a dissonance in that Britain can be celebratory of its former role, as though it bears such world-leading qualities still, whilst at once mourning their passing.[65] A large swathe of contemporary Britain appears to believe that the country's status remains equal to that of its imperial past whilst simultaneously decrying its diminished influence and exhorting the need to recapture its lost standing.[66] In this post-imperial, postcolonial sense, the idea of writing back is not simply something enacted by authors from former colonial states but rather an ongoing process of exchange in which the Empire replies to the Empire that wrote back. Porter's approach is thus too instrumentalist, and too literal. The legacy of the end of Empire on the British is not to be found necessarily in things and material traces, but in actions, attitudes, myths, stories and beliefs; often intangible forces with more power than any building or statue, more complexity than the cause–effect relationship he suggests, and, as a consequence, infinitely harder to challenge.

The interpretive status of such textual legacies resists closure, instead acting as a kind of perpetual contact zone, as Mary Louise Pratt argues, in which both parties remain forever altered by their interaction.[67] Yet it is the imbalanced terms of the original contact zone that remain in the psyche of post-imperial Britain, aided by the selective historiography of Nigel Biggars and Jeremy Black, who have sought to exonerate Britain of its more shameful legacies by re-inscribing the myth of the 'civilising mission' and the supposedly 'benevolent' Empire.[68] As Fintan O'Toole argues, such feelings provide succour to the diminished Britain of the post-1945 world, convincing it of its status, colouring all its actions and continuing to fuel the interest in the grand narrative of Empire expressed in literary and cultural representation.[69] Their existence and popularity is, as William Faulkner observed, testament to the notion that the past, far from being dead, is not even past. Rather, it continues to exist within and shape the present; to paraphrase, for some readers of Anglo-Indian fiction or adherents of Empire, it is always, whenever they want it, fifteen minutes to midnight on 14 August, and perhaps this time the clock will not strike.

In addition to their shared turn towards history and the legacies of Empire, a further crucial element in these novelists' reappraisal of colonial past is their decision to include recurrent motifs of illness throughout their work. Farrell, Jhabvala, Scott, Rushdie and others all identified medicine and illness as key to imperial authority and colonial experience, a constant presence amidst the broad sweep of colonial life they sought to depict, and a means through which the juxtaposition of the personal and the political might be achieved effectively in their novels. This recurrence of medicine, illness and health in Anglo-Indian fiction has not gone unacknowledged in existing criticism. John McLeod notes that 'illness and its consequences are prevailing issues' throughout Farrell's career as a writer, and that in each of his seven novels, 'key characters often suffer from debilitating or fatal conditions'.[70] Similarly, in *Troubled Pleasures: The Fiction of J. G. Farrell* (1997), Ralph J. Crane and Jennifer Livett recognise that 'sickness (has) occupied a central position in Farrell's novels', describing it as 'omnipresent' in the later *Empire Trilogy*.[71] Rebecca Ziegler makes reference to the significance of bodies and their fragility as a significant aspect of Farrell's depiction of the human condition.[72] Farrell, after periods of ill health due to polio, recorded in his unpublished diary that he became 'interested in writing, largely I suppose as a sort of self-therapy'.[73] The allegorical significance of birth in *Midnight's Children* features in critical approaches to Rushdie's work, especially given its relevance to postcolonial discourses used to consider his writing, and there are similar acknowledgements of how the principles of Ayurvedic medicine underpin many of his themes.[74] Aside from his diagnosis of Farrell's interest in illness, Ralph J. Crane has observed similar symptoms in the novels of Jhabvala too, again identifying birth and rebirth as an ordering leitmotif of *Heat and Dust*.[75]

Despite this identification of medical matters arising throughout criticism of Anglo-Indian fiction of this period, as well as the interweaving of medicine with the way these novels approach and appropriate history, the implications of these stylistic choices remain largely unexplored and under-theorised beyond their thematic and generic functions. Scholarly focus has not, to date, included sustained analysis of the significant presence and often narrative predominance of medicine and health within Anglo-Indian fiction, nor has the critical field addressed the utility of medicine more broadly as a means through which to read Anglo-Indian fiction produced after the end of the British Empire, or, further still, that of European colonialism.[76] As such, this book is the first to place these authors and their work within a critical framework of literature and medicine, and consider the connections between their shared literary approach to colonial medicine and history in their contemporary moment. I argue that their work exists within the frame of what Anne Whitehead terms the critical medical humanities, the 'broad, interdisciplinary perspective' offered by the application of a more 'critical, analytical, and politicized' approach to the human experience of medicine, illness and health.[77] Exploring the presence of medicine and medical themes within these authors' work, and their wider proliferation within the genres of post-imperial and postcolonial literature, from the perspective of medical humanities adds much to the existing critical discourses of race, power and identity that have so far been applied to Anglo-Indian fiction, and augments understanding of the experience of British India and the history and legacy of Empire.

The history of British India reveals how health and medicine were defining preoccupations of Anglo-Indian society that have, in turn, influenced the representation of India within fiction. The British experience of India and its representation in print cultures both factual and fictional has always involved medicine and health. Ill health whilst in India is near universal in memoirs, journals, travelogues and diaries, with numerous medical texts, pamphlets and guides available on how either to avoid sickness or remedy it.[78] Drawing on such sources, E. M. Collingham argues that the experience of India was intensely physical, marked by the centrality but also the transience of the body, with ill health and death central to Anglo-Indian life.[79] Others, such as Mark Harrison, have explored the entrenchment of medical topography within colonial medicine and the response of British and European bodies to the inhospitable spaces and places of India, itself acting as an allegory for the imposition of British society upon the subcontinent.[80] Jharna Gourlay, meanwhile, argues that concern over the health of British bodies in India was always connected to power; the greater the number of healthy soldiers and administrators, the tighter the grip of imperial rule over the subcontinent.[81]

Such currents of medicine and health exist in thematic and narratological forms within Anglo-Indian fiction, with Rushdie, Farrell, Jhabvala and their contemporaries employing a wide spectrum of approaches to the medical history of Empire. Their work contains multiple instances of illness, sickness and medical themes throughout their pages, from the recurrence of doctors, disabilities, the importance of birth, to the struggle with addiction. In order to

consider this disciplinary intersection of medicine, history and literature within Anglo-Indian fiction, this book reflects and engages with
the medical history of colonial India as these authors did. Some,
such as Farrell, employ archival material near verbatim in their
work, viewing period sources themselves as a form of documentary
legacy or representation of the Raj, and composing key subplots
and dialogue directly from source material. Others, like Scott, Rushdie and Jhabvala, take medical matters such as fever, alcoholism
or pregnancy as metaphorical or allegorical themes through which
to enact their critique of Empire, exploring the process of renewal,
healing and change after Indian independence. Whatever their methods, these authors acknowledged health and medicine as a vital part
of the colonial British past, a legacy for good or ill, and sought
to fold it into the broader literary approach to history that they
undertook within their novels. The fact that this group of writers,
in addition to their other means of post-imperial critique, choose
to interrogate the legacy of Empire through a medical lens further
places them in connection with each other, and medicine and the
critical medical humanities offers the opportunity to read Anglo-
Indian fiction produced during this period anew. To engage with
medicine and health in a literary context, as these authors do and as
medical humanities allows, is to continue to explore the history and
social make-up of Britain's colonial Empire, as well as the relationship between coloniser and colonised, from an alternative yet no less
significant perspective.

Treatment and prognosis: how will the book look?

At its heart, this book adopts a simple premise, namely that any
exploration of the Anglo-Indian literature produced throughout the
period of Britain's post-war decolonisation must be understood in
the context of the history and legacy of colonial India. In order to
appreciate the fullness of that history and its effect on these literary
responses to the end of Empire, such analyses must, in turn, appreciate the predominant and defining presence of medicine and health
within it. In the chapters that follow, I argue that these themes exist
in interrelation to one another within the pages of the Anglo-Indian
novel. Literature, history and medicine form a virtuous circle of reciprocity, exchanging, augmenting and occasionally subverting form,
literary and poetic technique, idiom, metaphor, knowledge, opinion
and belief, as well as historical record.

In light of these considerations, the book is ordered and structured thematically and addresses a range of medical matters represented by its component authors across its five chapters. It does not examine every author in each chapter, but instead draws focus on their works where relevant to the specific theme, thus offering close reading of its texts alongside the effort to situate them more broadly within Anglo-Indian fiction and twentieth-century literature. Chapter 1 develops the concerns of this Introduction to examine in detail the literary links between medicine, illness and Anglo-Indian fiction, and illustrates not just the ways in which specific authors engaged with the history of British India through a medical lens but also, crucially, why they did so. Grounding the critical theme of the book as a whole, the chapter argues that fictional imaginings of India published in this period continually configured British presence in relation to the experience, possibility or treatment of illness and the risk to health; it examines the variety of diseases, illnesses and medical conditions represented throughout key examples from Anglo-Indian fiction, the significance of being ill within individual narratives, and what the use of medicine as means of engaging with the history of the British Empire in India offers these authors and postcolonial approaches to literature in this period.

Chapter 2 focuses on the representation of medical men and women within post-imperial fiction, their social significance and the recurrent literary engagement with Anglo-Indian practitioners. Doctors are a significant presence within the pages of these novels, not simply because of the frequency with which medicine and ill health themselves appear, but also in their function as an embodiment of colonial medical authority; the chapter will explore how their representation within these narratives offers these authors the means of considering how that authority might be affirmed, subverted or resisted. The chapter examines the various treatments, remedies and examples of medical expertise included within fiction of the period, exploring how conflict between practitioners and their beliefs is representative of wider social divisions inherent to colonial India and to decolonisation in general, across national, ethnic or gendered lines.

Chapter 3 focuses on the importance of space, place and environment both within Anglo-Indian fiction and medical history of colonial India, recognising the connection between literary and physical representations of space and territory. The chapter is divided into two main sections – exteriors and interiors – and considers a range of spaces in the course of its analysis. For example, as a means of examining the authority of the British presence in India, the chapter approaches the spatial emplacement of colonial and medical authority through-out post-imperial fiction, considering the way in which Anglo-Indian writers depict colonial hospitals, clinics, medical schools and public places within their narratives, and the way in which these spaces are repeatedly pathologised or act as the setting for the application of British power.

Chapter 4 considers the juxtaposition between the political and the personal in Anglo-Indian fiction through an examination of health and well-being in relation to diet. The chapter argues that a range of authors explore the history of colonial India by using lifestyle and diet, and alcohol and alcoholism in particular, as lenses through which to explore the cultural, political and medical legacies of Empire. Through analysis of literary texts as well as a range of medical sources related to diet, alcohol and inebriation, it will illus-trate how drinking and eating are central to Anglo-Indian approaches to satirising, subverting and undermining the supposed benefit that Empire presented to India and Indians, or even the alleged danger with which India threatened the European constitution. The final chapter brings together the currents of history and medicine that run throughout the book, focusing on those post-imperial novels that deal directly with the demise and aftermath of Empire. Examining recurrent themes of memory, amnesia, hauntings, mortality and memorial culture, it explores the lasting traces of colonialism's effect on both the coloniser and the colonised, and argues that the medi-cal idiom with which the Empire is repeatedly assessed represents a desire to alternately diagnose Britain's contemporary sickness or conduct a post-mortem of the British Raj.

Notes

1. In his diaries of the handover, Prince Charles noted a sense of 'exasper-ated sadness' to the events, as well as a little bathos: 'It took me some time to realize that this was not first class (!) . . . I then discovered that others (politicians) were comfortably ensconced in first class imme-diately below us. Such is the end of the Empire, I sighed to myself.' Anon., 'Edited Extracts from Prince Charles's Travel Journal'.
2. Popular British interest in India remains as strong as ever. For example, connections between Britain and India was a major theme of the National Trust's 2017–22 strategic plan, and joins projects such as the Two Centuries of Indian Print initiative at the British Library (<https://www.bl.uk/projects/two-centuries-of-indian-print>) and the Open Univer-sity's 'Beyond the Frame: Indian British Connections' project (2007–12,

<https://www.open.ac.uk/arts/research/asianbritain/>, last accessed 11 September 2020).

3. Crane, *Inventing India*, 4–5. Corroborating and extending Crane's analysis, Máire ni Fhlathúin's *British India and Victorian Literary Culture* (2015) details the extent of the literary marketplace and the artistic extent of representations of India at the Raj's height.

4. This limited (and limiting) argument continues via the work of Nigel Biggars' 'Ethics and Empire' project, hosted by the McDonald Centre (<https://www.mcdonaldcentre.org.uk/ethics-and-empire>, last accessed 11 September 2020).

5. Teverson, *Contemporary World Writers*, 7.

6. See <https://www.imdb.com/title/tt0086711/> (last accessed 3 July 2018). The sweep of Kaye's story and its lavish HBO adaptation – the first of its kind – set the precedent for a kind of 'cinematic' TV miniseries for which HBO would come to be known.

7. An international addition to the Raj Revival would be Steven Spielberg's *Indiana Jones and the Temple of Doom* (1984), which is set in the fictional town of Mayapore in the Pankot district, both taken from Scott's *The Raj Quartet* (1966–75).

8. The India Office Archives in the British Library holds an extensive collection of unpublished manuscript sources written by European residents in India during the last twenty years of British rule. Many of these memoirists acknowledge in their prefaces or opening chapters that they have been personally invited to write up their recollections by 'V. C. Martin' at the India Office Library, or by Hookway himself. Each correspondent was sent a template with suggested subheadings and key themes, producing a uniformity of composition to these memoirs and thus an orthodoxy of narrative too. See for example BL, Barnes, Mss Eur F226/1: 1929–1940.

9. One such diarist, Colonel Basil Amies, formerly of the 14th Punjab regiment, observes when writing his memoir in 1977 that there are 'barely, I think, half-a-dozen left of the 100 cadets of that first batch at Quetta' when he began his career in 1915. BL, Amies, Mss Eur E418: 1914–1947, 2.

10. Fleming, 'Echoes of Britannia', 1–22.

11. Turner, *Crisis? What Crisis?*, 200.

12. Incidentally, one of the defining critical texts on nationhood of the decade, Tom Nairn's *The Breakup of Britain: Crisis and Neo-Nationalism*, was published in 1977, the same year as Scott's *Staying On*, illustrating the parallel discourses of Britishness extant in this period.

13. Spurling, *Paul Scott*, 369.

14. Rushdie, 'Outside the Whale'.

15. Fleming, 'Echoes of Britannia', 7.

16. The film ends with a grieving Karim kissing the feet of Victoria's statue in Agra.

17. Such plotting is evocative of Jhabvala's short story collection *A Stronger Climate* (1968), in which she identifies two types of Briton or European on the subcontinent: the 'seeker', who is heading to India in search of something (a theme she returns to in *Heat and Dust*), and the 'Sufferer', those who stayed on and are forced to live out their days in India. See Crane, *Inventing India*, 151.

18. The currency of imperial fictions is, of course, more widespread than these few examples suggest, and has been bolstered by the similar growth in neo-Victorianism over the same period. Further examples include Bernard Cornwell's enormously successful *Sharpe* novels (1981–present), featuring three set in India, Alan Moore's *League of Extraordinary Gentlemen* series (1999–2007), or 'The Raj' theme park in HBO's *Westworld* (2016–); but there are real-world contexts also, including Bombay Sapphire's 'Empire Bar' (the 'Jewel in the Crown' of their Laverstoke distillery, according to their website: <https://distillery.bombaysapphire.com/venue-hire/the-empire-bar>, last accessed 7 June 2021) and the abundance of imperial and nationalist iconography in British beer culture, including Fuller's 'Bengal Lancer' and Marston Brewery's 'Old Empire' India pale ales, replete with Indian elephants on the label.

19. Noor, 'Beecham House is a "flipping radical thing"'. Despite Chadha's claims of radicalism in her portrayal of the colonial India of the Company rather than the Raj, the programme was full of the familiar tropes of historical fictions of India, and did not return for a second series.

20. Ramaswarmy, 'A Suitable Boy review'.

21. See Koegler et al., 'Writing Brexit: Colonial Remains'.

22. See *YouGov*, <https://yougov.co.uk/news/2014/07/26/britain-proud-its-empire/>; <https://d25d2506sfb94s.cloudfront.net/cumulus_uploads/document/95euxfgway/InternalResults_160118_BritishEmpire_Website.pdf> (last accessed 11 September 2020).

23. Smith, 'How Unique are British Attitudes to Empire?'

24. Verma, 'Colonial Countryside'.

25. David Lammy (@davidlammy), Twitter, 30 April 2018. Lammy's words echo those of Ambalavaner Sivanandan, who first used the formulation 'we are here because you were there' as director of the Institute of Race Relations in the UK. See Younge, 'Ambalavaner Sivanandan obituary'.

26. Though slavery was abolished in India at around the same time as it was in the Caribbean, the system of indentured servitude that succeeded it remained in place, and asserted through a range of formal and informal practices and sanctions, for the remainder of the British colonial period. Empire was responsible for various migrations of people between its territories, such as the movement of Indians to Africa in the late nineteenth century, which would later produce the Ugandan Asian diaspora forced to flee to Britain in the 1970s. See Greenwood and Topiwala, *Indian Doctors in Kenya*.

27. Hall, 'Soft Brexit will be biggest "national humiliation"'. Mogg's one moment of insight here is his recognition of the importance of Suez, though not for the reasons he identifies; rather than the nation adopting a false consciousness of helplessness as he asserts, Suez was the watershed moment of imperial collapse, where the pretence of Britain's global power could no longer remain tenable.
28. Gilroy, *After Empire*, 98; Gill, 'Brexit'.
29. Coates, 'Ministers aim to build "empire 2.0"'.
30. Sara Wasson identifies Lennard Davis' coinage of the term 'teleogenic' as a means of assessing how some forms of writing are expressed in a way that directly reflects their ending. Wasson, 'Before narrative', 106–12.
31. Byatt, *On Histories and Stories*, 9.
32. Jhabvala and Rushdie would illustrate their complementary perspectives in their collaborative volume of short stories *Homeless by Choice* (1992), alongside V. S. Naipaul.
33. Boccardi, *The Contemporary British Historical Novel*, 2.
34. Another contemporary, Graham Swift, though shortlisted but ultimately unsuccessful in 1983 with *Waterland*, would go on to be awarded the prize for *Last Orders* (1996), itself dealing obliquely with the changing nature of British life in the aftermath of Empire through its focus on a group of working-class Londoners.
35. Strongman, *The Booker Prize*, 4.
36. See Goodman, 'Everything Must Go'. Scholarly interest in the middlebrow has increased in the last decade, especially in the work of Faye Hammill and Kristin Bluemel, and the Middlebrow Network: <https://www.middlebrow-network.com> (last accessed 21 March 2021).
37. Huggan, *The Postcolonial Exotic*, 115.
38. For a variety of approaches to *Midnight's Children* and Rushdie's work in general, see: Gurnah, *Cambridge Companion to Salman Rushdie*; Goonetilleke, *Salman Rushdie*; Eaglestone and McQuillan, *Salman Rushdie*; Cundy, *Salman Rushdie*; Mishra, *Annotating Salman Rushdie*.
39. As a range of commentators have noted, the historical novel experienced a boom in popularity in the decades after the Second World War; whilst contextually driven by what Frederic Jameson called the 'nostalgia industry', the desire to engage with the past through narrative or literary means seems acutely British and correlative to the decline of Empire. See Boccardi, *The Contemporary British Historical Novel*, 17.
40. Cronin, *Imagining India*, 5.
41. Rajan, 'Indian Writing in the West', 84.
42. Although Rushdie has argued that his writing is not autobiographical, analysis of his archive at Emory University offers evidence to the contrary; as an aside regarding *Midnight's Children*, Rushdie notes that he regrets 'making Saleem like me'. MARBL, Fiction, MSS/1000 Box 17/8, 'Midnight's Children Notes'.

43. For example, Farrell's work forms part of Hywel Dix's analysis of post-modernism in *Postmodern Fiction and the Break-Up of Britain*, and in my own work; see Goodman, 'A Great Beneficial Disease', 1.
44. Hilary Mantel joined J. M. Coetzee, Peter Carey and Farrell as a multiple Booker winner for her novel *Bring Up the Bodies*, published in 2012.
45. *The Hill Station* was published in its incomplete state, prefaced with introductory chapters by Margaret Drabble, Malcolm Dean and John Spurling. Because it is incomplete, it is not always considered canon by all critics of Farrell's work, but it is treated as such here.
46. Waugh, *Harvest of the Sixties*, 201. Such misconceptions have most recently resurfaced in relation to the ITV adaptation of *The Singapore Grip* (2020), which was criticised by BEATS (British East and South East Asians working in the Theatre and Screen industries) as 'harmful (non)representation' for its focus on the consciousness of the white coloniser. Whilst such observations are both long-standing criticisms of Farrell's work and entirely accurate, the perspective of Asian characters beyond how they intersect with the lives of the colonial British was not Farrell's objective for the Empire Trilogy, and nor could he have represented such a perspective faithfully. *BBC.co.uk*, 'The Singapore Grip: ITV drama called "harmful"'.
47. Jhabvala's life, work and archive are currently the subject of a long-term process of analysis and cataloguing; see McGonagle, 'A Transnational History of a Writer', 28–33.
48. Crane, *Jhabvala*, 1.
49. Ibid. 2–7.
50. Ibid. 27; 89.
51. Ibid. 5–6.
52. Alberto Fernández Carbajal is one of the few contemporary scholars to engage with Scott's fiction and argue for an appreciation of its complexity in matters of identity and sexuality; see Carbajal, *Compromise and Resistance*.
53. Spurling's biography of Scott details the complex family interrelations of the Scotts and his mother Frances' family, the Marks, implying that their inherent competition and petty rivalries stemmed from differences in class, with the Scotts belonging to the genteel artistic lower middle and the Marks' the poverty of the South London working classes; see Spurling, *Paul Scott*, 9.
54. Ibid. 94.
55. Crane, *Inventing India*, 4.
56. Goodman, 'Everything Must Go'.
57. Linda Hutcheon's formulation of historiographic metafiction outlined in *The Politics of Postmodernism* (1987) comes chronologically later than the novels discussed in this volume; however, it is nonetheless useful in analysing the stylistic and thematic choices of these authors.

58. Gurnah, *Cambridge Companion to Salman Rushdie*, 2–3.

59. Chakravarty, *Indian Mutiny and the British Imagination*, 4–5.

60. Dix, *Postmodern Fiction*, 25.

61. Boehmer, *Colonial and Postcolonial Literature*, 12–13.

62. Defining legacy is often as contested as legacies themselves, especially in relation to determining the after-effects of colonialism; see L'Estoile, 'The Past as It Lives Now', 267–79.

63. Widespread protest in June of 2020 in support of the Black Lives Matter movement subsequent to the death of George Floyd in the United States resulted in the spontaneous toppling of the statue of slave trader Edward Colston in Bristol, and a vote by Oriel College, Oxford, to finally remove its statue of Cecil Rhodes after years of activism. Similarly, the memorial to the women and children killed at Cawnpore in 1857 was removed in 1947 and replaced with a bust of Tantia Tope, a general of the Indian Rebellion. See Forty and Küchler, *The Art of Forgetting*; Buettner, 'Cemeteries, Public Memory and Raj Nostalgia', 5–42.

64. Addressing the work of Farrell, Scott and Jhabvala, Alberto Fernandez Carbajal argues for the influence of Forster's work as a form of legacy; see Carbajal, *Compromise and Resistance*, 27–8.

65. Porter, *Absent-Minded Imperialists*, 299.

66. O'Toole, *Heroic Failure*, 8.

67. Pratt, *Imperial Eyes*, 6.

68. For instance, Black's *Imperial Legacies* repeats the usual myths of Empire with little in the way of primary research to support them; see Black, *Imperial Legacies*. For a more critical examination of such imperial nostalgia, see Rasch, '"Keep the balance"', 212–30.

69. O'Toole, *Heroic Failure*, 86–7.

70. McLeod, *J. G. Farrell*, 5.

71. Crane and Livett, *Troubled Pleasures*, 126.

72. Ziegler, *J. G. Farrell's Empire Novels*, 153–4.

73. Farrell (Trinity), Box 9155: 'Unpublished diary', 69.

74. Byrne, 'Salman Rushdie and the Rise of Postcolonial Studies', 30.

75. Crane, *Inventing India*, 87. As later chapters will illustrate, birth and rebirth are continual metaphorical themes of Jhabvala's literary canon.

76. Such approaches that do exist are limited in scope. Alberto Fernández Carbajal mentions Jean M. Kane's assessment of Western and Ayurvedic medicine acting as a physical metaphor for the clash of nations and traditions within the novel, as well as Clare Barker's work on the recurrence of disability. See Carbajal, *Compromise and Resistance*, 222. Arthur Rose and Jessica Howell have both separately acknowledged the importance of a postcolonial health humanities, and their work has contributed significant advances in scoping what this field would look like. See Rose, 'Combat Breathing in Salman Rushdie's The Moor's Last Sigh', in Rose et al., *Reading Breath in Literature*, 113–34; Howell, *Malaria and Victorian Fictions of Empire*.

77. Bates et al., *Medicine, Health and the Arts*, 119.
78. These vary from specialist publications on health, such as Edmund C. P. Hull's *The European in India: or Anglo-Indian's Vade-Mecum, with Medical Guide for Anglo-Indians* (1874), to more general works combining medical information with practical details of travelling and recommendations for tourists, such as *The Imperial Guide to India, Including Kashmir, Burma and Ceylon* (1904).
79. Collingham, *Imperial Bodies*, 1.
80. Harrison, *Climates and Constitutions*, 19–20.
81. Gourlay, *Florence Nightingale*, 27.

Chapter 1

Colonial Conditions: On Being Ill in the Anglo-Indian Novel

'It is so curious about illness and health. Small things, little things, they make all the difference.'

Paul Scott, *Staying On*[1]

In exploring the intersection of medicine and twentieth-century literature, it seems necessary to begin with Virginia Woolf. Just as *A Room of One's Own* (1929) influenced feminist criticism, Woolf's *On Being Ill* (1926) has been instrumental in helping to justify the advent, existence and importance of the literary medical humanities.[2] Its regular recurrence within the scholarship of literature and medicine (my own included) has rendered it almost commonplace; however, the currency of Woolf's call for fictive works to address the totality of experience through acknowledgement of illness and its ever-present influence on human actions, behaviours and experience remains as a result of its ineffable truth. Even so, whilst Woolf's astonishment as to why illness was not among the 'prime themes' of literature (outside of poetry) is reasonable to some extent, this does not mean, as it is often taken to, that medicine and health were absent from the intention, plotting and literary aims of novelists and writers either contemporary to Woolf or who preceded her.[3] When considering the context of Woolf's own life and work, it is evident that she was acutely aware of the connections between ill health and literature and, more importantly, those between ill health and the experience of Empire. Along with Leonard Woolf's short career in the Ceylon Civil Service, the work and travels of fellow Bloomsbury Group authors such as E. M. Forster or Lytton Strachey influenced her thinking and her writing, and the links between Empire and health are expressed in her fiction. *Mrs Dalloway* (1925), for example, foregrounds British anxieties over bodily health in the wake of the Boer War and First World War, and it is particularly telling that the returned Anglo-Indian Peter Walsh struggles to keep pace with some passing soldiers whilst walking London's streets, the implicit suggestion being that his stamina, and the vitality of the men of his generation, is not what it once was, either weakened by age or, in his case, the enervating effects of his time on the subcontinent.[4]

Peter Walsh's degeneration is in part an acknowledgement of the belief in the debilitating effects of colonial space on British, and European, bodies that originated in the eighteenth century and lingered long into the twentieth.[5] Such beliefs were not unfounded, especially given the propensity of nineteenth-century Britons in India to attempt to continue to live in the manner they had at home with regard to dress and diet, and were indeed propagated by Anglo-Indian fiction and other publications of the period.[6] A key ingredient of the hold India had over the British mind, as Ralph J. Crane suggests, was the established literary culture of biography, memoir and travelogue that had grown exponentially in popularity over the course of the nineteenth century. As Rebecca Steinitz, Cynthia Huff and Felicity Nussbaum have all argued, the diary was a chief means of recording and propagating the colonial experience of Britons as the extent of the Empire grew, and various waves of publication followed key conflicts and periods of expansion.[7] Alongside the more exceptional events recorded in these diaries, many recorded the changeable circumstances of their authors' health too. Experience of ill health whilst in India is universal, and no diarist escapes illness entirely. This ubiquity of ill health speaks to the general infirmity of the human body, especially in an era of poor sanitation and rudimentary public health knowledge. However, the implication is always that it is India itself that is inhospitable. Such beliefs grew more pronounced as these print cultures established themselves, and in time the threat to health presented by India became a further aspect of the 'burden' of Empire.

Alongside the widespread popularity of memoir in the late nineteenth century, Anglo-Indian fiction was increasingly popular throughout this period as a result of the work of authors such as Flora Annie Steel and the literary dominance of Britain's best-known colonial writer, Rudyard Kipling. As Jessica Howell has illustrated, diseases such as malaria were a constant presence and recurrent plot device in Anglo-Indian fiction of the period, taking their place alongside a range of other conditions, maladies and illnesses throughout the pages of these works.[8] Nor was the focus of such works confined to bodily health alone. In Kipling's short story 'At the End of the Passage' (1891) he describes the effects of loneliness, isolation and too much alcohol on the psychological health of British residents, along-side the more common corporeal threats posed by heat apoplexy and cholera. These publishing cultures of fact and fiction should not be thought of as discrete; numerous diaries produced around the Indian Rebellion mimic language and style more closely associated with fiction, and, as Claudia Klaver has suggested, reflect and strengthen the extant overarching narratives of British imperialism from the period, in particular that of fortitude and endurance in the face of adversity.[9] In turn, the kinds of imperial adventure fictions popularised by G. A. Henty, H. Rider Haggard, Kipling and others used such events as the basis for their own plotting, something that the novelists of the late twentieth century examined in this volume would go on to criticise and engage with in their return to the genre after the Empire's end.[10]

Post-imperial authors were not only responding to the precedent set by Anglo-Indian publishing cultures of the nineteenth century, though. Shortly before Woolf wrote *On Being Ill*, E. M. Forster published *A Passage to India* (1924), his first novel in over a decade and the last he would publish during his lifetime. *A Passage to India*, drawn from Forster's own travels and experiences as a private secretary to the Maharajah of Dewas, openly criticised the attitudes, prejudices and inequalities he saw in Anglo-Indian society, winning Forster the criticism of those who believed his was the view of an outsider who did not, and could not, appreciate the reality of the Empire in India.[11] As well as the questions the novel raises around social inequality between Indians and Britons, *A Passage to India* anticipates Woolf's desire to see sickness recognised as one of the prime themes of literature and human experience. Whilst not a novel that focuses on illness in its entirety, health and medicine are nonetheless pivotal within the narrative of *A Passage to India*, from the effects of the hot weather that cause Adela and Aziz to venture into the Marabar Caves without Mrs Moore (and the heatstroke that is supposed to have killed her as she returns to England), through Aziz's profession as a doctor and the constant dangers of fever. The novel is not *about* illness directly, but illness is about the novel; it acts, as Scott observes, to make all the difference, shaping the actions and personalities of characters, driving the events of the plot, and influencing how they are perceived by the reader. Moreover, that Forster chooses to bring together the relationship between health, medicine and Empire within literary modernism is important, as Alberto Fernández Carbajal notes, in considering the novel's effect on anti-colonial and anti-imperial writing, and the cultural response to the end of Empire after the Second World War.[12]

Half a century after Forster, Scott, Jhabvala, Farrell, Rushdie and others are writing in response to the questions *A Passage to India* raises regarding the equity of the coloniser and colonised in India, and the extent to which modernism is a form sufficient to address them.[13] In returning to Empire and to the Anglo-Indian writing that preceded them, these authors thus engage with another legacy of the British past: its literary history.[14] In the process, they employ the styles, methods and subject matter of their predecessors with the self-reflexivity of postmodernism, to create what they intend to be a fuller, more searching critique of both past and present. As Farrell remarked in an interview with Malcolm Dean: 'I hoped to say something . . . about how we, in our thriving modern world of the 1970s, hold our own ideas.'[15] It is notable then that so many of the novels by Scott, Farrell, Jhabvala and others are indebted to the diary as well as the adventure novel in their composition, bringing together the concerns of historical record and literary narrative. In *The Siege of Krishnapur* (1973), Farrell plunders real accounts of the Siege of Lucknow for source material and his plotting; Jhabvala's *Heat and Dust* (1975) juxtaposes the diary its narrator keeps in the contemporary present with Olivia's letters from 1923; whilst Scott's *The Jewel in the Crown* (1966) is an amalgamation of various forms, part diary, part epistolary account and part historical novel.[16]

Their linkage of the past and the present through these various forms is key, and suggestive of the numerous contextual reasons as to why these authors all arrived at medicine and health as the manner through which to conduct their reappraisal of the colonial past. As observed above, the representation of a progressive serious illness has evident resonances with the trajectory of Empire and its terminal resolution. As Sara Wasson outlines, narratives within the medical humanities, just like those historical fictions of Empire, are informed by an awareness of the ending towards which they move, influencing the representational strategies adopted by Anglo-Indian writers and their inclusion of 'modes of being ill that have moral authority within particular cultural milieux'.[17] As this chapter illustrates, the illnesses and conditions that appear within the works of Farrell, Scott, Jhabvala and others all serve narratological and metaphorical functions, simultaneously driving their plotting and serving to make broader allegorical points regarding the end of Empire. In doing so, they correspond to Kenneth M. Boyd's consideration of the differences between disease, illness and sickness, which explores how some conditions possess a degree of social potency above that of others and signify an experience worthy of record or acknowledgement.[18] Some of these diseases, such as cholera and malaria, dominate Anglo-Indian fictions past and present, and re-engagement with them in the decades after Empire allows these authors to interrogate their connotations of hardship and suffering and the meta-narratives of colonial India that were generated around them. Other illnesses and sicknesses, meanwhile, might be seen as commonplace or, in the case of some conditions, even shameful or subversive, and their inclusion by Farrell, Scott, Jhabvala and others is a means of engaging with the quotidian experience of illness encountered by colonial Britons, or revealing a hidden history beneath the dominant one.[19]

Medicine, illness and health had an acute significance within the context of the literature and society of the particular period in which these authors were writing, just as it did for the nineteenth-century authors that preceded them. The post-war period was characterised by rapid changes in medical technology and in the state of medical care available in Britain, from the advent of the National Health Service in 1948 through to declining mortality rates from disease thanks to advances such as the mass production and widespread availability of penicillin and other antibiotics.[20] Healthcare was also deeply entangled with both the broader geopolitical history of Empire and the modern context of decolonisation. Julian Simpson argues that there had long existed a community of South Asian medical practitioners within the UK before Indian independence; based predominantly in London but also found in other major cities, Simpson suggests that this community of mostly Parsee origin were able to practise and build careers within Britain throughout the late nineteenth and twentieth century.[21] Parvati Raghuram states that in the years after the creation of the NHS, this presence became a dependence, with errors in 'manpower planning' by the Ministry of Health during the early 1950s necessitating increased reliance on migrant medical labour from South Asia.[22] The extent of this reliance leads Simpson to argue that the NHS should be acknowledged as 'a typically post-colonial institution; run by white people and dependent on labour from parts of the world that Britain had colonised', with over 3,000 doctors from India or Pakistan working within the NHS in 1965 and nearly 10,000 by the end of the 1970s.[23] Additionally, many former Indian Medical Service (IMS) personnel returned to Britain after Indian independence and continued in medical practice, however, some stayed on to work in the medical services of newly established Pakistan or in existing roles in mission hospitals.

The post-war period was also significant in terms of the development of medical humanities. As Therese Jones and others have argued, the term medical humanities and the active process of 'humanising' healthcare professionals within medical education grew in prominence and scope in the mid-twentieth century, before ultimately coming to encompass the consideration of medicine, healthcare and culture more generally and outside of medical training alone.[24] As critics including Michel Foucault drew attention to the 'dehumanising' apparatus of modern biomedicine that had grown from the professionalisation of healthcare, writers and artists explored the value of literature in reasserting human experience of ill health.[25] Recognition of the long-standing interplay between literature, language and medicine led to groundbreaking interdisciplinary work by writers such as John Berger, another contemporary of the authors examined here and another Booker winner, whose collaboration with photographer Jean Mohr, *A Fortunate Man* (1967), recorded the experiences of the country doctor John Sassall.[26] Berger and Mohr's work is a landmark humanistic text amid a period of growth in medicalised consciousness within literature, as likewise expressed in the work of Scott, Farrell, Jhabvala and others during this period, but also in regard to the more general and philosophical application of medicine and human experience in a time of decolonisation and national decline. As the British economy suffered in the wake of the Suez Crisis and approached the devaluation of the pound in 1967, Britain began to be referred to as the 'Sick Man of Europe', representative of the portability of medical metaphor in the conceptualisation of national identity. As Jeffrey Meyers argues in *Disease and the Novel: 1880–1960* (1985), drawing on the same mythology that would later inform Arthur W. Frank's *The Wounded Storyteller* (1995), there exists a correspondence between literary representation and social strife, stating that 'the illness of the hero, who is both an individual and a representative of his epoch, is analogous to the sickness of the state'.[27]

Although Meyers concludes in 1960, his analysis seems particularly appropriate given the embattled circumstances of Britain during the years of decolonisation and post-war decline, and their intensification in the 1970s. Similarly, just as Steven Connor has argued that the novel is an especially useful vehicle for exploring ideas of nationhood (a process that likewise accelerates in the post-war period, as Mariadele Boccardi and others point out), so too is it appropriate for considering the human experience of national identity and Empire.[28] Linking Frank, Connor and Boccardi is the resonance of Frank's typology of narrative types with the ideals of nationhood, Empire and history; the chaotic presence of illness is a threat to British superiority, to the established order and to the stability of colonial rule, whilst the Anglo-Indian novel that ends with the comfortable restitution of the health of British bodies and that of the colonial order was undoubtedly the kind of reassuring fiction produced amidst the tumult of Britain's changeable fortunes after the Second World War and Indian independence.[29]

There are biographical dimensions to the medical material within Anglo-Indian fiction, too. For example, Farrell died relatively young, drowned off the Irish coast at the age of forty-four. A contributory factor to his death was a lack of mobility in his upper body, itself a lasting effect of polio contracted whilst at Oxford as an undergraduate.[30] Previously an outstanding collegiate rugby player, in 1956–7 Farrell spent a number of weeks in an iron lung, leaving him with lifelong poor health. John McLeod views this sudden and shocking experience as that which shapes Farrell's sense of the 'essential infirmity of human life', both in terms of physical well-being and social perception.[31] Scott, meanwhile, experienced colonial India first-hand, but not without cost to his health, suffering from persistent stomach complaints and bouts of amoebic dysentery during his time in India and recurrently for years afterwards.[32] Scott was thus no stranger to illness, nor its effects on the body and mind; alongside his alcoholism, he was diagnosed with colon cancer in the mid-1970s and died aged fifty-seven in 1978. Jhabvala too contracted jaundice whilst writing *Heat and Dust* in the early 1970s – the first endemic disease she experienced during her twenty-five years in India, but one severe enough to provide the final impetus behind her decision to leave not long after.[33] However, whilst the sudden and life-altering effects of Farrell's experience no doubt influenced the content of his writing as McLeod states, it would be too straightforward an analysis to suggest that Farrell's interest in medicine in his fiction was solely driven by these autobiographical motives. Likewise, though Scott and Jhabvala experienced some of the conditions of India directly, their inclusion of them in their novels is not merely the direct translation of real-life experience into fiction. Rather, as the work of the novelists that constitute this volume suggests, illness serves a vital narratological function in the depiction of the life and death of Empire, allowing for meaning-making to occur on various textual, contextual and intertextual levels.

Drawing on these critical and cultural contexts, this chapter examines the variety of diseases, illnesses and medical conditions represented throughout Anglo-Indian fiction and the ways in which these authors use medicine as a means of engaging with the history of the British Empire in India. It argues that fictional imaginings of

India published in this period continually configured the British presence in relation to illness and the perennial risk to health; beyond
the recurrent use of illness as a narrative device, the metaphor and
idiom of post-imperial fiction are repeatedly expressed in medicalised
terms throughout the work of the authors under study. The chapter is divided into three thematic sections; the first examines Farrell's
use of medicine and medical history as a means of interrogating the
accepted narratives of the Indian Rebellion and those self-justificatory
myths of Empire. The second engages with Scott's representation of
pathologies that affect the body, exploring how bodily metaphor is
used throughout his novels to draw together the personal and political experiences of colonial India. The final section engages with Jhabvala's representation of mental health, and the psychological effects
and legacy of Empire past and present. However, as the subsequent
analysis shows, many of the conditions these authors include within
their novels are not limited to one of these categories and instead
affect both physical and mental health, suggesting that illness, and by
extension the history of Empire, pervade both body and mind, and
that the legacies of Empire are felt just as keenly in either physical or
psychological terms.

'Fair skeletons!': cholera and Empire in the novels of J. G. Farrell

Given the weight of their contextual, biographical and literary circumstances, the appeal and the utility of medicine and health within
the work of Farrell, Scott, Jhabvala, Rushdie and other authors from
this period is abundantly clear. Their means of approaching the topic
as well as the history of Empire differ greatly, however, depending
on their intent. For instance, unlike Scott's *The Raj Quartet*, which
takes place across a five-year period in the 1940s, or the temporal
juxtaposition of past and narrative present that occurs in Jhabvala's
Heat and Dust, *The Siege of Krishnapur* takes place in a fictional East
India Company station during the seemingly distant Indian Rebellion of 1857. The plot, echoing the historical events of the rebellion
and the imperial fictions derived from it, concerns the efforts of the
British residents, particularly the Collector, Mr Hopkins, an adherent of progress obsessed with the Great Exhibition of 1851, and the
socially idealistic poet George Fleury, to defend the garrison long
enough for their relief to arrive. Despite the relative simplicity and
linearity of the novel's plot, Farrell was not, as has been argued by

critics such as Gautam Chakravarty, a straightforward adherent of the realist imperial adventure novel in the style of his near contemporary Norman Partington.[34] *The Siege of Krishnapur* was instead Farrell's attempt to create 'a novel of ideas which could be read at the same time simply as an adventure story', combining the narrative simplicity of his source material with the ironic and parodic aspects of postmodernism in an effort to use the popularity of the format to advance his critique of the Britishness it stood for.[35] Farrell's return to the past of Empire and its values is not presented as a curative for the social ills of the 1970s. Instead of the romanticised unity of Empire, *The Siege of Krishnapur* is a novel about the continual clash of opposites and widespread divisions; one of past and present, tradition and progress, and, most obviously, between the British Empire and India, Britons and Indians, and the sick and the healthy.

Given the context of the turbulent 1960s and 70s in which Farrell was writing, his decision to write a novel about the Indian Rebellion just twenty-six years after Indian independence suggests an awareness of the critical currents of politics, scholarship and historiography of the period. Indeed, Peter Morey argues that Farrell is a postmodern author deliberately returning to British India to criticise colonialism through the blending of comedy and pathos.[36] Given the politicised nature of Farrell's undertaking as well as the inherently unequal racial context of Empire and British India, *The Siege of Krishnapur* is to some extent a postcolonial novel as well as a postmodern one, suggesting an awareness and criticism of the casual racial stratification and the classificatory techniques of British colonial society. However, despite these elements, Farrell's work does not sit wholly within postcolonial discourses.[37] For whilst *The Siege of Krishnapur* is evidently more critical of Empire and its effects than other Anglo-Indian fictions of the period, the novel focuses near exclusively on the actions, thoughts and failings of the colonisers, that of the British garrison; Indian characters are either only depicted as an indistinguishable multitude, briefly glimpsed and nameless, as a source of humour, or used instrumentally to make particular points.[38] However, the focus on British characters, again with emphasis on the temporal duality of Farrell's novel, is intended as a synchronic critique of Empire and the popular conception of a key moment in imperial mythology, namely 'the effect of colonization on the colonising power itself' in both short and long term.[39] As a consequence of this focus, Farrell's writing sits somewhere between these various critical positions; it is too parodic to be sincerely postcolonial, and too sincere to be entirely postmodern.

Farrell's post-imperial return to the days of colonial India is not to validate colonialism's existence but rather to expose its limitations. In addition to postmodernism and postcolonialism, the other key theme of many historical novels of the 1970s was that of unrest, representing a direct response to the political turmoil of the decade.[40] Examining the root causes of contemporary British decline is the driving force of Farrell's narrative in *The Siege of Krishnapur*, and the novel illustrates a colonial culture preoccupied with notions of its own progress, primarily in medical, scientific and spiritual matters.[41] Farrell's choice of period, location and medium in which to conduct this examination are significant, as 1857 was a turning point in the British governance of colonial India and its supposedly civilising and industrialising intent.[42] Farrell's critical approach thus becomes an attack on British belief in its dominant mythologies of Empire, and how they inform understandings of nationhood. Farrell exploits the irony of the British extolling the noble principles of imperial uplift whilst under siege throughout, and his characters praise the Empire's virtuous intent as that world quite literally explodes around them under the cannonades.

Like Scott, whose efforts towards historical accuracy are outlined in the author's note that prefaces *A Division of the Spoils* (1975), Farrell took pains to be accurate in his portrayal of the Indian Rebellion. Reflecting the publishing cultures of colonial India, Farrell's choice of method is to use a range of eyewitness accounts, memoirs and factual medical material directly within the composition of his novels.[43] This underpinning research is indicated in the 'afterword' to *The Siege of Krishnapur*, in which Farrell describes his extensive use of memoirs, diaries and letters from the Siege of Lucknow (June–September 1857), parts of which are often repeated nearly verbatim in the text of the novel or whose authors serve as inspiration for many of his characters.[44] In addition to the narrative accounts of the rebellion, Farrell uses contemporary sources such as medical diaries, scholarly journals, scientific case studies and newspaper articles from the 1850s as the basis for his text, reflecting their tone, style and structure throughout. Malcolm Dean relates that he found nineteenth-century copies of the *British Medical Journal* among Farrell's papers, indicating the extent of his efforts to ensure his portrayal of disease was as authentic and period-specific as possible.[45]

Lars Hartveit argues how the appeal of documents naturally intersected with Farrell's literary intent and chosen genre. Hartveit notes a file card marked 'HEALTH' among many others within Farrell's papers at Trinity College, Dublin, that listed a variety of sources consulted during the composition of his novels. Such documents indicate that Farrell's inclusion of medical material was in no way an incidental detail of his writing, but rather a systematic and deliberate process.[46] In a further indication of the significance of medicine and health to his assessment of Empire, Farrell's reasoning behind such documentary faithfulness was his belief that history 'leaves so much out . . . it leaves out the most important detail of all: what being alive is like'.[47] Such concern illustrates Farrell's feeling that conventional, documentary history is deficient in so much as its 'factual' demands means it lacks the emotional and physical subjectivities that literature is able to provide. Rather, the novel is more readily disposed to represent the effects and subjective experience of living through history or, as Farrell put it, 'undergoing history', through the embodiment of experience; the positioning of the body, its deficiencies and its treatment at the centre of his novels.[48]

The effect of this process of inclusion is that through individual incidents, objects or identities Farrell is able to criticise more than the art form or profession in the foreground; the technique enables him to critique the wider ideology and values of Empire embodied within it in simultaneity, a process that Ralph J. Crane and Jennifer Livett call 'interdiscursivity'.[49] As well as his comparison of the representational strategies of differing media, Farrell also uses medical details as part of this process of interdiscursivity, moving his novels away from traditional historical fiction and towards medical humanities. By engaging with medical treatment and practice in an imperial adventure novel, Farrell not only criticises the historical record of the Empire but attacks the epistemological foundations of science and medicine on which the garrison of Krishnapur and the Empire base their worldview. For example, the language used to describe the perceived spread of Victorian enlightenment is commonly that of a medicalised, often physiological nature: as Farrell's protagonist Fleury, who has travelled to India to research a tract on how the Empire has hastened the development of Indian civilisation, states:

> [E]veryone I talk to in Calcutta about my book tells me to look at this or that . . . a canal that has been dug or a cruel practice like infanticide or suttee which has been stopped . . . and these are certainly improvements of course, but they are only symptoms, as it were, of what should be a great, beneficial disease.[50]

Farrell's use of medical idiom here is not just a literary motif, but rather establishes medicine as a key component of the British presence in India, its scientific knowledge and its legacies with regard to the lives of its Indian subjects, to be critiqued through literary means. As Farrell goes on to suggest, the notion of the 'beneficial disease' of colonialism is both illusory and inherently contradictory. Fleury's terms suggest the transmission of these qualities of progress from the British to India ahead of their subsequent spread, but he fails to recognise the invasive connotations of his metaphor and consider the natural resistance to disease that any host would mount in response. In an extension of this metaphor, the British residency is later described as a 'contagion' of the countryside isolated by fire during the siege.[51] Moreover, the condition of progress that the Empire imposes on India is a phantom one in which 'the symptoms are there, but the disease itself is missing!', suggesting that the intent of the 'civilising mission' to India is only superficial, and skin deep.

Given the context of the siege and in reflection of his source material, Farrell's characters encounter a range of ailments throughout the narrative, including scurvy, malnutrition, delirium tremens, erysipelas, dysentery and nervous exhaustion.[52] However, Farrell's concerted engagement with illness and medicine is enacted through focus on cholera.[53] Unlike some of the illnesses drawn from Farrell's source material, cholera is not simply an incidental subplot or straightforward authenticating detail. Instead, it is integral to his further consideration of the Imperial progress narrative through focus on nineteenth-century debates over infectious disease, as Farrell's personal papers and manuscripts make clear. Farrell's approach to cholera is representative of his literary methodology and his critical approach to Empire through the paradigm of medicine and health.

As a consequence of the first pandemic of 1817–24, in which the trade routes of Empire brought the disease to Europe, cholera was one of the defining diseases of British imperialism on the subcontinent, and it has a particular association with both the Crimean War of 1853–6 and the Indian Rebellion.[54] In recognition of this status, alongside the index card marked 'HEALTH' that Hartveit notes in Farrell's archive is one entitled 'CHOLERA', which contains sentences taken from an 1865 medical text and used in the novel, and various notes from the 'Med. Times and Gazette of 1854'.[55] In the same tranche of materials, Farrell provides a preliminary list of key scenes and plot points around which the narrative is structured. These include 'The Last Great Battle Scene', 'The Relief' and 'The Great Cholera Controversy Scene', indicating how important cholera was within the novel's structure and Farrell's critical intent with regard to form and genre, but also how engagement with medicine and medical practice enables his critique of imperial teleology.

It is clear from the extent of cholera's prominence in *The Siege of Krishnapur* that Farrell seeks to present a detailed examination of the minutiae of the disease supported with period-specific research. Whereas Pamela K. Gilbert argues that the representation of cholera in fiction is typically more euphemistic and generalised in order to generate associative meaning-making, Farrell's exactitude in his representation illustrates his efforts to subvert dominant narratives of the rebellion and Empire by including a surfeit of information, as well as how his writing can be considered under Linda Hutcheon's definition of historiographic metafiction, or the representation of fictionalised history with a parodic edge.[56] Indeed, the playfulness and parody of his satirical approach is visible throughout his engagement with cholera. Once the siege is under way and the garrison begins to suffer from the effects of disease, tensions of the provision of care arise between its two resident physicians, regimental surgeon Dr McNab and civil surgeon Dr Dunstaple. Making his case to the Collector, Dunstaple takes him on a tour of the makeshift hospital:

> Suddenly, he seized the Collector's wrist and dragged him across the ward to a mattress on which, pale as milk beneath a cloud of flies, a gaunt man lay shivering, stark naked. 'How d'you think I cured this man?' . . . the Doctor explained that he had used the best treatment known to medical science . . . the treatment . . . every physician worthy of the name accorded his cholera patients . . . calomel, opium and poultices, with brandy as a stimulant.[57]

The grim humour found in Dunstaple's confidence in his methods compared to the state of the patient validates Morey's observations regarding the tragicomic blending that characterises the novel. However, beneath the irony, Farrell's text here also illustrates the extent of his research. Dunstaple's approach is a composite drawn from two sources; firstly, the *Medical Times and Gazette* of 1854 contained within Farrell's private papers, and secondly, a report entitled 'On the Treatment of the Epidemic of Cholera', published in 1855 by the Royal College of Physicians. Of these, the *Medical Times and Gazette* comprises articles and reports that detail the contemporary debates, treatments and publications on cholera, including case histories of outbreaks in 1832, in London in 1849 and in Newcastle and London again in 1853; all of which are mentioned the novel. Further details of Dunstaple's approach to treating cholera are drawn from an article entitled 'Statistics of the cases of the Cholera Epidemic 1853' by J. S. Pearse and Jeffrey A. Marston. Pearse and Marston state that the treatment of cholera should involve 'a warm bath, a blister to the spine and calomel'.[58] In a later chapter Dunstaple states that 'we must consider means of counter-irritating the disease . . . Hence a warm bath perhaps, and a blister to the spine.'[59]

Likewise, the similarity between Dunstaple's treatment for cholera with those contained in 'On the Treatment of the Epidemic of Cholera' again highlights how Farrell's research becomes a productive part of his critique, and not just the basis of it.[60] 'On the Treatment of the Epidemic of Cholera' outlines four main treatments: alterative, astringent, stimulant and cathartic, concluding that 'calomel and opium stand highest in success' when used as part of the astringent method.[61] Dunstaple echoes almost exactly the report's conclusion, reflecting that calomel 'was an admirable aperient for cleansing the upper intestinal canal of the morbid cholera poison'.[62] Instead of using calomel and opium in the astringent method, though, he combines elements of alterative and stimulant forms, using chloroform, turpentine and brandy along with mustard-coated flannels.[63] 'On the Treatment of the Epidemic of Cholera' concludes that the alterative and stimulant forms of treatment have a 36.2 per cent and 54 per cent rate of death respectively, meaning that they are nearly double and triple the death rate of the recommended treatment. Incidentally, Crane notes that there is a further postmodern intertext here, in that Dunstaple's treatments echo those used to treat Caroline Langford in John Masters' *Nightrunners of Bengal* (1951), illustrating a further enmeshing of the fictional and factual within his work.[64]

Farrell's point here is to illustrate the gulf between the intentions and the effects of British colonialism, medical expertise and scientific knowledge in the nineteenth century as a means of reflecting on his contemporary moment. By combining postmodern and postcolonial concerns within the format of the historical novel, Farrell is able to parody and satirise the history of British colonial India as a means of exploring the contemporary crisis of Englishness brought on by the end of Empire after Indian independence.[65] Medicine thus becomes Farrell's means of effacing key boundaries, either of past and present, fact and fiction, or Empire and after. By using medicine in this way, Farrell is able to turn the satire back to face his contemporary audience in pursuit of his consideration of 'how we, in our thriving modern world of the 1970s, hold our own ideas'.[66] In an extension of how McLeod states that Farrell takes his Victorian characters to the limits of their knowledge, Farrell attempts the same thing with his

contemporary audience. In highlighting the shortcomings of Dunstaple's expertise, and by extension the authority and legacy of Empire,
Farrell is inviting his readers to examine more closely the knowledge
they hold of Britain's imperial past and its potential effect on their
own beliefs in the present.

Bodies of evidence: Paul Scott's *The Raj Quartet*

Whereas Farrell's approach to medicine and disease is primarily an
attempt to dismantle the foundations of British imperial authority and the legacies of its history, Scott offers a more intimate,
yet similarly allegorical, engagement with ill health in his writing.
Following from E. M. Collingham's assertion of the corporeality of
British India, the representation of the body within Anglo-Indian
fiction is overtly prominent, especially in works, such as Scott's,
which attempt to represent a cross-section of colonial British society instead of the more focused narratives of Jhabvala or Farrell.[67]
Meeting Woolf's challenge to reflect the importance of physical
subjectivity, Scott's novels are often intensely embodied, devoting
long sections to the interiority of characters and their thoughts
and feelings on Anglo-Indian society and their place within it. As
part of this embodiment, his characters experience a host of major
and minor conditions ranging from the persistent discomforts of
heat, dicky bowels and recurrent fever through to the more serious
circumstances of Merrick's amputated arm and ensuing disability,
Meg Reid's cancer, Barbie Batchelor's pneumonia, Tony Bishop's
jaundice and the various physical or psychological conditions,
deaths or other maladies that befall the Smalley, Layton and Manners families. Such focus on the fallibility of British bodily resolve
is quite deliberate and affirms the critical tenor of Scott's writing;
beneath the adherence to the ideals of Empire that his characters
profess lies an attempt to consider human responses to illness: the
shock of bodily frailty, fear in the face of mortality and sometimes
unanticipated strength in moments of adversity. The centrality of
the body in Scott's work similarly emphasises how he explores the
range of anxieties of colonial society and Empire around, but not
exclusively related to, health, including illness and wellness, but
also more diverse subjects such as ageing, memory and sexuality.[68]
Scott's symbolic rendering of the imperial body in this manner suggests that it is not possible to appreciate the history of British India
in its entirety, but rather it must be examined piece by piece via

diseases and conditions, and these minutiae used in turn to illustrate the subjective, embodied experience of Empire.[69]

Scott's tendency towards bodily symbolism and metaphor is a pattern again set from the first volume in *The Raj Quartet*, *The Jewel in the Crown*, and, as Spurling makes clear, is an integral component of his writing.[70] Spurling records that Scott remarked of his career that '[w]hen I write about the India of the raj . . . I'm using it, always have used it, as a metaphor . . . India is my extended metaphor.'[71] Indeed, Scott's writing variously concerns itself with the political and metaphorical significance of bodies, female and male, throughout, as well as the various conditions that assail them. Guiding his focus is the notion of generational change, occurring not only in concert with the decline of imperial authority but also as representative of it; alongside his efforts to reveal the weakness inherent to the masculine elements of the Raj as embodied in Merrick and others, Scott also considers the influence brought to bear by the various Memsahibs in Pankot, particularly those of the Layton family, Mabel, Mildred, Susan and Sarah, and also Edwina Crane and Meg Reid. Here, like Daphne Manners, these women, their fates and their health are used variously by Scott to make associations between the well-being of individual physical bodies and that of the wider social body of the British Raj, with Scott using the expanse of his novel's scope to include characters from across the social spectrum and reflect their differences in age and class.[72]

Much of Scott's fiction makes direct links between the health or fortunes of individuals and imperial society, using historical context and illness to illustrate how the personal and the political are deeply entwined. In the elliptical structure of *The Jewel in the Crown*, Meg Reid's terminal cancer is described as part of the recollections of her husband, Brigadier Reid, addressed to the narrator engaged in piecing together the events of the Bibighar some years later. Reid explains the context of her illness, namely that Meg had been moved to a nursing home in Rawalpindi in 1942 just as he was appointed to his post in Mayapore to address the public disorder of the Quit India movement, and the political ramifications of the assaults on Edwina Crane and Daphne Manners. The Reids are also subject to the additional strain brought on by the news that their son Alan has become a prisoner of the Japanese in Burma. The year 1942 was the low point of Britain's Asian Empire, then under assault by Japanese forces, and when the security of colonial society in India felt truly threatened by the nationalist movement.[73] Reid, with evident symbolism, is the embattled servant of Empire in the midst of this turmoil, assailed by the rapidity of change within both his professional and personal spheres. Reid's experience corresponds to the chaotic disarray that is often a hallmark of the cancer narrative within medical humanities, and in which individuals and their worldview are disoriented by the sudden and often irreparable shift in their circumstances.[74]

Scott's use of Reid as an analogue to acknowledge the shifting fortunes of Empire in this period becomes apparent through Reid's account. Reid is given a pass to return to Rawalpindi, ostensibly to break the news of their son's capture to his wife; however, on arrival he realises that the visit is also to inform him of the severity of Meg's diagnosis. The senior medical officer informs him that Meg's prognosis is 'Perhaps six months. Perhaps three. Perhaps less. We shall operate but the end will be the same.'[75] Despite the offer of a post at Rawalpindi, Reid elects to return to Mayapore as planned and leave Meg to the attentions of the doctors. Reid's reaction is to meet the expected stoicism of his class and occupation but is also revealing of contemporary social attitudes towards terminal illnesses, and how Scott uses cancer to reflect and represent imperial decline. Scott illustrates the tension between a desire to take action on the one hand and the powerlessness of bearing witness to illness on the other, with Reid's frustration made apparent in his remark that 'Alan at least had the satisfaction of getting in a blow or two' against his enemy.[76] Instead, faced with the inability to bring any meaningful change to Meg's situation, Reid returns to Mayapore, where he is able to direct his energies towards quelling disorder. Although Reid's actions are successful, the irony inherent to Scott's conflation of Meg's cancer and the disturbances in Mayapore are evident. Recalling Wasson's arguments regarding the significance of telos within the medical narrative cited earlier, the same is true here of the post-imperial historical narrative; British efforts to halt terminal decline are ultimately in vain. Reid and the colonial authorities in Mayapore elect to operate and carry out their duties, just as the medical officer does on Meg's cancer; both do so with zeal and efficiency, buying time but essentially postponing the inevitable, and the reader knows the end will be the same regardless.

Reid's actions suggest how Scott's novel is subject to Susan Sontag's criticism regarding the use of illness as metaphor too. Unlike with other characters, Scott does not, in the case of Meg Reid, offer any insight into the subjective reality of her experience of cancer (she never has the opportunity to speak for herself), but rather uses her condition as a vehicle for narrative meaning-making around the end of Empire.[77] Such efforts, however, given Scott's intention at least in this first novel of the series, are not without significance. Michael Hanne and S. J. Hawken rightly call Sontag's 'absolutist demand' that we abandon the use of metaphor as a means of understanding or talking about illness and disease unrealistic, recognising that such repeated metaphors can remain deeply influential on social attitudes towards illness, and deeply revealing of them also.[78] Scott uses illness and Reid's reaction towards his wife's cancer to comment on the circumstances of British India at this point in the war, the relationship between colonial society and the individual's role within it, as a means of speaking to the beliefs and attitudes of his contemporary post-imperial readership. In the political context of Mayapore in 1942 and in light of Reid's military background, the desire to fight, evocative of the familiar 'warlike metaphors' associated with cancer, are a transposition of his worldview to the circumstances of illness.[79]

In so doing, Scott employs Reid's suppression of the Quit India disturbances as an extension of the medical metaphor found in Farrell, Jhabvala and his other contemporaries. His suggestion is to imply comparison between an individual body and a social body at war with themselves, either through the spread of malignancy affecting Meg or, in Reid's view, the 'cancer' of Indian nationalism in colonial society. To Reid, responsible for public order and representative of that small group of authorities composed of the military, the police and the Civil Service, anything outside of the boundaries of Anglo-Indian community is seen in terms of an invasion and is to be resisted, irrespective of the irony that it is the British who are the 'invaders' in a colonial context. Reid, Merrick of the police and Robin White of the Indian Civil Service (ICS) are charged essentially with maintaining the purity of the colonial social body, and so the language of the fight and the emplacement and defence of boundaries is the natural result of their social function, which in turn results in a reciprocity with the way in which they encounter and understand illness.[80] Reid and the colonial consciousness he represents view such medical encounters thus in the absolute terms of victory and defeat, a reflection of Mayapore society's rejection of Hari Kumar's own racial and cultural ambiguity as well as their typical coldness towards outsiders more generally. However, the actions of Reid, Merrick and the British authorities are in effect a cancer of their own, and the resentment they cause within the Indian community of Mayapore eats away at the authority of Empire from within.[81] Scott's overarching suggestion is that the riots themselves are a manifestation of the deeper underlying illness of colonialism; they are the surface symptoms treated with tremendous energy and solemn recognition of incumbent duty by Reid and the others, but their root causes cannot be cured.

As *The Raj Quartet* continues, it is apparent that Scott's engagement with medicine and illness in his fiction develops in both complexity and nuance. In the *Quartet*'s final novel, *A Division of the Spoils*, Scott finds an effective means of coupling his broad use of metaphor with greater attention to the detail of human experience of illness. It is significant too that such progression occurs in relation to a condition far less outwardly dramatic than that of Meg Reid's cancer in *The Jewel in the Crown*, instead focusing on the privations of amoebic dysentery or amoebiasis, the effects of which take place on a far more quotidian scale and which Scott had experienced first-hand as a result of his own Indian service.[82] As noted above, stomach and bowel complaints are one of a number of recurrent conditions recorded in the travelogues and diaries produced throughout the heyday of British India, and most authors include advice or recommend remedies to be tried if (or, more likely, when) they strike. Some complaints were evidently acute and related to improperly stored or cooked food, but others could linger for decades after they were contracted – such as in Scott's case – with tangible effects on general health, both mental and physical.

As a consequence, amoebiasis occupies a position of socio-medical contradiction and tension in so much as it is common, but not necessarily an ailment that can be acknowledged openly. Returning to Boyd's implied hierarchy of ill health and disease, too, amoebiasis is pathologised and in some cases could be a deeply grave condition. However, whilst also chronic, amoebiasis does not necessarily have the same terminal outcome as cancer, tuberculosis or cholera did throughout the history of Empire, despite being as prevalent in nature.[83] Moreover, it lacks the same cultural connotations of noble suffering found in other diseases of Empire. Amoebiasis is widespread, if not ubiquitous; however, given the nature of its effects and symptoms, it is remarked upon as a cause of social embarrassment and something that an individual would wish to keep private. As always with debilitating conditions in India, there is the additional anxiety of the British appearing weak or incapacitated in front of Indians, either professionally or in public.[84] Rushdie recognised the *lèse-majesté* of a condition like amoebiasis and included it in his early drafts of *Midnight's Children* in relation to the British withdrawal from India in 1947. Rushdie writes of how Partition had served to diminish the British colonists, and that the post-war lack of stomach for Empire had reduced them to retreat aboard their boats and back to England, 'spraying the fish of two oceans with liquescent brown proof of their fall'.[85]

Scott's main engagement with amoebiasis occurs in the first part of *A Division of the Spoils*, when the newly arrived protagonist, Guy Perron, meets with his commanding officer, Leonard Purvis, on arrival in Bombay. Invited to Purvis' apartment for drinks and to be briefed on his new duties, Perron observes Purvis' behaviour and deduces his illness immediately: 'Purvis caught his breath, placed one hand on the left side of his abdomen and then slowly breathed out. Inflammation of the colon, Perron decided. Amoebic in origin, almost certainly.'[86] Purvis is revealed to be taking pills recommended by an acquaintance 'when I first arrived and she saw I'd already got the trots. They're supposed to cement you up. Sometimes they do. Sometimes they don't.'[87] As this first part of the narrative develops, Purvis' condition, exacerbated by an evident dependency on alcohol and a deep unhappiness with India and his posting there, grows progressively worse, eventually leading to his suicide.[88]

Although the episode is a minor one in context of *The Raj Quartet*'s wider plot, Purvis and amoebiasis nonetheless serve various functions. Within the narrative, they induct Perron to the realities of Anglo-Indian society, its absurdities and its formalities, and facilitate his meeting with the Laytons and Merrick, which develops into the last act of the series. Beyond the diegesis of the novel, Purvis and Perron's encounters with amoebiasis suggest that Scott's writing corresponds to what Angela Woods and Anne Whitehead call 'first wave' narrative medicine, the transmission of illness experience in prose, as well as a means of advancing his more critical views of colonialism.[89] Although the origins of such medical humanities methodologies lie in non-fiction, they are also productive when used to read a text informed by an author's personal experience. By weaving his own experience of amoebiasis into *The Raj Quartet*, Scott is able to bring some measure of order to his illness through narrative and writing and thus reflect on its meaning, as well as continuing his use of metaphor to criticise Empire. Purvis allows Scott to continue the kind of broad approach to illness within the narrative that he enacts with the Reids, here showing how the service of Empire is not the glorious endeavour of popular myth but rather could be profoundly isolating and miserable, but also enables him to bring that approach to a far more quotidian, banal, and more human level. Purvis is a pathetic character and the reader is invited to feel pity for this man who, outmanoeuvred by his rivals in Whitehall, is effectively banished to India, where he grows ever more physically and mentally ill. As Perron reflects, '[a]t home Purvis might well have been . . . the most mild-mannered and considerate of men'; however, in the context of Empire he is rendered tragic and embittered by his experience of suffering seemingly for no discernible benefit.[90]

As their conversation continues, it becomes apparent that Scott configures the two characters into a divided representation of his own experience in India. Critics such as Spurling and Morey have noted that Perron is Scott's fictional analogue of himself; however, it is notable that Scott assigns both of his connected conditions, amoebiasis and alcoholism, as well as his mental breakdown, to the character of Purvis, who is then described by Perron through the focalised narration of *A Division of the Spoils*.[91] Much like the overarching project of his writing career, that of distilling the breadth and expanse of the Raj into fiction, Scott attempts to achieve something similar here through a process of two removes: the initial act of representing illness in fiction, and then the further separation of illness from the fictional self to enable reflection.[92] Again, the principles of first-wave medical humanities and narrative medicine are visible in Scott's efforts to achieve this separation, with prose fiction offering Scott the means to isolate and consider his behaviour, and that of illness more generally, with sufficient critical distance. Observing Purvis, Perron reflects that despite:

> an almost valetudinarian attention to the medicinal needs of his body . . . [he] had even so not been free of the shortness of temper that was one of the side-effects of an overworked and easily discouraged digestive system. The insight this had given him into the possibly important part played in Anglo-Indian history by an incipient, intermittent, or chronic diarrhoea in the bowels of the raj was one of the few definite academic advantages he felt he had gained by coming to India.[93]

Scott's point is to assert the significance of health and medicine in understanding the history of Empire and the actions of its various figures. Again, he suggests how the seemingly trivial can play a part of great and long-lasting significance within the life of an individual and those around them.[94] Indeed, Perron's ethnographic insight into the effects of amoebiasis throughout history is a transposition of Scott's own auto-ethnography, expressed in his contribution to Anglo-Indian literature. Moreover, it suggests Scott's belief in the interconnectedness of physical and mental health. Amoebiasis and the views of these characters become Scott's means of considering how illness cuts across the social dichotomy of body and mind and how medicine is an inherent legacy of Empire.

Later in the same novel, Scott considers further how illness of the body affects the mentality of the colonial Briton through a conversation between Captain Nigel Rowan of the ICS and Dmitri Bronowsky, wazir to the Nawab of Mirat. Bronowsky mentions how the Nawab's court physician believes that illness has been the motivating factor behind British rule, and as soon as 'medical science finds a way of rendering the English bloodstream and the English bowel system immune to the attacks of Indian microbes and amoeba, then the English will all perk up, look around and wonder what they are doing out here'.[95] By using this condition as his lens, Scott suggests that the physical events and experience of India and colonialism cannot be separated from their effects on the mind, and the British understanding of its colonial past in the contemporary present are likewise bound up together. Rather than limited to their corporeal or memorial forms, the legacies of Empire, like amoebiasis, affect body and soul, and with a sense of reciprocity and exchange. Instead of binary divisions, Scott's writing asserts, they must be considered as a whole, almost as an extension of Gestalt theory, in order to be sufficiently treated in the post-imperial present.

As if to underline the significance of bodily metaphor as a means of framing *The Raj Quartet* and addressing this connection of past and present through illness and medicine, Scott returns to the series' beginning in order to bring the story to a close. Late in *A Division of the Spoils*, Perron attempts to find Harry Kumar after he learns of his release from prison. Though Perron fails to meet with him, the novel implies that Kumar has returned to journalism and is now writing for the *Ranpur Gazette* under the pen name Philoctetes. Philoctetes, as Perron later discovers, refers to the wounded archer mentioned in the *Iliad* who, due to the suppurating stench from his wound, was abandoned on Lemnos.[96] The use of Philoctetes in this fashion is again significant both within the diegetic world of the narrative and in terms of reading the legacy of Empire from the time in which Scott is writing. In the narrative, Kumar selects the name as a means of acknowledging the injustice and actual bodily harm done to him by colonial authority; within the saga of the Manners and Layton families, who are leaving India convinced of the goodness of their intent, Kumar remains the reminder of their complicity and guilt in Merrick's abuse of power, his presence the unhealed wound in their community. Symbolically, Scott's use of Philoctetes signifies the psychic wound of racial injustice that remains associated with the history and legacy of Empire and the supposedly beneficent ending of the Raj. Kumar's treatment is representative of the widespread injustices done to members of the Indian National Congress, possessing evident resonance with notions of *habeas corpus*, suspended during wartime under the Defence of India Act 1939 in favour of the preventative detention that effects and maintains Kumar's imprisonment, as well as an acknowledgement of the body as a repository of memory and site of traumatic remembrance in relation to Partition.[97] Kumar, like Purvis, signifies the violent, destructive legacies of Empire both great and small, either in its quotidian, individual sense or in their greater, historical form.

Empire state of mind: Ruth Prawer Jhabvala and psychological illness

As Scott's writing on amoebiasis suggests, understanding the effects of illness, and in turn the legacies of the British relationship to India expressed in these novels, cannot be confined to the body alone. Close attention must be paid to the representation of psychological health and the nuanced relationship between the body and the mind, represented in historical fictions of Empire alongside that of bodily illness. Such attention is fitting given that concern for the effects of colonial service on psychological health were constant throughout the life of the Raj. As evinced by the extent of correspondence between the India Office in London and authorities in India regarding individual cases, or the various reports commissioned by the Indian Medical Service and its Sanitary Commissioners, colonial service could place considerable strain on individuals who were overworked or who were already ill – just as Scott reflects in his characterisation of Purvis in *A Division of the Spoils*, or as illustrated in the work of Kipling. Memoirs and personal accounts again corroborate the potential dangers of isolated postings where, compounded by other issues such as physical sickness or alcohol dependency, British personnel might experience short- or long-term difficulty with what would now be termed their mental health.[98] Though it could be presumed that struggles with mental well-being might bring stigma or shame within close-knit colonial society, records suggest that such difficulties were seen as largely part and parcel of colonial life, especially when linked to physical ailments such as sunstroke, heat apoplexy or exposure, and as much a perennial threat of the subcontinent as cholera or malaria. As a consequence, care for those affected by psychological disorders, both temporary and long-term, was a provision of the colonial government across each of the Indian presidencies, and a recognition that the debilitating effects of Indian service were not limited to the body alone.[99]

In reflection of this history, the literary representation of illness and medicine in historical fiction produced after Empire extends to psychological health and treatment. Mental health becomes another long-lasting legacy of Empire and a potent means of examining the mindset and psyche of post-imperial Britain. Jhabvala's *Heat and Dust* is particularly interested in the psychological interiority of its characters and the legacy of emotional feeling associated with Empire. For such a deceptively slight novel – compared to Scott's output, at any rate – *Heat and Dust* is ambitious in its scope, and often as beguiling in its depth of detail and the range of its themes. Like Scott, the narrative tells two stories at once: the first takes place in 1920s Satipur and relates how Olivia, an Englishwoman married to a civil servant, begins a relationship with the local Nawab, supposedly in order to escape from the boredom of her marriage and the stifling nature of Anglo-Indian society. The second narrative, told in parallel to the first, is set in the contemporary present and focuses on an unnamed narrator (revealed to be Olivia's step-granddaughter) who retraces Olivia's steps and travels to India. Jhabvala's narratives are linked by the fact that both Olivia and the unnamed narrator fall pregnant, but where Olivia aborts her pregnancy and lives in exile in India, the unnamed narrator decides to keep her child and ends the novel on the verge of giving birth, making the journey to the remote house in which Olivia once lived.

Although its evocation of the colonial romance genre might suggest a surface degree of superficiality, to consider the novel in these terms alone overlooks its more ironically playful elements as well as its sincere meditations on postcoloniality. Ralph J. Crane has argued that Jhabvala's novel sits comfortably within postmodernism, containing numerous examples of its defining elements such as intertextuality, self-reflexivity, textual production and non-linear narrative.[100] Beyond its intertextuality, Luke Strongman and Justin D. Edwards argue for Jhabvala's work to be read in direct dialogue with Forster and, moreover, suggest that it goes as far as to fictionalise him (as the Nawab's sickly and highly strung secretary, Harry) directly within the narrative.[101] As such, in terms of its form and themes, Jhabvala's novel is in many ways a bridge between Farrell's *The Siege of Krishnapur* and Scott's *The Raj Quartet*, in so much as it offers a similarly critical reworking of a popular format and engagement with the literary middlebrow as Farrell, with the same temporal juxtaposition offered by Scott. Of greater significance for an assessment of Jhabvala's relationship to illness and the 'spiritual change it brings', though, is the manner through which Jhabvala presents the complexity of Olivia's and the narrator's shifting interiorities. Whilst the effects of Scott's approach to illness are typically embodied and Farrell's more philosophical, Jhabvala shows them as psychological in nature and based around focus on her characters' change in identities and self-hood as a result of illness and their Indian experiences. Rather than the banality suggested by her characterisation as a 'beautiful, spoiled and bored' housewife, Olivia's actions are prompted by a range of psychological stimuli, including allusions to depression and stress and Jhabvala's recurrent theme of sexual self-awakening.[102] It is significant too that Jhabvala, as the major female figure in the group of writers this book explores, chooses to write about the female experience of India with a focus on mental health, marking a departure from the typically male-dominated nature of colonial fiction. Jhabvala's personal experiences in Indian society of the 1950s and 60s, as well as the broader context of contemporary feminism, are relevant here, with Ralph J. Crane observing how Jhabvala's novels regularly feature idealistic women who feel oppressed by their experience of India.[103] As such, the novel and Jhabvala's approach is concerned with the importance of interiority, not just as a means of exploring the consciousness of Britons under and after Empire (Jhabvala satirises the hippie-esque 'finding yourself' motivation of the European in India throughout her novels too), but rather as a way of exploring their mental processes and how they are linked to the variable state of their psychological and bodily health.

Given the generic fluidity of *Heat and Dust* that comes as a result of Jhabvala's postmodernism, examining how her approach to psychological instability is influenced by other forms of popular genre fiction is equally revealing of her intent. In Samantha Walton's analysis of Golden Age detective fiction, she calls attention to the genre's use of insanity as part of a narrative of detection and resolution. Drawing on the work of Alison Light, who calls detective fiction a 'literature of convalescence', Walton argues that 'the certainty of a resolution to a problem' in the turbulent circumstances of post-war Britain had therapeutic advantages for readers and authors alike.[104] Though of course there is a contextual difference between the circumstances of British society after the First World War and those of the end of Empire, the notion of how a literary genre might respond to the shared feeling of 'tremendous social upheaval' that

Walton identifies remains applicable, given the rapidity and arguably more politically destabilising experience of decolonisation. The
further similarities between how Jhabvala's narrator is on a mission
of detection to uncover the truth of Olivia's life and what became of
her, alongside other hallmarks of detective fiction such as its cast of
upper-class or privileged characters, the gradual revealing of secrets
and the 1920s setting, further emphasise such a connection. Walton's
suggestion of how insanity is used to affirm but also critique the
social structures in place within a novel's diegesis is also relevant to
Jhabvala's efforts in *Heat and Dust*.[105] Jhabvala presents us with resolution, albeit a deferred one enjoyed by the narrator and not Olivia,
but is similarly clear on how the social strictures of colonial life, marriage and paternalistic society produce the unhealthy circumstances
responsible for mental illness.

　　Illness is present throughout Jhabvala's novel in various physical
and psychological forms. Almost immediately on her arrival in India,
the narrator is told how the Europeans in India are all 'a derelict
lot . . . You see the state they're in. They're all sick, some of them
dying,' and the novel addresses a general sense of illness through particular conditions such as jaundice, ringworm or dysentery, or in its
various subplots, such as Harry's mother, slowly dying of an unspecified disease back in England, or Leelavati, the homeless woman
that the narrator attempts to help without success.[106] From the very
beginning of Olivia's parallel storyline, too, she is confronted with
ill health in the form of Mrs Saunders, wife of the local medical
superintendent, who is recovering from the loss of her infant child
and the subsequent effects of the experience on her mental health.
Olivia, newly arrived in Satipur at this point in the narrative and
unused to the realities of illness, reacts with some disquiet, noting
that she 'was by no means a snob, but she *was* aesthetic and the
details Mrs Saunders gave about her illness were not'.[107] Jhabvala
also suggests how the perception of illness is influenced by the social
divisions present within the Anglo-Indian community, and, crucially,
the manner through which the experience of illness is shared; in conversation with two of the other wives on the station, Olivia is told
that the Nawab's wife does not live with him because 'She is not very
well . . . mentally.'[108] Again, the novel's interest in truth and mystery,
either around the events of Olivia's narrative, her relationship with
the Nawab, or in the veracity of certain illnesses, is apparent in the
way such information is obliquely conveyed. However, these mentions also serve to illustrate how mental health is treated within the
context of colonial society to which Olivia belongs, where it is often

dismissed either physically or figuratively. Later in the novel, when their apparent inability to conceive begins to strain her marriage to Douglas, already tense as a result of her secret relationship with the Nawab, Olivia grows irritable, prone to mood swings and occasional weeping; rather than confront the evident issues in their relationship, Douglas' response is to blame the heat.[109]

Jhabvala's concerted engagement with psychological illness in the novel, however, focuses on the narrator's encounters with Ritu, the wife of Inder Lal, her landlord in Sitapur. In her conversations with Lal, the narrator learns that Ritu's intense homesickness when she and Lal were first married greatly affected her health in general, and notes that '[T]here is something frail, *weak*, about her . . . I have the impression that her mind, or do I mean her will, is not strong either, that she is the sort of person that would give way quickly.'[110] During the narrator's stay with the Lals, Ritu's condition grows to the point where she experiences nightmares and screaming fits in her sleep and has to be forcibly confined. Concerned by Ritu's worsening state, the narrator remarks:

> But I can't get used to the screams. I kept telling Chid 'But she ought to have treatment.'
> One day he said 'She's going to have treatment today.'
> 'What sort?' I asked.
> 'One of their people is coming to do it.'
> That day the screams broke out again, but in an entirely different way. Now they were bloodcurdling as of an animal in intense physical pain. Even the neighbours in the courtyard stopped to listen. Chid remained calm: 'It's her treatment,' he said. He went on to explain that she might be possessed by an evil spirit which had to be driven out by applying a red-hot iron to various part of her body, such as her arms or the soles of her feet.[111]

Jhabvala's representation of Ritu is significant for what it suggests about mental health in an Indian context, and how it relates to the physical illnesses and conditions seen elsewhere in the novel and wider genre. As part of her wider theme of cultural comparison between Europe and India, Jhabvala suggests a divide between the way in which both societies conceptualise and treat mental health. Alongside the reaction to other physical conditions, the community's disinterest in Ritu reinforces Jhabvala's points regarding the commonplace nature of illness in India (made through Leelavati) and the general indifference with which it is often met. Alongside the spiritual diagnosis of her condition, Ritu's treatment is likewise noteworthy within Jhabvala's approach to a medical and social context in which women's suffering is diminished or overlooked. Jhabvala's description of Ritu's response to treatment attests to Elaine Scarry's analysis of the human body in pain and the capacity illness has to narrow the division between the human and the animal, further illustrating how approaches from the medical humanities can be used productively to read fictional texts.[112] Scarry's argument that pain is a destruction of language, that it reduces the individual to a pre-linguistic state in which biological existence is reaffirmed, finds expression here in Ritu, whose screams are the only utterance she makes in the course of the narrative. Such characterisation conforms to the gendered dynamics of mental health within literature and society, illustrating how the passive female body is the site of further trauma once diagnosed.[113] Ritu effectively suffers twice; once as a result of her condition, and again as a result of her 'treatment'. The commonplace nature of such suffering is further emphasised by Chid's remark that 'he has been in India long enough to have got used to everything'.[114]

The lack of available care, as well as the lack of interest given the widespread ubiquity of sickness, exacerbates the perceived divide between Indian and Western attitudes towards medicine and health suggested throughout the novel. In her continued conversations with Inder Lal, the narrator suggests Ritu would benefit from psychiatric treatment, explaining it as a 'sort of science of the mind'.[115] Lal's reaction, the 'wistful' regarding of anything scientific as representative of progress and therefore positive, is again couched in terms of the imperial teleology and the benefits of Empire.[116] However, despite his admiration, Lal does not elect to (or cannot afford to) provide Ritu with this treatment. Instead, Ritu is again confined and then latterly sent on pilgrimage, reminiscent of how the Nawab's wife is treated, and serving to reinforce Jhabvala's suggestion that mental illness in India is subject to dismissal or disavowal. Ritu's spiritual exile is thus a resolution to the problem of her insanity, but illustrates how social attitudes produce and contribute to her illness at the same time. Indeed, Ritu's alienation, removal and effective displacement by the narrator recalls Franz Fanon's analysis of the link between the effects of colonialism and madness, and the violence that accompanies it.[117] Ritu is figuratively and literally forced from the narrative by the presence of the (white) narrator, who, despite her concern for Ritu's welfare, then begins a relationship with Inder Lal. Again, like Farrell's characterisation of Indian characters, the episode conjures an uncomfortable current of neo-colonialism in Jhabvala's otherwise nuanced novel.

Just as she suggests with the discrepancy between Western and Indian medicine and the human and the animal, a great deal of Jhabvala's novel appears to be concerned with splits, divisions and binaries, either those that underpin the novel thematically as part of its parallel narrative structure, or those of direct oppositions within each of the storylines themselves. For instance, the novel invites the reader to consider the synchronic metaphorical relationships between Olivia and the narrator, the Nawab and Inder Lal, Harry and Chid, and the Nawab's wife and Ritu. Each character acts almost as a temporal analogue to the other across the novel's fifty-year divide, serving as a counterpart to illustrate the similarity between the past and the present in terms of human nature and human relationships, but also suggesting the capacity for change and growth over time and the possibility of a different outcome the second time around. Such inclusions bring Jhabvala into the same postmodern orbit as Farrell, in terms of her efforts to replay the intimate history of Empire if not that of its grand narrative, as well as illustrate the difference between imperial and post-imperial Anglo-Indian relations in answer to Forster.

However, they also act as Jhabvala's sincere attempt at considering those other divisions which structure social interaction, identity and understandings of health and well-being through her writing. Jhabvala's corporeal representation of Ritu's mental illness highlights the division between mind and body as another arbitrary line, just as the novel does between that of Europeans and Indians or past and present. In the same way as the separation of her two narrative time periods collapses as the novel progresses, so does the division between physical and psychological health. However, this is not in the pathological sense of Scott's illustration of how amoebiasis affects the mind, but rather an acknowledgement of a shared validity and a holism to bodily and mental conditions. Rather than reading these divisions and binaries as split across the separate time periods, then, Jhabvala's parallels are to emphasise instead their harmony and the shared humanity of individuals separated by nationality, ethnicity, time or sickness and health. Such sentiments are echoed by Scott and Farrell, both of whom include characters that cast doubt on the divide between the physical and the psychological. Barbie Batchelor from Scott's *The Towers of Silence* (1971) muses that 'people don't only die because of diseases you know', whilst Farrell's McNab spends much of *The Hill Station* (1981) hovering at the fringes of modern psychiatry, considering that illness and wellness are determined by a combination of moral, psychological and physical factors in another of Farrell's deliberate anachronisms.[118]

Heat and Dust thus reveals how Jhabvala's approach to the representation of physical and mental health complements that of Farrell and Scott. Though their terms may differ depending on their individual interests and critical intent, what unites them is the same identification of medicine and health's applicability and utility in representing the subjective experience of Empire through fiction, and a means of considering its long-standing legacies into the contemporary present. As well as suggesting that a more holistic critical and literary understanding of illness and its effects is at work in these texts, the analysis here illustrates that to represent the arbitrariness of illness and wellness, of physical and mental health, Farrell, Scott and Jhabvala use medicine as a means of effacing other key boundaries, either of past and present, fact and fiction, or Empire and after, as part of a shared, concerted critique of their contemporary postcolonial moment. For each of these authors, medicine thus provides narrative tension and change, a degree of realism with regard to reflection of the Anglo-Indian colonial experience, and an incisive means of commentary on the post-imperial world. In their use of embodiment, Farrell, Scott and Jhabvala draw together the personal and political with regard to Empire, illustrating the critical function of medical humanities alongside that of postmodernism and their ability to return the mythologised, idealised grand narrative of Empire to a more human scale.

Notes

1. Scott, *SO*, 70.
2. See Woolf, *On Being Ill*. Woolf's opening line is often held up as a cornerstone for the medical humanities themselves.
3. Hilary Mantel views Woolf's claims as 'schoolgirl piffle' that overlook the enormous vocabulary of illness extant for centuries. Mantel, *Ink in the Blood*, 6.
4. See Woolf, *Mrs Dalloway*. Woolf's novel is filled with references to Empire, embodied in Peter and his Indian affair, but also captured in the variety of wares offered in the Army and Navy store visited by Elizabeth and Miss Kilman.
5. See Chapter 3.
6. After the end of Warren Hastings' tenure and 'Nabobism', colonial Britons greatly re-entrenched their taste for the trappings of home, especially in cuisine, architecture and diet; see James, *Raj*, 166.
7. Goodman, 'Lady Amateurs and Gentleman Professionals'.

8. See Howell, *Malaria and Victorian Fictions of Empire*, in which she addresses how various conditions are represented in the work of Henry James, Charles Dickens, H. Rider Haggard and Olive Schreiner.
9. Klaver, 'Domesticity under siege', 28.
10. Perhaps the most explicitly self-reflexive example of this is in the work of G. M. Fraser and his *Flashman* series, which places its titular character (a fictional bully from *Tom Brown's Schooldays*, written by Thomas Hughes and published in 1857) at nearly every major imperial crisis, intrigue and conflict of the late nineteenth century.
11. Gilmour, *The Ruling Caste*, xiv–xv.
12. Carbajal, *Compromise and Resistance*, 14–16. Ralph J. Crane argues Forster's work is a 'prime text', stating that 'all writers, European and Indian, who write about British India do so in the shadow of Forster'; Crane, *Jhabvala*, 64.
13. Luke Strongman notes the influence of *A Passage to India* on Jhabvala, and Ralph J. Crane her connection to modernism and postmodernism through adoption of intertextuality, setting the past sections in 1923, and at the zenith of high modernism; Strongman, *The Booker Prize*, 15; Crane, *Inventing India*, 87–8. In Farrell's drafts of *The Siege of Krishnapur* (1973) the final sentences of the book focus on Fleury 'at the very end of his life, in 1910', whereas the published version ends with the Collector's thoughts in 1880: a point just before the New Imperialism of the 'Scramble for Africa', in which all the pretence of his kindly, paternal view of Empire was stripped away. The 1910 setting places the novel in dialogue with modernism as well as imperialism, referencing that significant year in which, for Woolf, all of human nature, religion, conduct, politics and literature changed. See Farrell (Trinity), Box 9142: Index cards, notes and photocopies, n.p.
14. Justin Edwards asserts that Jhabvala's *Heat and Dust* rewrites Forster's own journey, as well as playing with those of his characters. Edwards, *Postcolonial Literature*, 57.
15. Dean, 'An Insight Job', 12.
16. Of Scott, Peter Morey argues that *Jewel in the Crown* is essentially mediated by a historian's consciousness and is an attempt at reconstruction both on a narrative level, where it tries to fathom the events of the Bibighar (the rape of Daphne Manners and not the massacre of 1857, though the allusion is deliberate) and the Quit India Riots, and a meta level, where Scott tries to reconstruct British India in fiction in 1965; Morey, *Fictions of India*, 141–2. Crane, meanwhile, sees *Heat and Dust* in terms of its intertextuality, playing games with genre and authenticity; Crane, *Inventing India*, 87.
17. Wasson, 'Before narrative', 106–12.
18. Boyd, 'Disease, Illness, Sickness, Health, Healing and Wholeness', 10.

19. Sexually transmitted infections were a particular concern of colonial authorities throughout the existence of the Raj; see Levine, *Prostitution, Race and Politics*, 37.
20. See Hardy, *Health and Medicine in Britain Since 1860*. For a full timeline of key developments within the medical humanities see Bates et al., *Medicine, Health and the Arts*, 281–4.
21. Simpson, *Migrant Architects*, 64.
22. Raghuram, 'Thinking UK's medical labour market transnationally', 5.
23. Simpson, *Migrant Architects*, 9. Such experiences find expression in a range of modern cultural contexts, from Sandhya Suri's *I is for India* (2007) to the arrival of Commonwealth nurses within the cosy community of BBC's *Call the Midwife* (2012–present).
24. Bates et al., *Medicine, Health and the Arts*, 281–2.
25. See Foucault, *The Birth of the Clinic*. This process would continue through texts such as Sontag's *Illness as Metaphor* (1978), Scarry's *The Body in Pain* (1985) and Charon's *Narrative Medicine* (2006).
26. Berger credited an Indian friend, Victor Anant, with the inspiration behind the book. Francis, 'John Berger's A Fortunate Man: a masterpiece of witness'. Berger would win the Booker for his postmodern work *G.* (1972).
27. Meyers, *Disease and the Novel*, 4–5. In another link between the postmodernists and their modernist forbears, the myth of the Fisher King that structures Eliot's *The Waste Land* (1922) is a clear example of the long-standing associations between the health of a nation and its representative.
28. Connor, *The English Novel in History*, 44.
29. See Frank, *The Wounded Storyteller*.
30. See Greacen's *J. G. Farrell: The Making of a Writer* for further detail on Farrell's early life.
31. McLeod, *J. G. Farrell*, 5.
32. Scott references his own condition at various points in *The Raj Quartet*, such as in *The Day of the Scorpion* (1968) with the character of James Layton, Colonel John Layton's father, who died 'unexpectedly in 1917 after a short illness caused by an abscess on the liver – the end result of a long-standing amoebic infection which had never been properly diagnosed or treated'. Scott, *TDotS*, 79.
33. Crane, *Jhabvala*, 7.
34. Chakravarty, *Indian Mutiny and the British Imagination*, 4–5.
35. Dean, 'An Insight Job', 11.
36. Morey, *Fictions of India*, 110.
37. Francis B. Singh notes the generally poor presentation of Indians in the novel and as such does not categorise Farrell as postcolonial; Singh, 'Progress and History', 23–9.
38. Like Singh, McLeod calls attention to the uneasy implications of the scene in which Fleury fights an unnamed sepoy towards the end of the

novel. After much slapstick and farce, Fleury kills him with a fifteen-barrelled gun which obliterates his top half; McLeod suggests that the audience reaction is not horror as it should be, but relief. McLeod, *J. G. Farrell*, 66.

39. Crane and Livett, *Troubled Pleasures*, 99.
40. Tom Nairn asserts that rapid decolonisation, economic 'stagflation' and the social and political conflict that characterised the 1970s were representative of a society undergoing a 'slow-motion landslide' of disintegration; Nairn, *The Break-Up of Britain*, 62. Farrell's first instalment of the Empire Trilogy is of course called *Troubles*, a title with a particular relevance and resonance in the 1970s. Intending to continue this trend, *The Siege of Krishnapur* was originally entitled 'Difficulties'; see Johnson, 'Ghosts of Irish Famine', 275–92.
41. Bart Moore-Gilbert has argued that British fiction of the period gives 'the impression of a society on the verge of social disintegration, or civil war', a statement that seems particularly applicable to Farrell, whose novels of the period all feature episodes of violent unrest and upheaval. Moore-Gilbert, *Cultural Closure*, 152.
42. For an overview of the 'civilising mission' in the early nineteenth century see Harrison, *Climates and Constitutions*, 154.
43. In his 1973 interview with Malcolm Dean, Farrell expressed how he 'had thought of constructing the novel entirely from contemporary nineteenth-century insights and observations'; Dean, 'An Insight Job', 11.
44. McLeod, *J. G. Farrell*, 61. Chief among the accounts Farrell employs are those of the Reverend Henry S. Polehampton and Maria Germon, wife of an Army officer, both present during the Siege of Lucknow, and the testimony of Mark Thornhill, Company Collector at Muttra. See Farrell, *SoK*, 314. Germon and her husband both survived Lucknow. Polehampton's journal states that he succumbed to 'fever' in July 1857, though it is strongly implied by the editors of his diaries that it was most likely cholera that killed him, a fact later corroborated by G. W. Forrest in *A History of the Indian Mutiny*.
45. Farrell, *THS*, 197.
46. Hartveit, 'Imprint', 458.
47. Ibid. 452. Hartveit's analysis is based on the work of metahistorian Hayden White and he views Farrell's decision to construct fiction from historical detail as a matter of ordering material in a different way, thereby equating the novelist and historian as two sides of a narrative coin.
48. McLeod, *J. G. Farrell*, 37.
49. Crane and Livett, *Troubled Pleasures*, 87. Crane and Livett relate interdiscursivity to the novel's penultimate chapter, in which the relief force arrives at Krishnapur and the survivors are led away from the compound, comparing Farrell's portrait with the real-life painting 'The

Relief of Lucknow' (1859) by Thomas Jones Barker. The quotation in this section's heading ('Fair skeletons!') is indicative of Farrell's constant appreciation of the line between life and death; Farrell, *THS*, 42.
50. Farrell, *SoK*, 38.
51. Ibid. 127.
52. Farrell's manuscripts contain various scenes removed from the final version, including those where erysipelas convinces the Collector that he is a tiger, and where he and Fleury discuss anti-masturbation pills in a catalogue from the Great Exhibition. Farrell (Trinity), Box 9139: *The Siege of Krishnapur*, agent's copy, 364–7.
53. Farrell also uses phrenology as a means through which to satirise imperial scientific knowledge, alongside that of medical expertise. See Goodman, 'A Great Beneficial Disease', 141–56.
54. For more information on the history of cholera, see Harrison, *Climates and Constitutions*; Hamlin, *Cholera: The Biography*; and Gilbert, *Cholera and Nation*.
55. Farrell (Trinity), Box 9142: Index cards, notes and photocopies, 1–98.
56. For further analysis of the representation of cholera in nineteenth- and twentieth-century fiction see Gilbert, *Cholera and Nation*, and Goodman, 'Literature and Disease'.
57. Farrell, *SoK*, 165–6.
58. *Medical Times and Gazette*, 130.
59. Farrell, *SoK*, 254.
60. Dunstaple later mentions the report by 'Dr. Baly' directly; it is also referenced in the article by Paris et al. and reproduced in the *Medical Gazette* of 1854 referred to in Farrell's papers.
61. Paris et al., 'On the Treatment of the Epidemic of Cholera', n.p.
62. Farrell, *SoK*, 166.
63. Ibid. 166.
64. Crane, *Inventing India*, 42–3.
65. Crane and Livett, *Troubled Pleasures*, 99.
66. Dean, 'An Insight Job', 12.
67. As noted in Chapter 4, although Hari Kumar and the Kasim family are the subject of Scott's focus, he restricts his narrative viewpoint largely to that of the white British community. Such a decision prompted Rushdie's justifiable critique of Scott in 'Outside the Whale' (1984) with regard to the marginalisation of Indian characters within their own history; however, at the same time, it is a logical choice for a series of novels that seek primarily to represent and criticise the shortcomings of British actions in the last decades of the Raj.
68. The body is central to Scott's overarching narrative, the rape of Daphne Manners in the Bibighar Gardens. As well as the body acting as the site of Daphne's violation and suffering, of evidence obtained through medical examination, and as a locus of punishment in terms of the torture and imprisonment Merrick and the British inflict on Hari Kumar,

it is also a key metaphor for the racialised anxieties of the waning Empire. In *Natives: Race and Class in the Ruins of Empire* (2018), Akala argues that the reduction of non-white bodies to sexual organs alone is a recurrent historical hallmark of racial dehumanisation, citing examples from the Hottentot Venus through to Linford Christie. Rushdie also argues that Merrick's repressed homosexuality is another unsophisticated allusion to sexual dysfunction as Empire metaphor on Scott's part; see Rushdie, 'Outside the Whale'.

69. It is significant that of the writers examined here, nearly all take a serial approach to India; Masters' Savage family saga takes place over two centuries, Farrell writes nearly four novels about Empire, whilst Jhabvala repeatedly returns to colonial and postcolonial India throughout her work.

70. As Rushdie writes of arch-colonialist William Methwold, 'beneath this stiff English exterior lurks a mind with a very Indian lust for allegory'; Rushdie, *Midnight's Children*, 96.

71. Spurling, *Paul Scott*, 118. The comment was made as part of 'Scott's Raj', an unpublished autobiographical outline written for a 1975 career-retrospective television programme.

72. As Scott writes in *A Division of the Spoils* (1975), his examination of British India is 'a story that's really two stories': the personal and the political, the intimate and the allegorical. Scott, *ADotS*, 608.

73. See Gopal, *Insurgent Empire*. It is no coincidence that Farrell too chooses the fall of Singapore as the setting for the most extensive, and arguably incisive, of his Empire trilogy, *The Singapore Grip* (1978); one of the recurrent motifs of this novel is Ehrendorf's Second Law, which states that '[t]he human situation, in general and in particular, is slightly worse . . . at any given moment than at any preceding moment.' Farrell, *The Singapore Grip*, 284.

74. It must be recognised, however, as Angela Woods argues, that typographies of illness narrative are limited and limiting, and whilst perhaps unable to escape conventions of genre, not all pathographies follow similar narratives. See Woods, 'The limits of narrative', 73–8.

75. Scott, *JitC*, 351.

76. Ibid. 351.

77. Anne Jurecic distils Sontag's argument to the insistence that 'we must speak, write, and think about disease without using figurative language or mythical narratives'. Jurecic, *Illness as Narrative*, 68.

78. Hanne and Hawken, 'Metaphors for illness in contemporary media', 93–9.

79. Engaging with Sontag, Jackie Stacey takes a more equivocal view of metaphor, arguing that whilst it does not represent an honest or 'real' engagement with the disease in question or the biomedical experience, the pervasiveness of metaphor throughout culture makes its use inevitable, and sometimes more relatable to the individual.

Stacey, *Teratologies*, 60–3. The British government employed a variety of metaphors throughout the first six months of the COVID-19 pandemic, including a host of military terminology and colonial allusions such as the Nightingale Hospitals. See Christoyannopoulos, 'Stop calling coronavirus pandemic a war'.

80. Hunsaker-Hawkins, *Reconstructing Illness*, 61. Such metaphors are also a legacy of Victorian culture, as expressed in the novel's contemporary present by Reid and the other characters; see Servitje, *Medicine Is War*.

81. Stacey, again echoing Sontag, notes how cancer is commonly seen as the 'cells in chaos, the body out of control', with medicine bringing order and stability. Stacey, *Teratologies*, 10–11.

82. Spurling, *Paul Scott*, 214–15.

83. Amoebiasis can develop into peritonitis if not treated, and also involves recurrent abdominal pain, liver abscesses and other debilitating effects.

84. The British Library India Office memoirs record various examples of this, such as the dismissal of G. A. Weston from the Punjab police for, among other things, appearing drunk and disorderly in public. BL, 'Compulsory retirement of G. A. Weston'.

85. Rushdie, MARBL, Fiction, *MC* MSS 'First Draught', 101.

86. Scott, *ADotS*, 38.

87. Ibid. 44.

88. See Chapter 4 for further details.

89. Whitehead and Woods, *Edinburgh Companion to the Critical Medical Humanities*, 3–4.

90. Scott, *ADotS*, 38–9.

91. Spurling, *Paul Scott*, 92–4. Spurling also records both of Scott's suicide attempts, related to his alcoholism; 253–4, 356.

92. Sidonie Smith and Julia Watson analyse the process of how the self is split within autobiographical and semi-autobiographical writing, arguing that the subject is split into various co-existing I's that represent various subject positions in the past, present, narrative and society. See Smith and Watson, *Reading Autobiography*, 72.

93. Scott, *ADotS*, 39.

94. Spurling believes that the same is true of Scott's writing, in so much as Scott's cure was the making of his career. After the amoebiasis was treated and cured in 1963, Spurling argues that Scott's writing style changes entirely, becoming robust and lucid where it was once pallid and weak. See Spurling, *Paul Scott*, 311.

95. Scott, *ADotS*, 195. Hamidullah, the court physician, further suggests that Colonel Dyer's decision to fire on unarmed protesters at Amritsar in 1919 was due to 'chronic amoebic infection', to which Rowan replies that Dyer's death was from arterial sclerosis, a condition that shares some symptoms with amoebiasis such as impact on decision-making.

96. Scott, *ADotS*, 662.

97. Kumar's experience is consistent with the embodiment of trauma; see Van Der Kolk, *The Body Keeps the Score*. As Patricia Novillo-Corvalán has observed, Scott was not alone in using Philoctetes to explore the history of Empire and postcoloniality in this way, and the character features in the work of Derek Walcott and Seamus Heaney. See Novillo-Corvalán, 'Reinterpreting the wound of Philoctetes'.

98. Jhabvala is dismissive of such claims of isolation, however; when Douglas remarks on being 'stuck out too long in a district all on your own' as a source of hardship, Olivia replies contemptuously: 'with only a few million Indians'. Jhabvala, *HaD*, 154.

99. The expression 'Doolally Tap' to indicate mental disorder comes from the number of shaking palsy cases taken to Deolali. See Martin, 'The Madness at Deolali', 94–5.

100. Crane, *Jhabvala*, 77–8. As I have argued in previous work on Jhabvala, *Heat and Dust* combines elements of travelogue, diary writing, the epistolary novel and the romance genre in its composition: Goodman, 'Everything Must Go'.

101. Strongman, *The Booker Prize*, 15–16, and Edwards, *Postcolonial Literature*, 57.

102. This description is taken from the blurb on my edition. However, it is likewise echoed by some critical writers on her work; for example, Ralph J. Crane, who notes how her later novels are about self-awakening. See Crane, *Jhabvala*, 57.

103. Crane, *Jhabvala*, 7; 58.

104. Walton, *Guilty*, 5.

105. Ibid. 7.

106. Jhabvala, *HaD*, 5.

107. Ibid. 27.

108. Ibid. 31.

109. Ibid. 108. Climate could often be a useful means of explaining away certain conditions, for example alcoholism or addiction, and would often result in a recuperative visit to a hill station such as Shimla; see Chapters 3 and 4 for more detail.

110. Ibid. 51.

111. Ibid. 81.

112. Scarry, *The Body in Pain*, 4. Morris and van Rysewyk (eds), *Meanings of Pain*, 389. Scott's depiction of Susan Layton's breakdown in *The Raj Quartet* adopts a similar approach to the mirroring of human and animal, setting up a parallel between Susan and the family dog, Panther, as they both become increasingly mute and lethargic toward the conclusion of *The Towers of Silence* (1971); see Chapter 3 for further detail.

113. Shahd Alshammari discusses this trope, alongside the compounding influence of race and ethnicity, within fiction; *Literary Madness*, 5. Given the postcolonial context, Jean Rhys' *Wide Sargasso Sea* (1966)

and its rewriting of the 'madwoman in the attic' trope is likewise relevant here.

114. Jhabvala, *HaD*, 81.
115. Ibid. 81.
116. There is an additional link to Farrell here in so much as one of Farrell's few Indian characters, Hari (an Indian princeling), becomes obsessed with phrenology, which he calls 'Frenla-ji ... Science of head'. Farrell's point is to use pseudoscience as a means of highlighting this similar, and misplaced, faith in all things Western as a mark of progress. See Farrell, *SoK*, 177.
117. See Mahone and Vaughan (eds), *Psychiatry and Empire*; Mills, 'The History of Modern Psychiatry in India', 431–58.
118. Scott, *TToS*, 363.

Chapter 2

Surgery for the Novel: Medical Practitioners in Anglo-Indian Fiction

As Susan Sontag notes in *Illness as Metaphor* (1978), illness is never an entirely singular experience.[1] It can frequently be isolating, and often inevitably severs some connections with those in the kingdom of the well, but it also produces and creates other meetings, facilitating new-found relationships both welcome and unwelcome between individuals and previously unimagined communities.[2] One of the more readily apparent groups that the ill individual encounters is that of the medical community, in the form of other patients, certainly, but more typically through contact with medical professionals. Illness demands treatment and treatment must be administered, at least in part, through contact with doctors, nurses and other practitioners in the context of the clinical encounter.[3] As Michel Foucault and others have argued, these meetings between patient and doctor or patient and nurse are perceived as necessary and essentially benign, as transactional exchanges in which the individual explains their illness, (possibly) pays a fee and receives care in return. However, for Foucault, they also represent a confrontation between the ill individual and the discipline of biomedicine, in which the unequal power relations of their subject positions are revealed, thus affirming the cultural and metaphorical power of the healthcare professional as a figure of scientific and social authority.[4]

In literary representations of illness and medicine, the figure of the medical professional is a perennial presence, and Anglo-Indian fiction is no exception.[5] Alongside the engagement with different kinds of illness offered by Anglo-Indian fiction, a continual current of the preceding chapter was not only how various physical and mental conditions were treated, but by whom. Doctors in particular proliferate throughout these novels; for example, John McLeod notes their regular inclusion in Farrell's writing from the very earliest of his published work, right up to his unfinished final novel *The Hill*

Station (1981).[6] It is no idle decision on Farrell's part either that Dr McNab is one of only two recurring protagonists in his Empire series of novels, but rather a deliberate choice of characterisation that supports his critical engagement with the medical culture of the British Empire.[7] The same is true of Scott, Rushdie and Jhabvala, and various doctors and nurses grace the pages of their novels too, from Aadam Aziz and Dr Narlikar in *Midnight's Children* (1981), Saunders and Gopal in *Heat and Dust* (1975) or the unnamed doctor in *A Backward Place* (1965), to the contrasting approaches of Sister Ludmilla and Dr Samuels in *The Raj Quartet* (1966–75). Indeed, so much of the meaning that Farrell, Scott, Jhabvala and Rushdie seek to generate through their inclusion of illness is likewise accomplished through this integral presence of medical personnel within their plotting. Just as these authors employ health and medicine as a means of reading thematic and political facets of imperialism, their novels also recognise, engage with and subvert the authority of the doctor as a representative both of Empire and of the science of professionalised medicine that the Empire represents in turn. Such an embodiment of imperial authority in a single character, their actions, and what their insights reveal about the colonial society of which they are a part, are as critical to the representation and utility of medicine and health within these novels as the conditions themselves.

This chapter engages directly with the figure of the doctor in his (for they are near invariably male) various forms and contexts within these novels, as the embodiment of the otherwise more diffuse imperial authority, expertise and power. Aside from the presence of doctors, however, the chapter also addresses various other medical roles within the Anglo-Indian novel, considering the narrative and contextual significance of nurses as well as lay practitioners and those practising traditional Indian medicine, who act as companions or subordinate counterpoints to the European medical apparatus of the Indian Medical Service or that of private practice. Following on from the confrontation with Western and imperial authority in the form of the doctor, the broader context of biomedical healthcare and treatment and encounters with its various representatives becomes a physical point of contact between citizens and representatives of Empire, coloniser and colonised, and ideal and reality. The clinical encounter is therefore also a 'contact zone', in which elements of European and Indian ideas and expertise meet and are reciprocally, and often again unequally, changed.[8]

The inclusion of doctors, nurses and the conflict over medical practice within Anglo-Indian fiction is driven by these authors' critical responses to two co-existing and complementary histories: the history of medicine within colonial society, and the literary history of the nineteenth and twentieth centuries. Again, and once more like their representation of ill health and disease, there is a tangible dialogue between the work of postmodernist and post-imperial authors like Farrell, Scott, Jhabvala and Rushdie and that of their modernist forebears when it comes to the representation of doctors and medical personnel within their plotting. Indeed, and again given Woolf's concerns, the extent to which medicine influences modernism and characterises the literature of the period is striking. As Vike Martina Plock, Peter Fifield and Ulrika Maude have all separately noted, Joyce and his modernist contemporaries were overtly interested in medicine, medical technology and the figure of the doctor within their work.[9] Plock, in particular, argues that Joyce 'consistently . . . [used] his fiction to interrogate some of medicine's theories and to criticize medicine's cultural authority at the beginning of the twentieth century', either through his own experience of medical training, characters such as Buck Mulligan in *Ulysses* (1922) or the novel's schema, with chapters corresponding to organs and body parts.[10]

Whilst less didactic in his form than Joyce, consideration of Forster's *A Passage to India* (1924) is again instructive when it comes to reading the post-imperial response to the history of Empire and the literature that it produced. For alongside Forster's general engagement with ill health noted in the previous chapter, Aziz's occupation as a doctor is a vital aspect of his approach to colonial society and his deconstruction of its hierarchies. As a member of staff at the local hospital in the fictional Chandrapore, Forster uses Aziz to illustrate the changeable social position of the professional Indian. On the one hand, Aziz is skilled, respected for his dedication to his work and respectable as a result of the social standing of the medical profession. On the other, he is subject to the disdain of Major Callendar, the Civil Surgeon and his superior, and subject more broadly to the institutional racism of the colonial society he tends.[11] When suspected of the assault on Adela Quested, his standing drops away immediately, suggesting that such professional respect accorded to Indians, within the broader context of the supposedly benevolent Empire, is only a surface affectation.

Such a demographic and such a disillusionment is echoed and intensified by Rushdie's own Dr Aziz, Saleem Sinai's grandfather Aadam, who witnesses the brutality of Empire at Amritsar first-hand, where Indians again are wrongfully accused and this time killed indiscriminately.[12] The disillusionment of both Drs Aziz in *A Passage to India* and *Midnight's Children* is another example of the dialogic relationship between these literary movements, as well as the close engagement with the historical conditions of colonial India by post-imperial authors such as Farrell, Scott and Rushdie.[13] Such examples as found in Forster and Rushdie offer all the more powerful a critique of Empire given the history of the IMS and medical education with regard to the growth of the Indian middle classes and the professionalisation of medicine. Mark Harrison and David Arnold note that most surgeons and doctors in India were originally employed by the East India Company in their different presidencies, with the first structured branches of what would become the IMS being founded in the 1760s.[14] Once control of India passed to the Crown after 1858, the IMS was made a single organisation, linking the different presidencies, finally becoming a centralised body in 1896.[15] Private practice existed alongside the IMS, of course, with doctors and other medical practitioners resident in most major towns and cities across India, whilst those 'unable to make headway down country' could find employment with organisations such as tea planting companies if unable to secure a position elsewhere, often alongside former IMS doctors who had elected to work after retirement.[16] Harrison notes, however, that the social standing of the mid-century Victorian doctor was still decidedly mixed, with the profession having 'not shaken off its status as a craft' and pay barely allowing doctors to live as 'gentlemen'.[17]

As medicine, like other scientific disciplines, gradually professionalised across the course of the century, and the remit of the medical service extended to public health as well as private and military practice, the perception, pay and social standing of the doctor began to improve. However, medical care across British India remained scant and often inconsistent well into the twentieth century and up until the ending of the British Raj in 1947. Margery Hall, wife of a British Indian Political Service officer, writes in her memoirs that when they were moved to Loralai in Balochistan (now Pakistan) she was told cheerfully that it was 'only 200 miles to Quetta, so you'll have a doctor not too far away'.[18] Even when medical personnel were on hand, experience of the care available was varied. John Orr describes how sub-assistant surgeons, the most junior rank in the IMS, were 'usually both enthusiastic and enterprising in their work' but began their careers having completed just three years of study of medicine, for which they were granted a licence to practice; their unofficial and less flattering title, Orr notes, was 'sub-assassins'.[19]

Though it did not place doctors and medical personnel as high in the pecking order of British Indian society as some roles in the Indian

Civil Service or the Indian Army did, medical service and possession of Western medical expertise nonetheless made for a potent symbol of colonial emancipation and uplift through its efforts to recruit from Indian and other non-European demographics. Harrison notes that elements of the IMS, such as the Subordinate Medical Service, were composed entirely of Indians, and that the IMS itself was open to Indians from 1855, when competitive examination was first introduced.[20] Medicine offered a means of advancement to elements of Anglo-Indian society who otherwise faced widespread discrimination or indifference, such as Eurasians, or castes outside of Brahmins, who had typically dominated Indian intellectual life. The employment and fulfilment found for women in nursing roles was similarly transformative for some. Although it was often in circumstances of great hardship, nursing in colonial spaces such as India offered a form of autonomy and pride from professionalisation that was often simply unattainable in Britain.[21] At the same time, Poonam Bala argues that biomedicine, and by extension medical education, was used as a tool of cultural domination, particularly as it displaced Ayurveda and traditional Indian medicine, and contributed to the growth of the Anglicised Indian middle classes.[22] Moreover, Sunil Pandya places much of early Indian medical education in light of Thomas Babington Macaulay's 'Minute on Indian Education' (1835) and its efforts to create its class of persons Indian in 'blood and colour, but English in taste, in opinions, in morals and in intellect'.[23] Such efforts were aided by encouraging Indians to attend British universities such as Oxford, Cambridge, Edinburgh and the School of Oriental and Asian Studies, a policy also practised by the Indian Civil Service up until 1939 and which likewise contributed to this Anglicisation of attitudes and methods.

Even if Indian doctors managed to qualify and set themselves up to practise, though, they could still face generalised discrimination when it came to the perception of their abilities. When pregnant at Loralai, Margery Hall is told there are two doctors nearby who can attend to her; however, when she discovers they are 'one army one who'd never delivered any babies, and one Indian one who'd "done", he said, "seven years in Edinburgh", and I wondered what for!', she decides that 'it's 200 miles to Quetta for me'.[24] Hall was not alone in her prejudice towards Indian doctors or the shortcomings of some elements of the IMS, though not all shared her misgivings; Alexander Redpath, also of the Indian Political Service, mentions that their station at Gilgit 'had an excellent doctor of the Indian Medical Service, who, aided by a first rate assistant and Indian Staff ran a hospital which was well attended by people from all parts of the Agency, many of them travelling hundreds of miles for a treatment'.[25]

As a consequence of these conjoined histories and their evident import of medical practitioners throughout Anglo-Indian literature and society, this chapter will examine the representation of medical men and women within post-imperial fiction, exploring how these authors continue their literary engagement with Anglo-Indian medicine, history and the legacies of Empire through use of these characters and their function within plot and narrative. The chapter is divided into two sections; the first addresses the representation of doctors, and the second that of nurses and other medical personnel. It will explore the critical use of doctors as an embodiment of colonial medical authority within Anglo-Indian fiction and the way in which that authority is affirmed, subverted or resisted through the use of the historical narrative. Just as with illness in general, the figure of the doctor or nurse is rich in metaphorical function and potency, used to allude to thematic meanings that characterise the history of Empire as well as specific concerns of the individual narratives. The doctors present in fictional settings as diverse as those of Rushdie and Farrell represent a range of divisions, such as those that broach race and class, past and present, the radical and the traditional, and those that engage with the cultural position of the doctor pre- and post-independence. As well as the distinctions between European and traditional Indian medicine, the chapter will consider the way in which post-imperial fiction is sensitive to representing internal divisions between British and Anglo-Indian medical practitioners both in terms of expertise and professional opinions; exploring the discrepancy between their methods, opinions and favoured treatments is a further way in which these authors and their novels engage with both the teleology of imperial progress and the limits of the Empire's intent. Further, this chapter will explore the gendered divisions inherent to medical practice in the form of the nurse and other lay practitioners, considering how nursing roles either serve to emancipate women working in a colonial setting, or further serve to limit women's expression by affirming their place only as caregivers.

Textual practice: the role of the doctor

As Plock identifies, modernism's engagement with medical, scientific and imperial authority gathers significance by being part of the movement's general anti-teleological concerns. In conformity with similar modernist approaches to other social phenomena, such as art and culture and religion, medicine likewise fits into a pattern of criticism of accepted or authoritative disciplines, iconoclasm, and radical reworking or rethinking of the contemporary world by modernist authors. However, such criticisms take place during a period when the Empire and its associated metanarrative of progress and the 'civilising mission' were very much still extant. Of course, the Indian nationalist movement of the 1920s and 30s, the devolution to diarchy via the Government of India Act 1919 and further autonomy granted by the Government of India Act 1935, and the ongoing decline of British industrial infrastructure in comparison with European nations and the United States cast a long shadow over the British Empire and made it clear that serious change, if not the end itself, was no more than a decade or two away. Even so, the reinscriptive properties of the Empire's wartime efforts, and events such as the Empire Exhibitions held in London in 1924 and Glasgow in 1938, were clear, and helped to create a feeling of solidity to British imperialism despite these threats to its existence.[26]

In the post-imperial period in which Rushdie, Scott, Farrell and Jhabvala were writing, however, no such grand narratives or structures exist for Britain, except as memory or nostalgia. In the period between 1965 and 1981, the broad temporal span in which the majority of the texts under discussion here were written, the postwar consensus and industrial prosperity Britain had enjoyed after 1945 was in decline, and the nation had yet to be admitted to the European Economic Area and experience the galvanising effect this would have on the economy in the late 1970s and early 1980s. The return to the history of Empire, its events, individuals or legacies through their novels in this period, then, is not simply the criticism of an extant system enacted by the modernists, but instead suggests a more searching critical process in which these authors seek to explore the postcolonial British psyche, the pre-history of the nation's modern circumstances and the limits of its contemporary and historical authority. The postmodern incredulity towards metanarrative is thus combined with the critical approaches to the colonial past offered through postcoloniality and mediated through the meaning-making inherent in the medical humanities. Whereas the continual criticism of postmodernism and its authors is that an adherence to irony precludes serious critique, the confrontation with power enacted through the engagement with illness and representation, and how imperial authority is encountered on an individual level through medicine and health, gives a human and

critical depth to these novels that transcends their playful and intertextual aesthetic.

In a similar vein to their use of illness as metaphor, explored in the
previous chapter, a key means through which Farrell, Rushdie and
Scott sought to engage with British cultural and medical authority
was through the figure of the doctor. Of course, alongside their contextual and colonial relevance outlined above, the place of doctors
within the metaphorical signification of storytelling and narrative is
evident. Margaret Healy argues that in doctor–patient interactions,
the doctor's role is to 'read the signs of the body' and interpret them,
thus conveying the 'story of his or her individual body'; in return,
continues Healy, the physician is expected to 'offer an authoritative
narrative which makes sense of, and gives meaning to, the patient's
troubling experiences; only then can tests and a cure be initiated'.[27]
The role of doctors as storytellers is particularly apparent in Farrell's
work, notably *The Siege of Krishnapur* (1973) and *The Hill Station*
(1981), where a great deal of both narratives are focalised through
the character of Dr McNab. Likewise with Rushdie's *Midnight's
Children*, where Saleem's narrative cannot be understood without
that of Aadam Aziz's own experiences, and the role of his profession
in the circumstances that would one day lead to Saleem's birth.

In light of Healy's analysis, for Scott and Farrell, employment
of doctors within their fiction is part of considering their own biographical health issues and efforts at self-healing and goes beyond
the importance of doctors as a form of narrative driver. Farrell in
particular notes in his unpublished diary that he became 'interested in
writing, largely I suppose as a sort of self-therapy'.[28] When connected
to his general desire, alongside that of his contemporaries, to consider
the circumstances of modern Britain (as expressed to Malcolm Dean),
the doctor in Anglo-Indian fiction of this period takes on new significance; by responding to the symptomatic nature of the cultural return
to Empire in British society, the function of the doctors in these novels, and indeed the authors themselves, is diagnostic; through their
emphasis on medicine and historical narrative, these books seek to
read the signs of the British social body and ascertain its ills in the
hope of initiating a cure. Responding to Britain's position as the 'sick
man of Europe', these texts are, like works from the same period
by Margaret Drabble, J. G. Ballard, Martin Amis and even John le
Carré, 'condition of England' novels; their inclusion and narrative use
of the doctor and other medical professionals is a further extension of
how their authors use medicine to explore the various divisions that
are affecting contemporary Britain.[29]

As outlined in Chapter 1, in *The Siege of Krishnapur* Farrell uses the conflict over cholera to illustrate a range of internal divisions and disagreements amongst the novel's British characters and undermine the perception of unity generated by the nation's imperial mythos. As the siege continues, the general rivalry between the garrison's civil surgeon, Dunstaple, and the regimental surgeon, McNab, culminates in disagreement over how best to treat cholera.[30] Farrell develops the dispute between Dunstaple and McNab from professional rivalry over miasma and water-borne theories of cholera into an open and public antipathy between the two men, their services and the differing philosophies of medical practice they come to represent. In the latter of two scenes set in the garrison's church, Dunstaple demands that McNab justify his hydration-based treatment of cholera patients. Farrell once again uses period sources, basing Dunstaple's arguments on the Royal College of Physicians' 'Report on Epidemic Cholera' (1854) and McNab's rebuttals on the research undertaken by John Snow in London between 1853 and 1854.

McNab fails to convince the garrison, and the treatments conducted by Snow in London are shown to gain little traction in an Indian context. Farrell thus reflects the opposition between the medical establishment in Britain and the IMS, which continued to support miasma theory into the early twentieth century, arguing that environmental pollution, bad air and poor sanitation as well as impure water were the source of cholera in India.[31] E. M. Collingham notes that European ideas and their proponents were not often afforded credibility by an IMS dominated by an older generation of doctors with outmoded understandings of physiology and treatment.[32] For instance, in the 1870s the Indian Sanitary Commissioner J. M. Cunningham condemned Snow's ideas as 'mere hypothesis' based on 'inexact and imperfect evidence'; in *The Siege of Krishnapur*, Dunstaple similarly derides McNab's convictions as 'rubbish' and charges McNab as unable to provide proof of his theories beyond these statistics.[33]

On the surface level, and akin to what Farrell does with phrenology elsewhere in the novel, this scene appears initially comedic as a consequence of its dramatic irony; for all Dunstaple's passionate conviction and criticism of water-borne theory, the reader knows that miasmatic transmission of cholera is eventually disproven and that history will vindicate McNab.[34] However, given the limitations of postmodernism, historical irony is not Farrell's sole intention. Instead of simply employing the cholera debate as a plot point to illustrate dramatic tension, Farrell uses it, alongside the pseudoscience of phrenology, as a lens through which to further satirise the adherents of Empire in Victorian society within the novel and contemporary society outside of it. As D. C. R. A. Goonetilleke has observed: 'when Farrell plays off the present against the past he is critical of both'.[35] Here, Farrell's split perspective on cholera seeks not only to highlight the divisions inherent to Empire both past and present, but to draw a parallel with contemporary debate on how best to treat the metaphorical ills of the nation; either through reliance on the familiar, traditional, but unsuccessful methods, or by disregarding the past and embracing something more radical.[36] By denying the analyses of McNab and by extension Snow, the garrison instead defers to the authority associated with Empire, again drawing comparison to Farrell's contemporary moment in which he suggests that the British public are likewise denying the evidence before them and are instead looking backwards to the perceived securities of the past.

By making them the polarities of this debate, Farrell expands his metaphor to the doctors themselves. Dunstaple is described as 'a kindly and paternal man' possessing 'authority and good humour . . . the more experienced, and hence the more reliable of the two'.[37] McNab, on the other hand, whilst similarly authoritative, 'seldom smiled' and 'seemed to take a pessimistic view of your complaint, whatever it was'.[38] Farrell suggests that the familiar, paternalistic view of Empire is preferable to the prospect of a post-imperial Britain facing the reality of its situation, allowing one of his characters, Mr Willoughby the magistrate, to observe of the garrison '[H]ow much more easily they were swayed by prestige than by arguments!'[39] The unsettling effect of the conflict between adherence to tradition and acceptance of an uncertain alternative is keenly illustrated by Farrell. As the bitterness of the cholera debate deepens, Farrell writes of how the garrison 'took to carrying cards in their pockets which gave the relevant instructions in case they should find themselves too far gone to claim the doctor they wanted'.[40] As both doctors hold forth on their respective theories, various members of the garrison cross out and rewrite their preferred choice of doctor multiple times. Farrell captures a picture of Britons, to paraphrase Homi Bhabha, caught uncertainly in the act of composing themselves; indecisively caught between their perception of comfort and familiarity in tradition and the hard logic of reason and fact.[41] Farrell intimates that a preference for tradition against all better judgement is equally applicable in a 1970s context; as he stated in his interview with Dean, 'I hoped to say something . . . about how we, in our thriving modern world of the 1970s hold our own ideas.'[42] By making his colonial Victorians ridiculous, Farrell strives not just to lampoon them and their views but also to make his contemporary audience consider how their own actions and judgements may one day too be assessed.

The Siege of Krishnapur was not the end of Farrell's engagement with medicine and health through his fiction, but rather the consolidation of that process of analogy between the health of individuals and that of their wider society that began with Angela Spencer's mysterious illness (later implied to be leukaemia) in *Troubles* (1970). Farrell returns to the setting of colonial India in *The Hill Station*, however, the novel's main narrative is much less overtly dramatic than *The Siege of Krishnapur*; set some twenty years after the events of the rebellion in the mid-1870s, it follows the journey made by Dr McNab, his wife Miriam and niece Emily up to Simla (now Shimla) for the summer season, and their various encounters with colonial society there. Despite the seemingly sedate setting, Simla is revealed as a more divided community than that of Krishnapur, riven by petty jealousies over social rank as well as more serious disputes over faith and theology. *The Hill Station* is set in the midst of the so-called 'Imperial heyday', that point between the Rebellion of 1857 and the First World War where imperial expansion into China, Africa, the Middle East and elsewhere continued apace, and the national narrative was one of a modernising, prosperous Britain unified in its pursuit of such goals.[43] Again, Farrell's objective is to unpick these metanarratives of Empire and complicate the more simplistic contemporary understanding of British history.

As the novel develops and Farrell exposes the rivalries and factions that exist beneath the surface of Simla society, he once again uses medical metaphor and the figure of the doctor as a means of enacting his criticism of Empire. The central dispute within *The Hill Station* is doctrinal in nature and concerns the contemporary debates over ritualism in the Church of England, and the fear of growing Catholicism within colonial society.[44] Juxtaposed against this is the tuberculosis of Reverend Kingston, the clergyman at the heart of the dispute itself, and a further subplot in which a rabies scare takes hold of the community. From the materials in Farrell's archives, the manuscript of *The Hill Station* is thought to approximate half of the planned novel.[45] It is notable then that so much of it is dedicated to the representation of Kingston's illness, one of Jessica Howell's 'scourges' of the nineteenth century, including an entire chapter in which McNab examines Kingston's symptoms at length and reaches his diagnosis.[46] In a tender, nuanced piece of writing in which the balance of power within the conversation passes back and forth between

McNab and Kingston (acting as representatives of their institutions and the wider nineteenth-century tension between medicine, science and faith), McNab voices his conclusions to Kingston:

> His illness was a secret he had had to carry alone for too long. McNab had seen this many times: the very bravery and self-control which a man or woman displayed when obliged to face the fear and suffering of death by themselves made the release of feeling all the more overwhelming once there was someone to confide in.[47]

McNab's expertise extends, again as Healy observes, to a narrative role in the diagnostic process as well as a medical one. Farrell suggests that McNab, and doctors in general, are not necessarily dispassionate representatives of an authoritarian or didactic biomedicine, but rather facilitate the recognition of the lived experience of illness and, moreover, as confidants, enable that story to be told aloud, or with resonances to the religious themes of the novel, through a sort of secular confession.[48] Doctors such as McNab are depicted as a conduit for meaning and change, either for the difference between sickness and health, between sickness and pathology, and through which treatment or remedy become cure. In this instance, and through McNab's measured yet respectful interactions with Kingston, Farrell illustrates how the doctor acts as amanuensis for a story that the patient is sometimes unable to write themselves. Farrell's novel thus brings the notions of narrative, medicine and the lived experience closer together, which belies the efforts of medical practice towards emotional and personal distance from the patient. Moreover, Farrell reveals that part of the reason McNab agreed to come to Simla is to find time to write a long-promised treatise on Indian medicine that will 'distil some order from the chaos of a life's work in medicine'.[49] Whilst McNab's narrative role conforms to McLeod's observation on how Farrell's novels are filled with instances of textual production, again supporting his inclusion within postmodernist discourses of fiction, such efforts again place *The Hill Station* within the frame of narrative medicine and the attempt to gain control over the disordered experience of illness, for both the patient experiencing ill health and the doctor treating it.[50] The mention of 'chaos', resonant of Arthur W. Frank's narrative modes of pathography, suggests that the role of the doctor, and the implications of their actions, extends beyond bodily treatment and affects the social existence and health of the patient too. The clarifying and ordering role of the doctor is emphasised in Farrell's manuscript drafts of the novel, where this encounter between McNab and Kingston is subtitled 'The Doctor of Confusion'.[51]

Farrell's novel also illustrates his concern for the necessity of humanism and empathy within medical practice. Indeed, Farrell's characterisation of McNab suggests that no doctor can proceed in a purely medical, professional capacity, and even that a degree of humanism is necessary for care to take place at all. McNab spends much of *The Hill Station* attempting to fathom what he calls the 'moral dimension' of illness and reflects repeatedly on his belief in how health can be affected by an individual's interiority, their social outlook and their spirituality.[52] Whereas in *The Siege of Krishnapur* Farrell uses the church setting to emphasise further conflict between faith in religion and faith in science and medicine, presenting them as antithetical structures, *The Hill Station* complicates this binary approach through McNab's ongoing philosophical and spiritual development. McNab's concern with affect and feeling makes him another of Farrell's temporal and contextual disjunctions within his fiction, in that he evokes a twentieth-century humanist doctor placed in the context of a professionalising nineteenth-century medical establishment more than he is an old-fashioned humanist at odds with the change in his contemporary moment.[53] Indeed, in *The Siege of Krishnapur*, the reverse is the case, and Dunstaple deplores McNab's adherence to less traditional methods of care.[54] Instead, and in a link to John Berger's *A Fortunate Man* (1967) and the work of John Sassall, McNab's actions and approach embody the efforts towards empathy sought by medical humanities and the humanising turn within medical practice after the Second World War.[55] Rather than use the doctor to enforce metaphorical divisions between reason and faith, Farrell instead argues that biomedical science and the lived experience of the patient are not two adversarial aspects of the process of treatment, but rather constitute the holistic experience of being ill and the disruption to the physical and ontological integrity of the subject that it incurs. McNab is thus part of Farrell's anachronistic approach to temporality and healthcare, with his speech-based, interlocutive approach to treating Kingston anticipating, as McLeod notes, the twentieth-century advent of the talking cure and Sigmund Freud's work in psychology.[56] Again, just as he does with Darwinian natural selection and the cholera cloud, Farrell deliberately blurs the temporality of his novels, emphasises an essential synchronic humanity to his characters across time, and closes the distance between his Victorian subjects and the contemporary present.

Like Farrell, Scott's *The Raj Quartet* is concerned with the juxtaposition of past and present. In the first novel of the series, *The Jewel in the Crown* (1966), this is made clear explicitly through its epistolary and documentary form; however, as the series progresses, Scott largely abandons this format in favour of a far more conventional historically set novel.[57] Even so, the comparison between the past of the narrative setting and the present of Scott's authorial moment is nonetheless made visible in the repeated clashes between the thoughts, opinions and beliefs of the older generation of Anglo-Indian society and those of various newcomers brought to India by the war that recurs throughout the remaining books in the series. Just as Farrell does with the division between the new methodologies of McNab and the comfortable paternalism of Dunstaple, Scott too uses developments in medical practice, and their contentious social reception, to illustrate the change in colonial society and the loss of its old securities.

Alongside the handful of practitioners who appear in the early novels, Scott focuses his engagement with the figure of the doctor in the third novel of his series, *The Towers of Silence* (1971), through the character of Captain Samuels.[58] Samuels is introduced as a Royal Army Medical Corps psychiatrist attached to the military wing of the hospital in Pankot, and is responsible for Susan Bingham's treatment after her bereavement and breakdown at the end of the previous novel, *The Day of the Scorpion* (1968). As a member of the socially prominent Layton family, daughter of Colonel John Layton of the Pankot Rifles, and widow of a former officer, Susan is entitled to care from the military hospital as opposed to only that of the Civil Surgeon, Dr Travers. Susan's mother, Mildred, the formidable memsahib of the community, directs her care, and whilst she appears glad that Susan gets both the greater attentiveness of the military hospital and the recognition of her rank, Susan's treatment causes her some consternation as a result of Samuels' involvement. Mildred dismisses Samuels as a 'trick cyclist' whose expertise is confined to 'slackers' who had been 'deprived of fish and chips' based on the fact that he is a newcomer to India, and used to dealing with military cases.[59] However, the main impetus behind Mildred's concern is the question of social propriety raised not by stigma associated with Susan's breakdown, but rather her interactions with Samuels. Illustrating how her class prejudice is supported by an evident antisemitism, Mildred believes that 'there was something disagreeable about Susan being talked to, questioned, by a man; particularly by a man like Samuels who might be considered clever at home where psychoanalysis was fashionable, but who was after all a Jew'.[60] Scott shows how the Anglo-Indian preoccupation with the maintenance of status ironically confounds itself in so much as, while Mildred accepts the treatment of the military hospital – as is Susan's entitlement and which affirms her social position – to do so means accepting that her treatment will be administered by Samuels, whose identity as dual outsider, by dint of his newness to India combined with his Jewishness, is at odds with the appearance of prestige she wishes to maintain.

Samuels' experiences in Pankot illustrate how Scott uses the figure of the doctor to highlight the divisions within Anglo-Indian society, but also to emphasise how that society resists change in favour of tradition and belief in an established, exclusionary order. Mildred denigrates Samuels' involvement, as she considers him to be outside their social and professional sphere. However, her antisemitism and resistance to what Samuels represents, just as with Farrell's *The Siege of Krishnapur*, extends to a suspicion of the doctor's methods and abilities as well as his origins. Scott writes that Mildred asks little about Susan's treatment and takes no interest in its detail because she 'distrusted the whole psychiatric process and had no time at all for the jargon'.[61] Instead she complains that Susan is not in the nursing home recommended by Travers, where 'a good rest, a change of air, and the company of young people' would put her right, evidencing her faith in the traditional rest cures and seclusion that were commonplace mental health treatments two decades prior.[62] Her attitudes towards the new methods of psychoanalysis likewise recall the approach of the IMS to bacteriology half a century earlier, marking a belief in conflict between British or European practice and the particular nature and requirements of colonial India. Such attitudes mean that Scott's novel likewise suggests a backwards-looking mentality, swayed by the prestige of the past and driven by a belief in exceptionalism.

Scott's characterisation of Samuels furthers the suggestion of how the doctor can broker a break between old and new. Having treated her for a short while, Samuels advises that Susan's readmittance to society take place at a social occasion, so she attends a farewell party for Nicky Paynton, the wife of an officer killed in the fighting at Arakan. Samuels' decision to permit Susan to attend, described as 'an extraordinary choice' and a 'bit cool' by the community, apparently fulfils part of Susan's treatment, but it also allows him admittance to Anglo-Indian society on a more equal footing under his professional duties, rather than as a disempowered outsider.[63] Samuels is revealed to be, like McNab, a disruptive presence, but in a way that is far more wilfully disdainful of colonial hierarchies than disagreements over cholera treatments. In conversation before he arrives, Samuels is criticised for not observing any of the social niceties of Anglo-India, such as calling, or making an effort to show deference to the local sahibs and their wives.[64] Indeed, when introduced to Nicky Paynton he shows no interest in impressing her or inviting Pankot society to like him: 'Captain Samuels was slender, fair-haired. He looked down on Nicky [Paynton] from above average height. He did not smile . . . The image of the Jew-boy trick cyclist was completely shattered. He was remote, patrician; in the opinion of most of the women present disturbingly, coldly, handsome.'[65] When asked whether he was a Freudian or a Jungian, Samuels instead and with a 'flicker of . . . amusement' professes an interest in Reich's theory of how the human orgasm is a 'major contributory factor to physical and mental health', clearly intending to puncture the atmosphere of emotional repression he sees in colonial society and provoke those present.[66]

Samuels' lack of interest in impressing his hosts does not come from the acknowledgement that they are unlikely ever to accept him, given his status and his Jewishness, but rather reflects his opposition to what Pankot society represents. Scott goes on to illustrate how Samuels is less disinterested in colonial society as much as he is openly critical of it, and, in particular, its psychological effects on the individual:

> As Samuels followed her his glance fell here and there upon faces as if he were looking for evidence of mental and emotional disorders of the kind he had presumed to uncover in *her* but blamed *them* for. He bore himself like a man taking someone out of an area of contagion.[67]

Through Samuels, Scott acts to criticise the psychology of the society he observed in India and its unhealthiness. In light of his opinions, it is significant that Susan is permitted to re-enter society through a kind of post-traumatic debutante ball, thereby evoking and satirising such outmoded traditions, but that she leaves again in the care of Samuels. It is another moment of the transition of power between the weight of social expectation inherent in the Old India of the Laytons and Payntons, and recognition of that of the new, embodied in Samuels and the professional authority and change that he represents. Scott shows that Samuels, and the doctor in general, can be a destabilising figure as much as they can act towards restitution, existing outside of the traditional dominant hierarchies of colonial military or government. Moreover, the metaphorical resonance of Susan's breakdown and Nicky Paynton's widowhood, which foreshadow the imminent trauma invoked by the loss of Empire and the bereavement of its passing, are likewise apparent. Teddie Bingham in particular dies as a result of his faith in the traditional values of the military, whilst the old guard like 'Bunny' Paynton, John Layton or 'Tusker' Smalley are killed off, retired, or shown to be irrelevant; Samuels' psychoanalysis thus appears, in light of Susan's place as inheritor of these outmoded Anglo-Indian values, as much a preparatory response to the impending end of Empire as it does a restorative treatment for her condition.

In foregrounding Samuels throughout this section, Scott suggests that the doctor and the treatment they provide can be unsettling and even destructive, recalling Sontag's analysis of the illness experience and its propensity to sever social connections. However, both Scott and Farrell further indicate that such destruction is necessary, especially when it intersects with the hierarchies and structures of the Empire. For Scott in particular, the breaking down of colonial authority Samuels undertakes through Susan (punning on her own breakdown) is indicative of Scott's critical approach to colonial society; through Samuels, Scott asserts that the outsider figure, a representation of how he himself felt in India, is vital to the narrative process of diagnosis, understanding and change, either within the fictional world of *The Raj Quartet* or within the wider discourses of the return to imperial narratives in the 1960s and 70s as part of the Raj Revival. Moreover, Scott implies, it is the feeling of detachment that makes these individuals effective in their criticisms, something he further compounds through Samuels' Jewishness; differing to McNab's humanistic care, a degree of remoteness and emotional distance are required for truly honest, dispassionate diagnosis to take place. Only then, Scott appears to suggest, can cure or healing occur, even if it equates to destruction.

The experience of change and destruction can also apply to the doctor themselves, especially if their outsider status pushes not only at the strictly enforced borders of colonial society but extends to their ethnicity too. Whilst Samuels' Jewishness places him partly within this category, he is shown to be able to pass sufficiently within British society as a result of his professional and national identity. The same is not the case for Indian practitioners. In Rushdie's *Midnight's Children*, Aadam Aziz undergoes repeated changes as a result of his medical training and profession as a doctor, either in social status, political worldview or in terms of understanding his own ontology in relation to the colonial hierarchy of the British Empire. Whilst Aadam's decision to become a doctor and his medical training in

Heidelberg occur before the point at which Saleem begins his retelling of Aadam's story, it is apparent that his experiences have already altered his identity and the way he is perceived by others by the time that the reader is introduced to him in the opening pages of the novel. As the chapter develops, Rushdie uses Aadam to illustrate a host of concerns around mutability of the Indian subject under colonialism and how the supposed benefits of European professional education, idealised as a form of imperial uplift, serve to isolate as much as they empower the individual.

Aadam's return to his home state of Kashmir is mixed; although armed with his new knowledge and professional standing, Rushdie writes that Aadam 'also felt – inexplicably – as though the old place resented his educated, stethoscoped return', setting up a legacy of disconnection and outsiderness that affects generations of characters across the narrative.[68] Rushdie suggests that medical education confers on Aadam a '[p]ermanent alteration: a hole', created by the different perspective his training and European experience gives him on politics, faith and selfhood.[69] His newly achieved medical knowledge ironically results in greater ontological uncertainty, prompting questions of self-knowledge, despite his deeper medical understanding of life and death. Led to a state of disbelief and agnosticism by the confluence of his Eastern religion and his Western education, the hole in Aadam Aziz is a spiritual wound that the techniques and methods of biomedicine cannot heal. Rushdie embeds the conflict of the split Indian subject through this satire of faith in medicine throughout this initial chapter and the rest of the novel, with doubt, difference and dislocation forming the roots of the Sinai dynasty.[70] The focus on the trappings and iconography of his profession likewise mimic and replace those of religion, with the stethoscope in particular, worn around the neck like a symbol of religious devotion, attracting scorn and derision from Tai the boatman and furthering the conflicts and oppositions between faith and medicine that recur in Farrell's writing. Likewise, the pig-leather medical bag Aadam carries becomes an object of concern, part icon, part blasphemy, and also representative of European colonialism and the shift in his being. Rushdie writes that 'the bag represents Abroad; it is the alien thing, an invader, progress', and its instruments, such as the stethoscope, serve to replace existing, more authentically Indian and organic, ways of understanding being.[71] Further, with its 'knives, and cures for cholera and malaria and smallpox', the bag is also a Pandora's box, signifying the threat enclosed within the change wrought by his medical training and the epistemological system it represents.[72] Aadam's return effectively mimics the incursion of a colonial missionary, carrying his outsider's knowledge into the local community and changing it forever.

As a consequence of his Indian ethnic identity, however, Rushdie goes on to illustrate how Aadam can never truly assimilate into British colonial society either, despite his adherence to its professional values. Reflecting the same currents of systemic racism experienced by Forster's own Dr Aziz, Rushdie uses Aadam to illustrate the indifference of the colonial system towards the altered Indian subject that it produces, regardless of how educated they may be or what social standing they may have achieved through their Westernisation.[73] Despite his initial association with European biomedicine and its implied place as an extension of the imperial project, however, what faith Aadam Aziz has in colonial British India is short-lived. Further to his conflict with Tai, the 'hostile environment' he finds on his return to Kashmir leads him, with dramatic irony, to accept work in Amritsar in early 1919.[74] Here he becomes involved in the nationalist disturbances that sweep the city, again ironically using his medical skills tending Indians who have suffered wounds in the rioting, treating the results of British colonial violence with its own medical practices, and returning home to his wife Naseem covered in the 'red medicine' of mercurochrome. His experiences at Amritsar culminate in his trauma at the massacre at the Jallianwala Bagh on 13 April, where, forced into the compound with other Indians, he is part of the crowd fired upon by Dyer and his men. In the midst of the bloodshed, Aadam's instincts reassert themselves, and as a result of the sneeze that saves his life he is thrown to the floor and onto his doctor's bag, which inflicts 'a bruise so severe and mysterious' that it does not fade until after his death, years later.[75] Crushed under the bodies that fall on top of him, Rushdie writes that Aadam's nose is 'jammed against a bottle of red pills' whilst his 'bottles, liniment and syringes scatter in the dust'; that the 'big shot doctor', though here unscathed by any bullets, suffers the indignity of being forced into the dirt like any other Indian recalls Aziz's loss of status after Adela Quested's accusation.[76] However, Rushdie goes further to confront Aadam with the implications of his profession, and how through medicine he is complicit in the colonial system that abuses him. With evident symbolism and in an ironic inversion of the previous scene, he returns to Naseem covered not in red medicine but in blood. Unwelcome in Kashmir and sickened by Amritsar, Aadam thus becomes stateless, again othered and caught between his two identities, aware that he is not part of British society but knowing too that 'with Tai in his head, [he] does not feel Indian' either.[77] Aadam's medical education thus dually others him, enabling his movement within British and Indian colonial societies but not allowing him to belong in either of them.

Beyond the religious resonances of Aadam Aziz's 'conversion' and his loss of faith, the altered state of his being has further secular resonances in relation to Kashmir and Rushdie's approach to nationhood, identity and the effects of Empire. In its juxtaposition of the newly fashioned, educated middle-class doctor and the peasant class of the long-lived (if not eternal) boatman, Tai, Rushdie presents his criticism of how colonialism not only sets Indians against each other in cultural contest and class conflict but disempowers them all further in the process. Aadam Aziz is raised up in social terms by his achievements but becomes the subject of their limitations also. For instance, though the sheet through which Aadam treats each of Naseem's illnesses is partly Rushdie's analogy for the partial recounting of history and subjectivity and the necessity of piecing together the whole from its component parts, it is also a criticism of the limits of Western medical practice as conferred through the doctor and its tendency towards reductionism when it concerns the human subject. In the same way that Aadam's treatments reduce Naseem to 'a badly-fitting collage of her severally-inspected parts', the figure of the doctor here is likewise reduced to his gaze, his hands and their function.[78] Whilst Aadam's social standing is increased by his profession, his personhood is inversely diminished. Moreover, the antagonism between Rushdie's characters here is further significant because of the legacy it has on Saleem, who is himself a signifier of the 'new' India, born at the stroke of independence. Saleem is a composite of both of these influences, that of the Westernised, professionalised, educated Indo-European family within which he is mistakenly brought up, and the instinctual, corporeal humanity represented by the peasant boatman, whose unwashed and scrofulous state comes to represent the apparently eternal poverty and disease of India and the class to which Saleem had truly been born before being switched. The divisions, distrust and internal doubts engendered by Aadam and Tai's antagonism are thus internalised and become integral to the new Indian subject. The incompleteness of the Indian subject after colonialism is likewise perpetuated, symbolised by the ongoing conflict over Kashmir between Pakistan and India; the absence of Kashmir from either country is a further hole that cannot be filled, yet both countries strive to complete it through further conflict.[79] Just as Saleem is incomplete as a result of various injuries and missing pieces, curing the wound and the void at the centre of the Indian subject is beyond the power of the doctor, and indeed the conflict over Kashmir is that which eventually kills Tai in 1947.

Ultimately, linking the doctor protagonists of Rushdie, Scott and Farrell is their adherence to and embrace of the new, whether in methods, the empathy of their outlook or just by the fact of their ethnic identity, in the face of an Anglo-Indian society committed to the preservation of tradition. Samuels, Aadam Aziz and McNab are all, in their differing ways, radical reimaginings of the colonial doctor who are confronted with a medical establishment that is stagnant and resistant to change. Colonial medicine becomes representative of the anti-progress narrative, experienced on both a social and individual level and used by these three authors to again question the adherence to the past in their present moments; the faith in the outlook and ideology of the past, here represented by the authority of the colonial medical establishment, is shown as misguided, limiting and occasionally dangerous. Rushdie, Scott and Farrell all use their doctors in the hope of diagnosing, questioning and remedying such misplaced faith in the British Empire, and in the hope of prescribing a new approach for the future. The doctor is no longer there to repair and restore the social body to its status quo, but rather prevent such a terminal relapse.

Midwives to colonial society: nurses, missionaries and the female caregiver

In tandem with, and sometimes in opposition to, the doctors that appear throughout these novels is the figure of the female caregiver. In the same manner that medical practice offered a means of social and professional advancement for Indians under British rule, so too did it appeal to women from across the social and ethnic spectrum of the Raj. Though East India Company and missionary hospitals existed in India from the seventeenth century onwards, nursing as a professional occupation began very much in an ad hoc fashion in response to the British wars of the 1850s. Fresh from her efforts in the Crimea, Florence Nightingale was instrumental in establishing similar principles of healthcare and treatment in response to the inadequacies of care experienced by British participants in the Indian Rebellion of 1857, leading to the development of the Nursing School at Netley in 1860.[80] Given the extensiveness of that conflict, and the fact that it involved not only military personnel but the civilian populations of British cantonments and stations across India, women from across the class spectrum were pressed into far more active service of Empire; the great boom in popular memoir that followed the conflict acts as testament to the involvement of women in a nursing or auxiliary capacity, with numerous accounts from the many sieges such as at Lucknow, Agra and elsewhere attesting to their fortitude, if not always their skill. Such narratives of collective British resistance in the face of adversity crystallised in the decades that followed and became one of the defining metanarratives of British India, as recognised in the slew of novels written across the life and aftermath of the Raj.[81]

In later decades, the efforts of the British Government of India, aided by the creation of the Countess of Dufferin Fund, to improve and expand the provision for women's healthcare through medical training, the opening of new facilities, and other public health measures were widespread, mirroring similar developments in Britain at that time and swiftly exceeding them.[82] Within the military context, the establishment of the Queen Alexandra's Imperial Military Nursing Service in 1902 bolstered the extent of nursing practice in India as well as the numbers of women engaged in practice.[83] The creation of the Women's Medical Service for India in 1913 added a professional branch to complement the work of the charities and missions. Alongside the expectation, if not necessity, for women to manage the health of their families as part of the domestic economy – especially where they were often many miles from a trained professional, as in the case of Margery Hall at Loralai – nursing and female medical practitioners eventually became commonplace in British India. Though H. Hervey, writing in 1913, alleged that female doctors were generally disliked by their male counterparts (seemingly as a result of the latter's sexism rather than any fault of the former), the accounts by ICS officers regarding the medical facilities in their districts have nothing but praise for the efforts of female medical practitioners of all ranks and the benefit of their work to Anglo-Indian society.[84]

Such gendered divisions inherent to medical practice are visible in Anglo-Indian fiction, with authors such as Jhabvala and Scott in particular seeking to represent female medical practitioners in their work, either as counterparts or in comparison to the male doctors already identified above, or as a means of exploring how the paternalism of the Indian medical establishment is encountered and experienced by female subjects. Additionally, their novels explore alternate means and methods of medical practice through Indian and European female characters, illustrating that although the British Raj became increasingly more orthodox and professionalised in its practice and apparatus as described above, there were still opportunities for women to play active and significant roles within medical practice. Even so, Scott and Jhabvala do not offer a picture of unproblematic female empowerment through medicine; differing from Farrell's McNab, treated with scepticism but respect by Simla society, or Scott's own Samuels, the disruptive outsider who forces change on an ossified Raj, female practitioners evoke mixed feelings and experience mixed fortunes within Jhabvala and Scott's narratives. Their novels repeatedly offer a contradictory portrait of how nursing and associated practice can serve to emancipate women either working or receiving treatment in a colonial setting, whilst also serve to limit women's expression by affirming their roles as caregivers to the exclusion of other possibilities.

For Jhabvala, whilst illness and health are continual currents that run throughout her novels, her focus on medical personnel is seemingly more limited and selective than her counterparts. For the most part, the doctors that populate her novels are academic rather than medical by background, such as Hochstadt in *A Backwards Place* or Sarla Devi in *Get Ready for Battle* (1962), who are both economists.[85] Those medical practitioners that do appear are those who seem either disconnected from the profession, such as the unnamed doctor in *A Backwards Place*, who, having 'long since ceased to practise', is now a landlord, or disconnected from their patients, as Jhabvala's representation of the aloof Saunders in *Heat and Dust* (1975) suggests.[86] For Jhabvala, her novels are less about considering the exercise or break from the paternalistic power invested within doctors as explored by Scott, Farrell and Rushdie, but rather the consequences of a confrontation with it, as experienced by disempowered female subjects such as Ritu, Leelavati or Olivia. Given how pregnancy and birth are seemingly Jhabvala's leitmotif, as observed in the Introduction, the medical experience of women around pregnancy recurs across her narratives, on each side of the Indian and European divide her novels often impose. In doing so, her work again recalls Foucault's analysis of the inequality of the clinical encounter and the hierarchical relationships implicit within biomedicine. Her response then, through the representation of Indian medicine in particular, is to offer an equitable alternative to the norm of female experience at the hands of European doctors.

In *Heat and Dust*, the prevailing juxtaposition of these medical systems and their practitioners comes towards the close of the book, when Olivia elects to have an abortion rather than bear the Nawab's child. Through an arrangement made by the Begum, the Nawab's mother, Olivia is taken to a 'tumble-down' house in Khatm and attended by 'two homely, middle-aged midwives'.[87] There she is made to lie on the floor whilst the two women induce an abortion through vigorous massage of the stomach. Jhabvala's inclusion of this procedure, a much older alternative to the medical and surgical abortions of the modern era, illustrates the difference between the coldness of Saunders' approach and the human connection offered by more traditional medical practice.[88] Despite the shabbiness of the house, Olivia notes that:

> . . . this was not in any case unpleasant. They were massaging her abdomen in an enormously skilful way, seeking out and pressing certain veins within. One of the women sat astride her while the other squatted on the floor. Their hands worked over her incessantly while they carried on their conversation. The atmosphere was professional and relaxed.[89]

As well as the difference in her surroundings to those of European medical practice, the method and manner of her treatment vary considerably in terms of their intent and what they signify. Rather than the hierarchical gaze of biomedical practice, where the patient is rendered vulnerable by being laid prone on the operating table whilst practitioners stand above them, here the three women are all on the same level. As opposed to examination or inspection, here the midwives engage in physical contact and affective touch, delivered with a professionalism and skill at odds with the 'tumble-down' context of their surroundings, and also counter to the assumptions and expectations made about Indian or non-European medicine, which are evident in the focalised perspectives of Olivia and the narrator. Further, no medical instruments are used; instead, the means of enacting the procedure come from within Olivia's body or through natural remedy, such as the insertion of the twig smeared with 'the juice of a certain plant', presumably one of the various herbs or flowers such as tansy or pennyroyal that can be used to induce miscarriage.[90] In so doing, the novel is extending its underlying meditations on the idea of naturalness to the context of medical practice. In the same way that she contrasts the natural actions, emotions and instincts around Olivia's romance with the Nawab to the unnatural formality and disconnection within the relationships of the British community, Jhabvala follows this thread through to the subject of health and medicine, and employs this ancient practice to further explore the clash of cultures in Anglo-India. The division over naturalness

becomes one of the novel's central conflicts, with considerable resonance around the use of a natural method and means to induce what
is perceived as unnatural within Olivia's social context, namely the
act of deliberate miscarriage.

Jhabvala contrasts Olivia's gentle treatment by the midwives
with that of the dehumanising approach of Saunders and his staff.
When Olivia becomes ill as the procedure takes its course, she is
taken to the European hospital where Saunders immediately recognises her condition as being the result of an abortion, noting that
he 'had extracted many such twigs from women brought to him
with so-called miscarriages'.[91] Here, Jhabvala reinscribes the status
of the European doctor not just as professional authority but also
as a figure of social power, noting that Saunders often 'confronted
the guilty women and threw them out of the hospital. Sometimes
he slapped them – he had strong ideas about morality and how to
uphold it.'[92] Jhabvala illustrates how European medicine is not the
dispassionate, clinical profession that it purports to be, but rather a
means of mirroring and consolidating the prevailing moral values of
Anglo-Indian society, especially when it comes to sexual and reproductive health. Recalling the same currents of medicine and religion
that occur in Farrell's work, rather than the rational application of
treatment based on physical or mental need, medical practice reveals
itself to be guided as much by emotive and faith-based beliefs as
it is by legal responsibility and scientific expertise. Of particular
note in this section too is that Saunders relies on the support of his
hospital matron, who 'stood grim-faced behind him . . . outraged'
by Olivia's behaviour.[93] Jhabvala's contrast in the medical roles of
women in this section is clear, suggesting a shared humanity and an
empathy between patients that crosses ethnic lines (just as it does
with the narrator and Ritu in the narrative present) but no similar
depth of feeling when it comes to professional responsibility, with
the matron's attitude serving to compound the disempowerment
of women within European biomedical practice as well as wider
Anglo-Indian society. As Kristine Swenson states of Victorian doctor
Mary Scharlieb's *Reminiscences* (1924), a desire to offer care does
not displace the racism of the Anglo-Indian community.[94] Having
availed herself of Indian medical practice, Olivia is no longer part
of the Anglo-Indian community and is treated as suspect; the diagnostic function of the doctor is again apparent here, with Saunders
noting that alongside his outrage, he was 'somewhat triumphant'
that his assumption that there was 'something rotten' about Olivia
had 'been proved right'.[95]

Even so, it is important to note that Jhabvala's depiction of the Indian midwives is not necessarily the corrective to this picture of paternalistic European medicine that it might initially suggest itself to be. Though the women are professional, skilled and possessed of a greater degree of humanity and warmth than any of their Anglo-Indian counterparts, they are never really developed into meaningful characters in their own right, and instead function as a medical means to an end. The reader is likewise given no detail or translation of their conversation, nor any real sense of them as individuals. This lack of depth might be a conscious decision by Jhabvala to remain focused on the European experience of India, especially in this latter phase of her Indian novels where she was writing with this goal explicitly in mind, and to likewise illustrate Olivia's detachment as a result of the language barrier and ethnic distance between them.[96] Such a decision also emphasises the difference between Olivia's time and that of the narrative present, where the narrator also initiates the same procedure with an Indian friend, Maji, but interrupts her before it is completed. Maji is a much more developed character; the two women forge a greater connection, converse and interact beyond their immediate instrumental relationship. In this sense, the abortion and the midwives past and present become another aspect of Jhabvala's juxtaposed temporal settings; her novel's defining message is that for all the aspects of India, medical practice and human relationships that stay the same, there is the potential for positive change, growth and development.

The representation of medical practitioners such as the Ladies of Khatm and Saunders adds a further layer of complexity to Jhabvala's engagement with illness and health. Whereas in the case of Ritu's psychological health the narrator makes the case for Western psychiatry, here the implication of the text is that Olivia is much better treated by Indian and non-biomedical practitioners. Questions of professional expertise intersect with notions of ethnic or gendered identities and empathy in each instance here, with Jhabvala seemingly advocating compassion over the perception of professional skill or cultural authority in some cases. Her novels recognise that biomedicine requires submission to power, which produces and perpetuates male medical indifference towards female suffering, as illustrated by Saunders' attitude to Olivia in the past and by Inder Lal and Ritu's relationship or Dr Gopal's attitude towards Leelavati in the present. However, Jhabvala offers a degree of hopefulness through the narrator's resistance to the stigma associated with the expression of her sexuality that broke Olivia, and through the potential for a more humanistic form of healthcare that combines knowledge and skill alongside empathy as embodied in the Ladies of Khatm and Maji.

Scott, meanwhile, takes a characteristically broad approach to the representation of nurses throughout his novels. Just as he does with nearly all elements of colonial society and its hierarchies, nurses appear in various forms, contexts and roles throughout *The Raj Quartet*, and thus fulfil a host of narrative and metaphorical functions. Again, medicine is entwined directly with the central premise of the series too, as Scott explains how Daphne Manners' reason for being in India in the first place is as a result of being 'dismissed the service' from her position as an ambulance driver in the London Blitz through ill health.[97] Scott further uses Daphne to echo and evoke the intergenerational colonial connections between India and Britain that characterise medical practice, as well as the ongoing British fascination with its Empire occurring in his own contemporary present. Daphne's journey to India relies on the legacies of her father's time there, when he was a respected member of the IMS at Mayapore, and the resumption of the friendships he left behind on his departure. Whereas he left India for private practice in Britain, Daphne arrives in India and seeks employment at the local hospital as part of the Voluntary Aid Detachment (V. A. D.). In her interview with the matron there, it is impressed upon her the status that nursing, as well as her family background, confers on her, with the matron emphasising that Daphne is joining the '*British* general hospital' (italics in original) rather than one of the other missionary or charitable establishments.[98] The scene also foreshadows the disputes over the maintenance of colonial hierarchies described in relation to Samuels in the later novels, with Daphne observing how the Queen Alexandra nurses and the V. A. D. 'rule the roost' and inflate their standing, noting that 'at home they'd simply be ordinary ward nurses, or staff nurses at best. Here they rank as sisters' and that all menial tasks are left to the 'poor little Anglo-Indian girls'.[99] Scott suggests that doctors like Samuels are content (and able) to destabilise such hierarchies, but that nurses and auxiliaries, in their supporting functions, mainly conform to existing regimes, and thus perpetuate social divisions for their own advancement.

As well as being relevant to the overarching plot, Scott's characterisation of nurses beginning in *The Jewel in the Crown* sets a precedent for the novels that follow, with such questions of rank, social mobility and personal freedom within the otherwise restrictive atmosphere of colonial British society recurring repeatedly throughout the series. In particular, and aside from Daphne Manners, Scott focuses his attention on three main characters: Sister Ludmilla, Sister Prior and Sarah Layton. Just as Farrell does between *The Siege of Krishnapur* and *The Hill Station*, Scott returns to many of the themes first broached in *The Jewel in the Crown*, developing and refining them as *The Raj Quartet* progresses and his intentions, and his facility with medicine as a critical frame, coalesce.[100] However, whilst his approach to using medicine and healthcare as a means of troubling the existing state of the Raj through the doctor drew on Samuels' status as outsider and subsequent ability to force change on colonial society, Scott's approach to nursing illustrates instead how colonial society changes the lives and identities of these individuals.

Aside from Daphne Manners' experience at the hospital, Scott's other concerted focus on nursing in *The Jewel in the Crown* centres on Sister Ludmilla and her clinic in Mayapore, known as the Sanctuary. As well as being the landowner and financial benefactor of the Sanctuary, Sister Ludmilla is one of its principal practitioners, alongside Mr de Souza and the various orderlies and temporary staff they employ. When Merrick comes looking for Hari Kumar the morning after the rape of Daphne Manners, he arrives at the Sanctuary, whereupon he is received by Sister Ludmilla and demands that she explain the function of their practice, ostensibly under the suspicion that they provide shelter for criminals. As Sister Ludmilla explains:

'The clinic receives only in the evening. Only people who cannot afford to lose a morning or a day's work come to our clinic.' 'And your medical qualifications?' 'Mr de Souza is in charge of the clinic. He gave up paid work as a lay practitioner to work with me for nothing. The health authorities of the municipal board sometimes come to see us. They approve of what they find. As District Superintendent of Police you must know most of these things.' 'And the dying?' 'We have the voluntary services of Dr Krishnamurti, and also Dr Anna Klaus of the purdah hospital. You can of course also inspect my title to the land and buildings.'
'It is a curious arrangement,' Mr Merrick said.
'It is a curious country.'[101]

Sister Ludmilla's observation that Merrick already knows the answers to his questions is dually significant here. On the surface level, it is an early indication of Merrick's sadistic authority, later revealed in full during his interrogation of Kumar; Merrick questions Sister Ludmilla principally because he can, and in anticipation that he might be able to turn her answers against her if he needs to incriminate her later, as he is shown to do with other characters throughout the novels of the series. The further purpose of this expository exchange, and the chapter in which it sits, is that it allows Scott to make a point about the shortcomings of healthcare and palliative care, both during and after the British Raj. Sister Ludmilla's function, and the work of the clinic, offers care to those unable to afford or unable to access the other medical facilities available within colonial society. The charitable, voluntary nursing that Sister Ludmilla engages in, with the support of de Souza, discounted medical supplies courtesy of Krishnamurti the pharmacist, and Anna Klaus' expertise, make up the shortfall in provision by the British medical establishment and government of India, thus undermining the familiar narrative of the benefits of British rule to Indian subjects. The apparent tacit consent of the health authorities further emphasises this failure of Anglo-Indian society to provide healthcare to those Indians in greatest need of it, with Sister Ludmilla's (and Scott's) most intense criticism reserved for the fact that India was, and still is, a place where people die without being given the 'dignity' of care.[102]

Scott makes a further point regarding nursing through how it affects Sister Ludmilla's identity and social standing. Whereas volunteer nurses come in for criticism from Daphne, Sister Ludmilla and the Sanctuary demonstrate how their existence is not as straightforwardly self-serving as first presumed. In the course of the chapter, it is revealed that 'Sister' Ludmilla is neither a nursing or religious sister, but rather Mrs Ludmilla Smith, originally of obscure Eastern European origin, now a holder of both French and British passports, and the widow of a British engineer who died whilst in the employ of an Indian princely state.[103] Recalling from her childhood how her mother had tried to donate to a passing congregation of nuns in Brussels, Sister Ludmilla explains how she came to dedicate her life and wealth to the running of the Sanctuary, swapping the privilege of her married life for the selflessness of medical practice. Nursing thus sublimates her previous identity and remakes Sister Ludmilla as the ideal of the female caregiver, exchanging the association with female sexuality in her past for one of feminine sanctity. Her title of 'sister', given to her by the Indians she treats, also takes on a broader significance; whilst apparently conferred on her as a result of her clothing and its resemblance to a nun's habit, there is a further humanistic resonance within it, referring to her acceptance and bond with the Indian community that she serves.[104] As a result, Scott shows how nursing impoverishes Sister Ludmilla by lowering her social standing, yet elevates her through her devotion to the lives of others.

Whilst Sister Ludmilla's presence and perspective are significant within the unfolding of the Bibighar plot, Sister Prior is a more minor character. However, she is just as revealing of the shifting identities of women within healthcare settings. Introduced towards the end of *The Day of the Scorpion*, Prior's exact role is unspecified, however, she appears to be a senior nurse at the officer's wing of the Military Hospital in Calcutta and is especially protective of Merrick whilst he is in her care. Sarah Layton encounters Prior when she visits Merrick on behalf of the Layton family, having received his letter after he was wounded in Burma attempting to rescue Teddie Bingham. Sarah, having made the long journey from Pankot to Calcutta, uses her family connections to arrange her visit, resulting in a confrontation with Prior when she arrives: 'Sister Prior made no move. They eyed each other levelly. The same height, Sarah thought, as well as the same age.'[105] Though seemingly expecting some sort of bond based around their shared connection to Merrick, as well as in their evident similarity, Sarah finds only veiled resentment from Prior, leaving her 'embattled behind the barriers of her class and traditions because the girl had challenged her to stand up for them'.[106] Such an encounter is not simply a confrontation between the two women, but an instance in which Sarah is confronted with the implications of her class; with her status enabling a privileged life without much responsibility or difficulty, Sarah's shock comes from having the usual actions of women of her class turned against her. Prior mimics the kinds of petty expressions of power visible elsewhere within colonial society by asserting her position over Sarah within the orbit of her control, namely the space of the hospital. Despite appearing cordial enough on a surface level, Prior treats Sarah with 'distant irony', keeps her waiting, and does not return to take her to Merrick, instead sending 'a dark-skinned Anglo-Indian nurse' in her place.[107] In the context of the novel and the generalised racism of the Anglo-Indian society it describes, such a decision is implied by Scott and recognised by Sarah as a deliberate snub, evocative of the same kind of exclusionary practice embodied by Sarah's mother, Mildred, and her coterie of memsahibs in Pankot. Sarah's encounter with Prior demonstrates the extent of medical authority in so much as Sarah is subjected to the effects of a power she usually wields.

In her refusal to express the class deference Sarah expects, Prior is Scott's expansion on the character of the matron that Daphne describes in *The Jewel in the Crown*, and a further consideration of nurses within the context of the Raj. Key to Scott's representation of Prior is the flexibility of her personality, and how she is able to alter it in the differing contexts of her role. For instance, in a later continuation of her challenge to Sarah, Prior returns, 'trim, capable, and asexually attractive', to brusquely eject Sarah from Merrick's room, once again asserting her power over her.[108] Sarah reflects on the changeability of Prior's personality, swinging between 'bitterness', 'professional coyness' with Merrick, and then as 'the talkative, informed and uniformed bouncer' that ejects her from the hospital.[109] In an ironic counterpart to Sister Ludmilla, Sister Prior does not lose her identity as a result of her profession, but uses it to recast herself in different contexts; it seems too that Scott deliberately names her 'Prior', alluding to her previous states and roles, as well as acting as a link to the religious context of a 'prioress' and how those values are seemingly absent in her identity. It is in the character of Prior that the difference between doctors and nurses is illustrated within Scott's work too; whilst Samuels attempts to shape society around his personality, nurses such as Prior shape their personalities to fit their role and their context, which affords them a greater degree of power than their class would otherwise permit elsewhere.

In her reaction to Sarah's connections, Prior exercises what power she has to challenge them based on her status as a nurse. These themes are foreshadowed on Sarah's train journey from Pankot, where she travels with a group of nurses on their way to Shillong; the nurses, and Sarah, proceed to drink too much gin and eventually have to be separated from some junior Army officers travelling in the next car.[110] Though again seemingly minor, like Prior's pettiness, such incidents suggest that the strictures of the Raj and its fiercely emplaced codes of propriety are beginning to loosen, allowing for social and sexual freedoms and the opportunity to push back against boundaries of class deference. Key to both examples is the role of the nurse, which brings professional standing but also geographical and social mobility and a degree of emancipation; Sarah in particular is not scandalised by the nurses' behaviour, but instead admits to how she envied them and their freedom.

Such actions are in fact not so much of a challenge to the status quo of colonial society, but an affirmation of it. Embodying the authority associated with doctors and the medical establishment, Prior asserts her status over Sarah in a similar fashion to Saunders and the matron from Jhabvala's *Heat and Dust*. Although the moral judgement inherent to Olivia's situation is absent here, the process is the same, and the female subject is subordinate to the authority of the medical figures in each instance, who draw their power from the status of the medical establishment composed of the IMS, the military and private practice within colonial India. Ultimately, Scott suggests that nurses such as Prior occupy a contradictory position in so much as they benefit from and therefore must enforce the very limits and boundaries that their actions push back against. Prior's parting speech to Sarah, in which she details the forthcoming amputation of Merrick's arm, shocks her because it is precisely what a person of her standing does not expect to hear from a perceived subordinate, as Prior is well aware. Prior's actions thus subvert social expectation through her understanding and recognition of its effects.

Sarah's experience with Prior is also significant in the context of her own personal development over the course of *The Raj Quartet*'s narrative. When introduced in the second book of the series, Sarah is characterised as a somewhat fey and shy young woman, uncertain of her place in India and beginning to perceive a clear difference between her own instincts, thoughts and values against those that are expected of her as a member of the prominent Layton family. However, as the series develops, it becomes apparent that Sarah's characterisation is also dependent on her relationship to illness and medicine, and, eventually, her decision to also engage in medical practice herself as a volunteer nurse at the Women's Hospital in Mirat. In the context of Scott's representation of female medical practitioners and how their selfhood is affected by their occupation, Sarah is a key character and prominent example of how nursing and medical practice affords fulfilment to otherwise dissatisfied individuals within the colonial society he depicts. In the early part of *The Day of the Scorpion*, Scott describes how Sarah is prone to suffering from what she calls her 'funny turns', in which 'everything went very far away, taking the sound with it'.[111] Though Sarah describes these episodes as largely invisible as they are without outward symptoms, they signify a distorted perspective, either personally, and pertaining to how her class influences how she sees the world around her, or on a metatextual level, in relation to how Empire is viewed across the recollected composition of *The Raj Quartet*, and also through the historical fictions of the Raj Revival more generally. Sarah further affirms the postmodernist leanings of Scott's novels, as it is explained that she once wrote an essay entitled 'The Effect of Climate and Topography upon the Human Character' on how the environments of India and Britain exert influence on health and physique, echoing the similarly self-reflexive practices apparent in the work of Farrell, Jhabvala and Rushdie.[112] Her essay, inspired by the same episode in which she first describes her 'funny turns', is largely a consideration of the merits of colonial service and British exceptionalism, but is also Sarah's personal reflection on the differences between the branches of her family and how life in India and Britain had caused them to diverge. Sarah, reflecting on this legacy at the end of the Raj, becomes Scott's representative of a particular class of colonial Briton and colonial woman, left seeking a purpose as the securities and certainties of the Raj collapse or come to an end.

Leading on from her essay, and inspired, or shamed, into action by her confrontation with Prior, Sarah first elects to work for the Women's Army Corps in Pankot. Her decision signifies a continuation of tradition (her family's military background) in one sense, but also an indication of how the war had opened up new possibilities for women that had previously been denied them in colonial society. The context of the war is an additional catalyst for Sarah's transformation, bringing her into contact with new arrivals to India such as Guy Perron and Leonard Clark, who have no investment in its restrictive codes of behaviour and social expectations. Over the course of the last two novels in the series, Sarah's new-found occupation occurs in conjunction with her sexual awakening, ironically confirming Dr Samuels' comments regarding Reich's theories of psychological health and sexual repression expressed at the end of *The Towers of Silence*. These various influences on Sarah transform her personality and her attitude to India; in *A Division of the Spoils*, when Perron mentions to her: 'You told me once that India wasn't a place you felt you could be happy in,' Sarah replies: '"Did I? Yes, I remember thinking that." She looked at him. "I've been very happy since."'[113] It is only revealed late in this same novel, however, that Sarah's happiness is in part due to the fact she has left military service for medical work, specifically volunteer nursing at '[t]he Mirat women's hospital . . . She's done a lot of voluntary work for them . . . She's been very popular with the patients and the nurses. . . . The hospital's one of the main reasons she stayed through the hot weather.'[114] Scott thus presents the reader with another echo of Sister Ludmilla, and an inversion of Prior, in Sarah's narrative; through rejection of her status and privilege, Sarah finds spiritual fulfilment through helping others, and even, at the very end of the book, a form of penitence and atonement through her work in volunteer hospitals in the aftermath of Partition.

There is, of course, a degree of the white saviour complex to Sarah's journey of self-discovery and personal growth, and the character fulfils various clichés regarding Europeans who 'find themselves' in the East. More critical novelists such as Jhabvala satirise such idealised imaginings directly, with a disillusioned hippie in *Heat and Dust* complaining that they had come to India to find peace, 'but all I found was dysentery'.[115] However, despite this 'physician, heal thyself' neatness, Scott's novels offer a significant approach to the representation of nursing by exploring its potential to permit movement across class boundaries, as well as reshape the personal and social identities of women involved in healthcare. It is notable too that Scott suggests through the varied characterisation of Daphne, Sister Ludmilla, Sister Prior and Sarah that those European women who choose nursing or caregiving roles in a colonial context are somehow aberrant or unusual. From Daphne's 'big-boned' awkwardness, Sister Ludmilla's rejection of status, Sister Prior's abrasive personality rendering her a 'bit off', through to Sarah's disaffection prompting her transformation and rejection of the Raj's values, all of Scott's nurses are at some point othered and exceptional within colonial society.[116] Within the lives of these unusual women, however, nursing provides each of them with a form of direction, distinction and self-determination, as well as crucial self-knowledge, either for good in most cases, or with more complicated or self-interested results in the case of Prior. Though, ultimately, their occupation in nursing conforms to the patriarchal and paternalistic character of British India and what is considered suitable for women of their time and place, their actions and small subversions gradually broaden those parameters, carving out further freedoms as a consequence. Whilst not acting with the assuredness or impunity of Scott's male medical practitioners, his female characters find in nursing a level of change and fulfilment that so few of their male counterparts do.

Notes

1. Sontag, *Illness as Metaphor*, 52.
2. Carel, *Illness*, 7. Carel describes how adjusting to illness forced her to 'reinvent' her life.
3. Foucault, *Birth*, xiv.
4. Ibid. 9.
5. See Surawicz and Jacobson, *Doctors in Fiction*; Arnold-Forster and Moulds, 'Medical women in popular fiction'.
6. McLeod, *J. G. Farrell*, 5. Ralph J. Crane counts at least six doctors in Farrell's published works; however, Farrell's papers held at Trinity College show evidence of a further doctor removed from the final version of *Troubles* (1970) and another in an untitled and unfinished play. Crane and Livett, *Troubled Pleasures*, 129; Farrell (Trinity), Box 9153: *The Hill Station*, 'Notes and Index Cards', 39.

7. The other is Major Brendan Archer from *Troubles* (1970) and *The Singapore Grip* (1978). Again, like the doctors, Archer fulfils a particular function; in this instance he is a genial, well-meaning everyman figure engulfed by the extraordinary events that unfold around him, both in Ireland in 1921 and Singapore in 1942.

8. Pratt, *Imperial Eyes*, 6.

9. See Maude, *Samuel Beckett and Medicine*, and Fifield, *Modernism and Physical Illness*.

10. Plock, *Joyce, Medicine and Modernity*, 3. The Linati and Gilbert Schemas were written by Joyce as guides for friends to understand the structure of his book, with the latter first published by Stuart Gilbert in *James Joyce's Ulysses: A Study* (1930).

11. Forster's book was not well received in Raj society, as Herbert Thompson (ICS) noted: 'Vernon was incensed by Forster's Passage to India . . . [it] had not yet appeared to rouse the wrath of my later Collector . . . His immediate verdict on the book was "wicked and mischievous. Grossly libellous to both Indian and Englishman."' BL, Thompson, 'Icarus went East', 73.

12. Teresa Heffernan notes the echo between the texts, but argues for a divergence between the characters based on their authors' approaches to Indian nationalism. Heffernan, *Post-apocalyptic Culture*, 101.

13. Rushdie's archive reveals that he was mindful of such connections between his writing and genres past and present, using them to make ironic allusions to literary and popular culture. An early draft of *Shame* (1983) states of Omar Khayyam that the character's name was originally 'Dr Fareed ("Freddie") Forsyte', recalling both Frederick Forsyth and John Galsworthy's *The Forsyte Saga* (1906–21). Rushdie, MARBL, Fiction, 20/6: *Shame*, 'Notes, Manuscript and Typescript', n.p.

14. Harrison, *Public Health*, 7. Arnold, *Science, Technology and Medicine*, 58.

15. Harrison, *Public Health*, 8.

16. Hervey, *The European in India*, 51.

17. Harrison, *Public Health*, 10. In Farrell's *The Hill Station* (1981), Emily reflects on how when seen with her uncle, Dr McNab, and his wife, 'she suffered a slight but perceptible loss of rank', not 'because Dr McNab ate peas off his knife or was anything but presentable . . . it was simply that he was a *doctor*'. Farrell, *THS*, 91.

18. BL, Hall, 'And the Nights', Chapter 8, 1.

19. BL, Orr, Mss Eur F180/22, 83.

20. Harrison, *Public Health*, 15–16. Even so, examination was held in England and further training at the Army Medical School at Netley, meaning recruits required a certain level of financial means in the first place.

21. Sweet and Hawkins, *Colonial Caring*, 8–9.

22. Bala (ed.), *Medicine and Colonialism*, 3–4. Harrison notes too that even if they did elect to join the IMS, recruits nonetheless faced overt or implicit racism; Harrison, *Public Health*, 33.
23. Pandya, *Medical Education in Western India*, 289–90.
24. BL, Hall, 'And the Nights', Chapter 8, 7.
25. BL, Redpath, 'Recollections of a Political Officer in India', 36. Moreover, Redpath notes that the doctor 'was not only a skilled surgeon but also a linguist who spoke excellent Urdu and the local language, a combination of attributes that was of considerable political value'.
26. See Stephen, *The Empire of Progress*; Gopal, *Insurgent Empire*, 376.
27. Healy, 'Bodies politic', 14.
28. Farrell (Trinity), Box 9155: 'Unpublished diary', 69.
29. The Condition of England novel, popular at points of perceived national crisis since the mid-nineteenth century, has experienced a resurgence in the last half decade as a result of Brexit and its convulsive nationalisms; see Ashbridge, 'It aye like London', 15.
30. There is a further intertextual link here to Farrell's literary forebears; Arthur Conan Doyle's John Watson, an assistant surgeon trained at the University of London, and who served with British forces in India, is often cast as the slower-witted of the pair, with the intimation that his former profession and limited intelligence are somehow linked. Farrell plays with this idea of the dull regimental surgeon by vindicating McNab's hypotheses. James Reed, however, claims this perception of Watson's intelligence is due to the films of Basil Rathbone and Nigel Bruce, rather than Conan Doyle. See Reed, 'A medical perspective on the adventures of Sherlock Holmes', 77.
31. Klein, 'Cholera', 30.
32. Collingham, *Imperial Bodies*, 90–1. Mark Harrison argues that Snow's analysis asked only a limited range of questions and excluded a number of factors pertinent to India and colonial space; Harrison, *Climates and Constitutions*, 191. Indeed, key figures within the IMS, such as Dr James Bryden, maintained that there were also distinct atmospheric and meteorological differences between Britain and India which affected the transmission and treatment of cholera; see Bryden, 'Epidemic Cholera in the Bengal Presidency', 14.
33. Klein, 'Cholera', 31.
34. The same is true of Farrell's depiction of phrenology, and the zeal with which both the Magistrate and Hari adhere to its principles; see Goodman, 'A Great Beneficial Disease'. See also John Spurling, 'As Does the Bishop', in which he discusses Farrell's use of dramatic irony; Farrell, *THS*, 155.
35. Goonetilleke, 'J. G. Farrell's Indian Works', 412.
36. Dix, *Postmodern Fiction*, 25.
37. Farrell, *SoK*, 250.
38. Ibid. 250.

39. Ibid. 253.
40. Ibid. 249.
41. Bhabha, *Location of Culture*, 70.
42. Dean, 'An Insight Job', 12.
43. Fischer-Tiné, 'Liquid Boundaries: Race, Class and Alcohol in Colonial India', 90, in Fischer-Tiné and Tschurenev (eds), *A History of Alcohol and Drugs*.
44. McLeod, *J. G. Farrell*, 75.
45. Ibid. 73. As Farrell's papers suggest, Kingston is modelled on an earlier character deleted from the original draft of *The Siege of Krishnapur*, the ironically named Reverend Brightwell, who is also suffering from consumption and being treated by McNab; Farrell (Trinity), Box 9141: *The Siege of Krishnapur*, 'Early fragments', 76–7.
46. Howell, *Malaria and Victorian Fictions of Empire*, 14.
47. Farrell, *THS*, 131.
48. Charon, *Narrative Medicine*, 1.
49. Farrell, *THS*, 72. Farrell's notes for *The Hill Station* suggest McNab would have encountered practitioners of traditional Indian medicine in the course of the narrative; see Farrell (Trinity), Box 9153: *The Hill Station*, 'Notes and Index Cards'.
50. McLeod, *J. G. Farrell*, 60.
51. Farrell (Trinity), Box 9152: Manuscript (typed) of *The Hill Station*, 157.
52. Farrell, *THS*, 73.
53. Hywel Dix argues that this is a technique that can be described as the 'deliberate use of anachronism' that engages (if not relies upon) the reader's knowledge of subsequent history in order to 'generate a specific trans-historical understanding'. See Dix, *Postmodern Fiction*, 23.
54. Farrell, *SoK*, 94.
55. It is perhaps not coincidental that Berger was Farrell's contemporary of course, winning the Booker the year before him for his novel *G* (1972).
56. McLeod, *J. G. Farrell*, 77. Farrell explores similar ideas in *Troubles* too. Sarah Devlin's interactions with the Major are essentially this, a talking cure, though are never explicitly named as such.
57. Scott's writing remains postmodern, however; the character of Major Tippet, a historian of India in peacetime, appearing within a historical novel seems deliberately self-reflexive. Scott, *TDotS*, 37.
58. Scott is one of the few authors here to include a female doctor, Anna Klaus of the Mission Hospital, who tends to Daphne Manners after her rape in the Bibighar in *The Jewel in the Crown*. Klaus is a minor and aloof figure; she is seemingly an excellent doctor, but appears unemotional and detached. One of her few lines of dialogue is to tell Daphne that she must 'learn to live without' (seemingly referring to Hari), but there is a deliberate ambiguity to this line, and Klaus' words imply the privations of her own life in medicine and what she too has had to live without as a German-Jewish refugee. Scott, *JitC*, 563.

59. Scott, *TToS*, 367.
60. Ibid. 367. Farrell also explores such prejudices in *SoK*, where a rumour that McNab is Jewish causes similar reaction; Farrell, *SoK*, 273.
61. Scott, *TToS*, 367.
62. Such attitudes are reminiscent of Virginia Woolf's *Mrs Dalloway* (1925), and the rest home treatment recommended for Septimus Smith by Dr Holmes.
63. Scott, *TToS*, 409.
64. Calling was strictly observed until the very end of the Raj, despite being seen by many as a relic of Victorian etiquette. See for example the memoir of Sidney William Cecil Dunlop, ICS Madras, who found it 'very tiresome, very hot' in 1937; BL, Mss Eur F180/51, 3. Scott, *TToS*, 416.
65. Scott, *TToS*, 414–15.
66. Ibid. 416.
67. Ibid. 419.
68. Rushdie, *MC*, 11.
69. Ibid. 12. There are similar currents of unexpected change as a result of medical training in Scott's *The Towers of Silence* in relation to the Indian doctor Lal; Scott writes that whilst Lal's training should 'have opened a world to him', his path had been blocked by British doctors, and overwork had left him 'tubercular', 'sanguine' and weakened. See Scott, *TToS*, 277.
70. Another process of cultural and spiritual dislocation occurs in relation to Ahmed Sinai's alcoholism; see Chapter 4.
71. Rushdie, *MC*, 21.
72. Ibid. 21.
73. Alberto Fernández Carbajal states that his education makes Aadam a 'suspected foreigner in his own nation'; Carbajal, *Compromise and Resistance*, 167.
74. Rushdie, *MC*, 11.
75. Ibid. 36.
76. Ibid. 36. Aadam's fall into the dirt also recalls the so-called 'crawling order' later issued by Dyer on 19 April; James, *The Rise and Fall of the British Empire*, 417.
77. Rushdie, *MC*, 33. Rushdie would continue to explore similar questions through the character of Omar Khayyam in *Shame* (1983), who wins a scholarship to medical college in Karachi, but is sent off with a pocket full of pawnbroker's banknotes after his family hock all their belongings lest the scholarship suggest he is from a poor background.
78. Rushdie, *MC*, 25–6. Such a reduction recalls Scott's *The Jewel in the Crown* (1966) where, in the midst of Daphne's rape, Scott writes of how the act itself diminishes the body, emphasising instead the vulnerability of the individual reduced to constituent parts; Daphne notes the pressure at her ankles and wrists, and her 'exposed nakedness'; Scott, *JitC*, 520. This powerlessness and smallness of the individual is later

echoed in the deliberate comparison with the caesarean section Daphne undergoes at the novel's close, where she is once again reduced to her stomach and womb; Scott, *JitC*, 562.

79. At time of initial research on this chapter, a state of emergency in Kashmir had been in operation for over two months, ahead of the formal division of the region on 31 October 2019. *BBC.co.uk*, 'Jammu and Kashmir: India formally divides flashpoint state'.

80. Best, 'Training the "natives" as Nurses'.

81. Gautam Chakravarty argues that the 1890s were the high point for 'Mutiny' narratives, with nineteen titles published in the course of the decade, alongside various memoirs; Chakravarty, *Indian Mutiny and the British Imagination*, 6.

82. Kristine Swenson argues that there was also much greater opportunity for female medical practitioners within colonial space, as opposed to that of Britain; Swenson, *Medical Women and Victorian Fiction*, 189. S. R. Collinson notes, for example, the opportunities afforded to Mary Scharlieb in Madras; Collinson, 'Mary Ann Dacomb Scharlieb: A Medical Life'. Scharlieb gained her licentiate of medicine in Madras and was later a student of Elizabeth Garret Anderson's London School of Medicine for Women. Alison Moulds argues that the issue was at the forefront of public debate, as indicated in the periodical press of the time; Moulds, 'The "Medical-Women Question"'.

83. Sweet and Hawkins, *Colonial Caring*, 9. The service continues to operate today, though 'Imperial' has become 'Royal'.

84. Hervey, *The European in India*, 169; BL, Paterson, Mss Eur F180/46, 30.

85. In another link to modernism, Ralph J. Crane argues that the character of Devi is drawn from Henry James' *The Bostonians* (1886), which features 'a wonderful woman doctor with a small but strong role'; see Crane, *Jhabvala*, 18.

86. Jhabvala, *A Backwards Place*, 15. Those instances where a doctor becomes a businessman, landlord or entrepreneur are often representative of the difference between the colonial and the newly independent India; Dr Narlikar, a former gynaecologist turned property developer from Rushdie's *Midnight's Children*, is a further example, and suggestive of how new opportunities for social advancement replace the old.

87. Jhabvala, *HaD*, 166.

88. Potts et al., 'Thousand-year-old depictions of massage abortion', 233–4.

89. Jhabvala, *HaD*, 167.

90. Ibid. 169.

91. Ibid. 169.

92. Ibid. 169.

93. Ibid. 170.

94. Swenson, *Medical Women*, 190.

95. Jhabvala, *HaD*, 170.

96. According to Ralph J. Crane, Jhabvala stated she eventually became no longer interested in India, but rather 'interested in myself in India'. Crane suggests that this is the same point where she becomes interested in the Raj; Crane, *Jhabvala*, 57.

97. Scott, *JitC*, 565. It is initially implied that Daphne may have left London due to combat fatigue, but later confirmed that it was on medical advice due to cardiac arrhythmia.

98. Ibid. 125.

99. Ibid. 126. Scott's novel likewise echoes a long-running perception of weakness or lower standards endemic to British personnel born in India; various documents from the military and civil authorities of India in the nineteenth and twentieth centuries expressed such prejudices, with a case file from 1919 stating: 'It must also be remembered that he belongs to the Anglo-Indian Community in which mental stamina is much below British standards.' See BL, 'Compulsory retirement of G. A. Weston'.

100. *The Jewel in the Crown* is essentially the blueprint for Scott's later character development in subsequent novels. For instance, the conversation between Daphne and Matron is developed into the exchange between Sarah and Sister Prior, and Sister Ludmila is echoed in Sarah's own decision to volunteer at the Zenana hospital.

101. Scott, *JitC*, 166.

102. Ibid. 160. The novel's historical frame suggests that Scott is likewise commenting on the fact that the situation remains unchanged in the narrative present of 1966, and after independence.

103. Ibid. 148. In her description of her childhood, it is implied that Ludmila and her family are originally from St Petersburg and that her mother was a sex worker, hence why the nuns refuse her money.

104. These ideas are later echoed in the closing sections of *A Division of the Spoils*, where Perron witnesses European and Indian nuns working as nurses, tending wounds that revealed 'the whiteness of the bone, and the redness of the flesh under the brown skin', implying Perron's realisation of the universal nature of suffering (and the superficiality of the racial differences that had underwritten British rule of India) during the violence of Partition. Scott, *ADotS*, 705–6.

105. Scott, *TDotS*, 436.

106. Ibid. 438.

107. Ibid. 438.

108. Ibid. 478.

109. Ibid. 478; 480.

110. Ibid. 434.

111. Ibid. 99.

112. Ibid. 142. See Chapter 3 for further consideration of Sarah's essay, and the relationship between climate and health in more detail

113. Scott, *ADotS*, 594–5.

114. Ibid. 648.
115. Jhabvala, *HaD*, 21. Sarah Layton also reinscribes Swenson's observation regarding the complex connection between Victorian feminism and imperialism, likewise applicable here, where such feminisms affirm the roles of Empire. See Swenson, *Medical Women*, 195. For a more contemporary example of the nursing-as-class-liberation trope in fiction, the storyline of Lady Sybil Crawley from ITV's *Downton Abbey* (2010–15) follows much the same pattern.
116. Scott, *JitC*, 407; *TToS*, 293.

Chapter 3

Know Your Place: Space, Environment and Medicine

In its chapters thus far, this book has concerned itself with the 'what' and the 'who' inherent to the representation of medicine and health in Anglo-Indian fiction, specifically the effects of illness on the individual or those treating them. When it comes to analysing the content of such works or their own specific historical and literary context, though, it is impossible to ignore the 'where', or the crucial importance of space, place and environment in relation to their narratives and their engagement with the medical legacies of Empire. Alongside the intrinsic importance of India to the novels under study here, in its very essence, colonialism itself is of course predicated on the idea of capture and control over space; Marcus Rediker argues that this preoccupation produces a sense of 'terracentricism', or a cultural primacy of landed spaces that underwrites the concepts of colonialism and Enlightenment ontologies during the age of empires, and which continues to exist within the politics and poetics of the postcolonial present.[1] Such thinking, as Tim Cresswell observes, informed widespread beliefs about the deleterious effects of tropical climates on European bodies, made all the more susceptible to disease and ailment by being figuratively and literally 'out of place' whilst in the East.[2] As a consequence of this connection between bodies and spaces, European medical practice in India was for a long time wedded to ideas of what Mark Harrison terms 'normative ecology' and 'medical topography', with some IMS doctors remaining adherents to the belief in the intrinsic relationship between climate, landscape and disease until the early twentieth century, often in spite of crucial new developments and techniques such as bacteriology and the germ theory of disease.[3]

This topographical understanding of health and medicine reflected the broader significance of space and place within the cultural and professional landscape of Indian society. The effect of space on Anglo-India, from governance and medical practice through to domestic life, was deeply felt, and influenced the history and development of its varied publishing cultures both during and after Empire. At the very foundational level of India's position within British cultural life existed an overriding romanticism of the East, expressed in a range of visual and print media.[4] Alongside its focus on health, the perennially popular genre of colonial travelogue and autobiography invariably contains extended descriptions of an author's passage to India and their journeys across it; given that before the opening of the Suez Canal in 1869 a voyage to India might take up to 160 days, depending on the route taken, accompanied by further overland travel on arrival, this concern with both space and time is understandable.[5] It is in these documents too that newcomers to India record their emotions as they first arrive on the subcontinent, further contributing to the production of the East through record of their shock or astonishment at its 'exotic' sounds, sights and smells.[6] Anglo-Indian social and professional life were likewise shaped by the relationships between individuals and space; strictly demarcated and enforced, understandings of access and exclusion from space, supported by distinctions of class, caste and ethnicity, dictated the movements of Britons and Indians alike.[7] For those in government and the military, life in India was often itinerant, suggesting an impermanence and transience to their experience of spaces and places within the country, or isolating, as Margery Hall's experience in Balochistan suggests. There was a clear hierarchy to space and place within the Indian Civil Service, where newly qualified officers competed for the coveted postings of the United Provinces, the so-called 'Old India' of Lucknow and Jhansi that brought with it the 'romance' of 1857, or the contrasts of the Punjab, boasting rugged country alongside historic cities like Amritsar.[8] Once posted, the practice of touring meant that some junior officers would be on the road for the majority of the working year, recording their movements and engagements in their ubiquitous tour diaries.[9]

Aside from diaries and travelogues, the representation of Anglo-Indian life in literary fiction was just as much characterised by the importance of space and place. In Anglo-Indian literature of the nineteenth and early twentieth centuries, nowhere was this more clearly articulated than in the works of Rudyard Kipling, whose descriptions of India's labyrinthine cities, teeming jungles and endless roadways, hills and plains cemented their position within the popular imagination of imperial Britain.[10] Kipling's choices should not be seen a passive component of plot and narrative or just an appealing backdrop. As Franco Moretti has argued, space is an active force within literature, intrinsic to character development and vital to the staging of narrative, shaping and enabling certain actions.[11] Consequently, this pervasive spatiality in colonial fiction should not be thought of as simply reflective of the conditions of Anglo-Indian life. Instead, as noted in preceding chapters, the relationship between colonial society, non-fiction and literature was an inherently reciprocal and co-productive one; many of those same ICS-men-turned-diarists arrived in India armed with expectations drawn from the reading habits of their youth, especially Kipling, and thus sought actively to realise them and experience the India of their boyhood imaginations during their service, before going on to record them in diaries, memoirs or fictional works of their own.[12]

The literary preoccupation with space and place was not confined to the duration of the Empire's existence either, but only took on deeper intensity and greater importance in its aftermath. As numerous authors, myself included, have argued, the literary imaginary of post-war, postcolonial Britain was directed, if not dominated, by the response to the end of Empire and the loss of its colonial possessions, with the nation's anxieties over its diminishing status, power and prestige expressed consistently in spatial terms.[13] Spatiality serves as a common thread that ties together the overlapping discourses of post-war, Cold War and post-imperial Britain after 1945, connecting the changes in landscape through contemporaneous efforts to rebuild those cities and towns destroyed by aerial bombing, the emergent rhetoric of the Cold War with its Manichean binaries and spheres of influence, and the ongoing process of decolonisation in which British overseas possessions diminished with increasing rapidity. The cultural preoccupation with space only intensified as decolonisation continued, exacerbated by the Suez Crisis of 1956–7, which would be Britain's last attempt at unilateral military action until the re-inscriptive efforts in the Falklands a quarter of a century later, and the nation's relegation to a supporting role as the Cold War rumbled on. In order to compensate for the increasing vicissitudes of this history, the narrative of the end of Empire was rewritten to become one of benevolent emancipation, of giving back and not giving up. Britain had generously and bloodlessly returned control of its colonies to their people, went the official line, having adequately prepared them for self-government. Such refashioning of the point and purpose of British imperialism was not only demonstrably untrue, especially in relation to Kenya, Malaya and Aden, but self-deluding, allowing Britain to convince itself that Empire had been, on balance, a force for good, and not like the violent and oppressive empires of other European states. This self-image served only to repress any meaningful national confrontation with the exploitative reality of Britain's colonial past and would lead to the creation of a seam of mythic nationalism within British politics and culture, the effects of which continue to be felt over half a century later.

In reflection of its pervasive presence, spatiality is a significant force visible in the production of post-war British fiction of all kinds. From the frustrated agents of the popular espionage novel, through the variously muted and furious responses of the Movement poets and Kitchen Sink playwrights of the 1950s and 60s, to the post-imperial obsessions of the Booker winners of the 1970s that make up this volume, space is a significant element of their response to the nation's identity crisis in the wake of Empire.[14] For Rushdie, Jhabvala, Farrell and Scott, space acts as further unifying factor, linking their fiction as well as their authorial intent. As noted in the Introduction, these writers did not constitute a school in the traditional literary sense; they did not meet socially or even share much in common by way of class or economic background. However, their experience of the disordered spatiality characteristic to the British post-imperial period, and their resultant focus on India, is a common element that brings them together.

That Jhabvala, Rushdie, Farrell and Scott all decide to return to colonial space, and specifically India as the 'jewel in the crown' of Empire, is redolent of such unity through spatial focus. Their shared effort to deflate the pretence of the supposedly noble intent of Empire in its efforts to ready its colonies for self-governance stretches across all of the texts analysed here, especially given the effects of Partition in India and the violence that ensued as a result of British inaction. Farrell and Rushdie in particular, as evinced in their choices of form and tone, seek to overtly undermine the perceived grandeur of colonial society through irony, pastiche and parody, satirising the orientalism of Anglo-Indian fiction as they add to it. The importance of spatiality of their novels is further significant when examined in relation to their engagement with health and medicine. That these authors seek to return to India in each instance supports Moretti's analysis that only certain spaces can enable particular literary narratives; simply put, the engagement with medicine and health, and the kinds of critical reflection on the legacy of Empire and contemporary British national identity that these novelists sought to produce, could only occur within the spatial context of the colonial Empire. The figurative return to colonial space through the historical novel allows Farrell, Rushdie, Jhabvala and Scott to explore the health of the nation past and present, historical and metaphorical.

In response to these concerns, this chapter focuses on the importance of space, place and environment within Anglo-Indian fiction and how Rushdie, Jhabvala, Farrell and Scott use spatiality, illness and their attendant metaphor to engage with the legacy of colonialism in their contemporary moment. The chapter is divided into two thematic sections in reflection of the spatial divisions within their novels, namely those of exteriors and interiors, further considering a range of macro, micro and meta-spaces in relation to health in the course of its analysis. In its focus on exteriors, the chapter draws on the historiography of medical topography as well as critical discourses of spatiality and health expressed within colonial medicine and society to explore the representation of the Indian landscape and its effects on health. Reflecting their engagement with the literary history of colonial India, the chapter explores the distinctions between towns, hills and plains throughout Scott, Farrell and Jhabvala's work and how these spaces are variously presented as conducive to health, or the ways in which they are pathologised. With a particular focus on the significance and recurrence of the hill station throughout the genre, it argues that on their surface level, these novels appear to mirror the beliefs of their literary forbears, and suggest a distinction between the dangers to health and well-being presented by the climate and environment of the plains in comparison to the relative safety of the hills. However, through close analysis of Scott and Farrell's novels, the chapter illustrates that India is never free of risk for the British body, and whilst these spaces may function as sites of physical recuperation, they are responsible for a moral and spiritual sickness within colonial society whose legacies linger into the contemporary present.

The chapter's second part approaches the spatial emplacement of colonial and medical authority and treatment throughout Anglo-Indian fiction, considering how Scott, Farrell, Rushdie and Jhabvala depict hospitals, clinics, nursing homes and domestic spaces within their narratives. The chapter argues that the representation of these interiors serves a variety of functions within these novels, illustrating that through the import of the gendered, racialised and hierarchal prejudices of colonialism, spaces of care become just as damaging, debilitating and restrictive as those that exist beyond their walls. Through analysis of the relationship between space and the classificatory practices of Empire in terms of race and ethnicity, the chapter demonstrates that these novels show how spaces of healthcare and convalescent environments become contested and liminal spaces of European and Indian encounter in which the good intentions of healthcare and the prejudices of Empire collide.

Exteriors: hills to die on

Reflecting on the long history of Anglo-Indian fiction since the nineteenth century, Ralph J. Crane observes that it is 'noticeable how many novels begin with detailed descriptions of the topography of India'.[15] This topographical focus is not simply an effort to set the scene for the narrative that will ensue, nor only a way to place a character in context. Rather, Crane's observations, and indeed the general premise of his analysis of the genre, indicate the bind in which so many Anglo-Indian writers have found themselves. At once over-awed by their experience and compelled by the expectations of the literary history of memoir and travelogue to call attention to the exotic, otherworldly nature of India's geography to the British visitor, Crane suggests that these writers are nonetheless unable to capture it in print in its entirety, nor with any objective clarity. Instead, Crane states that '[e]very novelist who has written about India has re-invented that country,' with their fiction producing a host of imaginary Indias that exist alongside one another, each representative of the intent of their intervention within the genre.[16]

Crane's approach suggests that for these writers, India is never simply just a setting, but instead an active presence throughout their novels and the wider genre, responsible for shifts in plotting, the shaping of character development and dramatic tension, if not arguably acting as a character itself. Such topographical openings to these novels are as much examples of liminal spaces, those in which an individual undergoes change and development, as the thresholds to the subcontinent represented by the docksides that recur throughout memoir and travelogue. Forster's *A Passage to India* (1924) again sets a fictional precedent with its description of the darkly portentous and forbidding Marabar Caves, the catalyst and site of much of the tension and destruction, but also spiritual and personal growth, to follow. Representative of the adversarial relationship between the British individual and the landscape of India, such beginnings often serve not only to throw the smallness of the individual into relief against the vastness of the country in which they find themselves, but also signify the beginning of the narrative journey that will follow. For Jhabvala,

Scott, Farrell and Rushdie, the significance of such journeys and their usefulness as metaphor is heightened and accentuated by their place within Britain's own postcolonial journey; these authors are situated in a state of liminality, as the nation undergoes its own process of change and transformation in the wake of the end of Empire. It suits their purposes to each feature a character for whom all of India is new, acting as a useful expositional device and narrative driver, but also as a way in which to puncture the ideals of Empire through sharp introduction to the realities of colonial life, as evinced in Farrell's Fleury, Scott's Perron or Jhabvala's unnamed narrator.[17] The journeys that their characters make are sometimes metafictive, representative of the journey into the nation's past that will take place through their postmodern historical fiction or in imitation of the form that they seek to mimic, but also psychogeographic. Guy Debórd's formulation of psychogeography as the collision of feeling and spatiality, of psychology and geography, seems particularly applicable to the postmodern return to colonial space enacted through the Anglo-Indian novel.[18] Farrell, Scott, Jhabvala and Rushdie all engage in a process of historical and narratalogical archaeology, whether personal or more broadly political, through their emphasis on the retracing of past journeys, travels and historical events. Their novels adopt the guise of the *dérive*, and drift through imperial history and Indian topography as their characters do, albeit with a sharpened sense of purpose as they seek to unpick the dominant or singular understanding of the British past. As such, their novels further echo the concerns of psychogeograpy in that they become palimpsests, attempting to write over the dominant narratives of Empire as the traces of the past return to the contemporary present.

This notion of the journey in the Anglo-Indian fiction of Scott, Rushdie, Jhabvala and Farrell takes on further critical and contextual resonance when examined in relation to the recurrence of medicine and health through their writing, as well as their own biographical circumstances. Their individual, personal experiences of the disordered spatiality of mid-century and post-imperial Britain were never passive, and all were affected by significant journeys throughout their lives that acted as formative backdrops to their use of the trope in their writing; Farrell's Anglo-Irish origins, Scott's military service in India, Jhabvala's flight from Nazism to Britain and married life in India, and Rushdie's education in England all found expression in their work. The medical experiences of Farrell and Scott in particular suggest how these authors' lives might also be read within the frame of the illness narrative and its inherent incorporation of the spiritual, physical and recuperative journey. Using Arthur W. Frank's taxon-omy of the illness narrative, the predisposition towards journeying in these novels might productively be identified with the restitution or quest narrative in which an individual undergoes a process of treat-ment that produces new knowledge and self-actualisation, albeit at a cost.[19] In their combination of Anglo-Indian literary history, personal biography and the metaphorical resonance of illness, these novels are thus literary journeys of self-discovery, healing and growth, as well as destruction, death and change.

The import of these critical contexts is apparent in the plot, nar-rative and aesthetic of Scott, Rushdie, Farrell and Jhabvala's work. Scott in particular often evokes the debilitating effects of the environ-ment of India on British bodies throughout his series, as indicated in various examples from across his novels noted in the preceding chapters. Of these, Sarah Layton's essay 'The Effect of Climate and Topography upon the Human Character' from *The Day of the Scor-pion* (1968) is perhaps one of Scott's most explicit considerations of the relationship between environment, health and character. The point of Sarah's work, as she recalls, was to highlight the differences she observed between her English family and her Anglo-Indian fam-ily, with the former having been made 'strong, active, energetic and self-reliant' as a result of England's climatic diversity.[20] In an echo of the kinds of essentialist thinking of 'normative ecology', Sarah goes on to consider that these qualities are those which have enabled the English to gain and keep control of their Indian territories, in tandem with her belief that the indigenous inhabitants of tropical spaces are more inclined to follow and be led.[21] Lurking amidst this story of British success is the fact, as she sees it, that to live in India represents 'the human struggle against nature', further evocative of the sugges-tion that imperial service is a burden to the Britons that choose to bear it. Continuing her train of thought shortly after this reminis-cence on her essay, Sarah reflects on how 'Once out of our natural environment . . . something in us dies.'[22] In one sense, this statement appears to affirm her socially inculcated belief in the degenerative effects of the Indian climate and the danger posed by cultural dis-location. However, when viewed within Sarah's own journey of self-discovery that occurs throughout the series, Scott suggests that whilst something may indeed die as a result of being taken out of place, new facets of personality also come to life as well, affirming the power of the journey to create change. Sarah's own journey is one of sexual and social awakening; she does not, like Daphne Manners, cross the ethnic boundaries of colonial India, but after her pregnancy and resultant abortion, she ends the series married to Guy Perron and living in England, where he lectures, noting that 'academic life is as itinerant as the one we used to live in India, or nearly'.[23]

Beyond the general threat that the tropics pose to British bodies and minds, these novels pay close attention to the specific distinctions between spaces in colonial India and the opinions of Anglo-Indian society with regard to their detrimental or beneficial effect on health. One of the key dichotomies that Anglo-Indian fiction preserves from colonial beliefs about health and environment is the distinction between the debilitating plains and the more salubrious hills. As noted above, a great deal of British life in India was mobile in nature, not only due to the circulation of personnel between provinces, but also in response to the seasonal conditions of the subcontinent. The government of India and the military, as well as much of Indian high society, split their time between winter residences, usually on the plains and in cities, and summer residences in the hills as a means of escaping the extreme heat of central and lowland India during the summer. Despite the administrative and practical effort involved in moving the seat of British power close to 1,000 miles, from 1864 Simla (now Shimla) became the summer residence of the government of India, which moved there from Calcutta each spring, 'files and all'.[24]

Simla was just one of the many hill stations of colonial India that served as summer retreats for the Anglo-Indian well-to-do. However, as a result of its association with the viceroy and the government, it became the centre of British social life and social intrigue for the duration of the Raj. Its status as a retreat existed not just for the maintenance of health away from the deleterious effects of summer, but extended to its function as a place for rest and recuperation all year round. This reputation was enhanced by the building of institutions such as the Ripon Hospital in 1885, which replaced the Simla Dispensary and offered care including medical attendance, diet, nursing and medicines for between two and eight rupees per day.[25] Simla's value lay not just in the care available from these professional facilities, but in the opportunity to rent a hillside bungalow and enjoy the restorative airs, views and cooler weather; in Jhabvala's *Heat and Dust* (1975), Douglas concludes that the source of Olivia's growing dissatisfaction in their marriage is the climate, so promptly sends her to Simla with the assurance that '[i]t'll be all right once you get to the hills.'[26] Given its temperate climate at 7,000 feet above sea level, its pine trees, and the British taste for neo-Gothic architecture in their development of the town, it was distinctly and deliberately evocative of Europe, thus offering a far closer (and cheaper) alternative to furlough in Britain for military patients as well as the more homesick members of Anglo-Indian society in general.

At the same time as it was considered a healthy space and used for convalescence, Simla also became notorious for its excesses. William Howard Russell, in India during 1858–60 initially to report on the suppression of the Indian Rebellion for the *Times,* visited Simla so as to recover from his own experience of an Indian fever and wounds sustained during his coverage of the fighting. Whilst there he noted the general atmosphere of high living, detailing his own visits to the Simla Club as well as the 'boisterous sick' of the military with a characteristically wry suggestion that the young officers there were benefiting so greatly from Simla's restorative powers that one would hardly be able to believe that they were unwell.[27] Along with this association with drinking, Simla was host to endless dinner and dancing parties stuffed full of 'grass widows' and young women of the 'fishing fleet', and, with the unwelcome assistance of Rudyard Kipling's Mrs Hauksbee and Mrs Reiver from *Plain Tales from the Hills* (1888), acquired a further reputation for the salacious and the scandalous side of colonial life.[28]

Drawing on this legacy of health tourism and hedonism, hills and hill stations are of particular importance to the novels of Farrell and Scott. For Scott, one of the key spatial contexts of *The Raj Quartet* (1966–75) is the relationship between the plains towns of Mayapore and Ranpur and the hills of Pankot and Nanoora, essentially standing in for the landscape of the United Provinces and Simla. Farrell's unfinished *The Hill Station* (1981), meanwhile, continues the narrative world of *The Siege of Krishnapur* (1973) through the reintroduction of Dr McNab and his wife, Miriam, some twenty years hence. This time Farrell focuses not on the conflict that faced them on the central plains but instead sets McNab and Miriam on a journey to Simla that begins innocuously enough as a vacation, but soon draws them into various disputes at the heart of colonial society. Whereas Scott creates a fictional Anglo-Indian world in which to explore his chosen themes, Farrell abandons the fictionalised setting of his previous Indian novel for an approach more in keeping with the historiographic metafiction of his prior book in the series, *The Singapore Grip* (1978).[29] With an eye on the language games and punning inherent to postmodernism, Scott's verisimilitude of Indian life offers environments comparable to those of the real Raj, whilst Farrell offers a version of Simla that is near but not quite exactly representative of the original; both settings are therefore not Simla, but similar to it. Instead, they offer environments in which to accentuate, recreate and reimagine the concerns of their real-life counterparts.

Farrell's approach to health and medicine in this novel comes not only with the casting of McNab as the doctor protagonist and questing hero of the narrative seeking an insight into medicine, spirituality and the British colonial psyche, but also through his representation of Reverend Kingston's tuberculosis, and the spectre of rabies that haunts both the existing narrative and the remainder of Farrell's draft chapter plan.[30] From his notes and research, it appears that Farrell's intention was for one of the characters, likely Mrs Forester's son Jack, to die from the disease later in the novel, thus providing the dramatic tension and tragedy that would work in counterpart to the social comedy that dominates the novel's first hundred pages.[31] John McLeod argues that Farrell's 'depiction of a small isolated community beset by disease' is in reference to Thomas Mann's *The Magic Mountain* (1924) and Albert Camus' *The Plague* (1947); however, it also has deeper thematic resonances within Farrell's approach to the representation of Empire as well as the intersection between spatiality and health.[32] Space and place are revealed to be key to both the narrative events and their meaning. McNab notes how he had developed an instinct which told him when a place 'was not of a kind that would favour a cure' and a belief in the importance of where a patient is treated and not just how, stating that 'if you removed a patient, preferably to a more salubrious spot', or if that was not possible, 'then *anywhere*', their chances of recovery were greatly enhanced.[33]

Farrell's inclusion of rabies in his plotting suggests that even in the supposedly ordered spaces of British high society such as Simla, the 'pathogenic' environment of India, as well as the orientalist animal element of the subcontinent, is still liable to prove deadly to the European body.[34] Farrell's decision to make Kingston tubercular affirms his general thematic approach to illness in so much as sickness pervades the pillars of Empire and British life, from the effect of rabies on the cohesion of the British family to the cholera that sweeps through the military and the civil government of Krishnapur, and through to the illness within the Church of England in *The Hill Station*. Farrell's inclusion of rabies thus provides a bodily counterpart to the spiritual sickness that pervades the disputes over religion as well as McNab's ongoing contemplation of the value and intersection of belief and medical practice. Moreover, the novel continues Farrell's general enquiry in that the (medical) authority of the imperial British is taken to its limit and rendered powerless in the face of both conditions. As McNab notes whilst gazing out on Simla's hillsides, '[he] felt uneasy here, as if beside the beautiful scenery, the prodigious vistas, the snow-capped mountains sparkling in the clear air, there lurked the malevolent presence of a disease he would be unable to control.'[35]

For McLeod, McNab's unease is the creeping change that is approaching Empire, noting not only the cameo presence of Karl Marx (pictured in the British Museum's Reading Room in London, presumably working on the second volume of *Das Kapital*), but also the observations of Ralph J. Crane and Jennifer Livett that the temporal setting predates the oncoming nationalist agitations of the 1890s.[36] In addition, the spatiality of the hill station in conjunction with the use of disease as metaphor gives this passage deeper thematic and critical significance. Most apparent is the way Farrell, as is typical of his fiction, inverts the usual meaning of his settings through the use of irony. Despite Mark Harrison's assertion that hill stations offered important refuge from politics and the climate, Farrell illustrates that all threats, whether political or physical, only become all the more focused and intensified there.[37] The hill station itself then acts as a counterpoint to the vastness of India that Crane identifies as a trope of the genre, illustrating not just the breadth of the Indian landscape versus the individual, but the smallness of the British and their concerns within it. The tightly localised narrative adds a feeling of claustrophobia, concentrating and exacerbating the elements of British disunity just as the siege conditions of Krishnapur did, illustrating how Anglo-Indian society, and Empire more generally, is always divided and riven by the pettiness of disputes over rank and status.

As Spurling notes, whenever Farrell is critical of the past, he seeks to criticise the present also.[38] The resonances of Harrison's notions of retreat and refuge from politics and climate within Farrell's contemporary 1970s present are evident. Faced with the cold light of British decline in the present moment, the appeal of a retreat to the comforts of the imperial heyday, when the sun never set, or the refuge to be found in the literature and culture of the Raj Revival, is Farrell's other target here; such a journey into the past is to find refuge in a fiction of a different kind via the mythology of British imperialism, and a retreat from reality. The malevolent presence and disease that McNab cannot control might therefore be read as that curiously British condition, and not one endemic to India: nostalgia. In an effort to treat such nostalgia, though, instead of the playground of the upper echelons of colonial society, there is instead only disease, division, social anxiety and rivalry to be found in Farrell's Simla.

Belief in the mythos of Empire also informs Scott's engagement with the space of the hill station at Pankot, which begins in earnest in *The Day of the Scorpion*, the second book in *The Raj Quartet* and the point at which his narrative moves away from Hari Kumar and Daphne Manners to explore instead the social world that surrounds the Layton family. Along with Sarah Layton's musings on topography and character, the novel similarly entwines the experience of landscape within the biographies of the various Laytons that litter the narrative, past and present, and the longer history of the British presence in the region. Scott is evidently cognisant, as Farrell is, of the contradictory qualities of the hill station, introducing Pankot as simultaneously exclusive and respectable, and as a place with the potential for scandal. On the one hand, Pankot is the hot weather station of the 1st Pankot Rifles as well as the summer residence of the provincial government; therefore, like all hill stations, it possesses a little of the cultural cachet that comes with its association with Anglo-Indian high society. Though not viceregal, the long-standing presence of military families like the Laytons and the Muirs marks Pankot out as a place of some distinction, even if it is only 'second class' in comparison to Darjeeling, Nainital or Kashmir, and not as popular with tourists and leave-takers.[39] On the other, however, Pankot is 'a place to let off steam in', 'thoroughly English' and representative of the clubbable, boisterous hill station society that William Russell identified in Simla.[40] Scott's Pankot is a summer retreat for the local military regiment and the British society that gravitates around it, and can be read, as Scott suggests, as the setting for a curious kind of Anglo-Indian theatre. Later in the novel and in reference to British India more generally, Ronald Merrick calls attention to how colonial life seemed to him 'unreal, like a play'; the nature of the Pankot community renders this state in microcosm and creates a static environment in which people play their parts on a continuous, seemingly permanent basis.[41] In this sense, Pankot, with its faux-Alpine and 'Indo-Tyrolean' architecture, is just as much a production and flight from reality as Farrell's Simla, with the power of Scott's novel likewise considering how removed such a community is in relation to the Britain of the contemporary present.

Scott's depiction of Pankot also addresses its role in the maintenance and restitution of health. Again with particular focus on the Laytons, Scott asserts the familiar dialectic between the hills and the plains, including the biography of John Layton's (unnamed) birth mother, who died as a result of double pneumonia coming soon after a bout of malarial fever contracted as a result of the 'ill effects of life in places like Mayapore and Dibrapur', which had become 'too deep-rooted for the healthier climate of Pankot to have made much difference'.[42] For most other concerns, however, Pankot is a destination for recuperation, rest and retirement, offering an atmosphere more conducive to the maintenance and preservation of health. Scott writes of how both Sarah and Susan Layton are born there given their mother's wish to escape the hot weather and give birth at the Pankot extension of the general hospital in Ranpur, illustrating a further connection between the careful management of treatment around the conditions of the plains and the hills.[43] Likewise, Susan Layton's convalescence after her nervous breakdown, whilst managed by the abrasive Dr Samuels, also takes place in the familiar surroundings of Pankot, and she benefits from her family's connections in order to receive treatment in the nearby military hospital.

Scott's description of the breakdown itself draws on the significance of its surroundings in order to generate meaning within the narrative. Released for a visit to her family's home in Pankot, Susan suffers a relapse and has to be taken back into care: 'her melancholy cries could be heard in the hills, scarcely distinguishable from the howling of the jackal packs'.[44] In describing Susan's condition in this manner, Scott not only brings together the human and the animal, just as Farrell does with the threat of rabies, but likewise emphasises the stifling and claustrophobic nature of the hill station: a space in which illnesses are experienced socially and publicly, with everyone knowing and reporting on each other's misfortunes in 'an air of furtiveness'. Described as 'damned embarrassing for the station', Susan's breakdown is a disruption of the surface-level orderliness and neatness of the hill station community, offering an indication, as Farrell's religious disputes do, of the disorder that lies beneath the façade of colonial society.[45]

Susan's mental illness, and Pankot itself, are both part of Scott's exploration of a similar aggregation of physical and spiritual health, and the relationship between people and place, within *The Towers of Silence* and the wider context of colonial India as that of Farrell in *The Hill Station*. As is his habit throughout the series, Scott begins *The Towers of Silence* with an extended introduction to a character previously only obliquely mentioned, in this instance Barbara (Barbie) Batchelor. Barbie is the paying guest of Mabel Layton, John Layton's stepmother, and instrumental to the plot of the third novel of the series, where the edifice of colonial society and authority begins to unravel. A former missionary and teacher at the Protestant Mission School in Ranpur, Barbie acts as Scott's lower-middle-class contrast to the upper-middle Laytons, whose history makes them part of the Pankot elite, and allows him to explore the hypocrisy of colonial society from another outsider's perspective. Over the course of the novel, Barbie accidentally discovers the long-running affair between Mildred Layton and Kevin Coley, one of the officers of the Pankot Rifles. Shocked by what she witnesses, Barbie runs from Coley's house out into a storm, catching a severe cold that develops into broncho-pneumonia, resulting in her admission to the civil wing of the Pankot general hospital.

Scott uses Barbie and this episode to bring together his concerns around the physical and spiritual threat posed by colonial India to the health of the individual. Whilst Barbie's illness is the result of physical symptoms contracted in an inhospitable climate, its origins, as well as her recovery, have a psychological as well as physiological bearing; Scott implies that Barbie's state stems also from the effect of discovering the unseemly truth of colonial society, and of a family in which she had placed so much belief and admiration. After over thirty years spent in service of the ideal of colonial India, it harms her faith as well as her health to witness what she considers a moral sickness beneath its surface. Knowing that she had been asked to leave the cottage, her doctor enquires after a place for her elsewhere in Pankot, recognising the implications a similarly inhospitable social climate might have on Barbie's health and stating darkly that '[p]eople don't die only of diseases, you know.'[46] Scott thus illustrates how people, health and place are again connected within colonial society. As he makes clear in *The Day of the Scorpion*, Scott states that the Laytons and Pankot are near synonymous and therefore intrinsically linked; Mildred's actions and Susan's breakdown signify their gradual unravelling as colonial India comes to an end, with Scott suggesting that its culturally emplaced values are undermined from the very top of the social hierarchy. As if to underline the ending of the colonial India of her imagination, *The Towers of Silence* concludes with Barbie accepting an offer to return to missionary work in a school at Dibrapur. However, as she alights in a cart to leave, she is the victim of an accident and is once again returned to convalescent care, this time permanently. She dies on the same day as the atomic bomb is dropped on Japan, thus signifying the end of the old world order of Empire and the beginning of the new.[47]

Linking Scott and Farrell's novels is the similarity in their representation of Anglo-Indian society and the effects of various illnesses within the localised environment of the colonial hill station. Both *The Hill Station* and *The Raj Quartet* offer an indication of how the connotations of illness are altered by space and place, particularly in terms of their intensity and concentration as a result of the confines of the hill station community. As both narratives progress, what begin as localised conditions develop to the point where their effects threaten the existence of the station community, colonial India and even Empire as a whole. When read together, Scott and Farrell's novels seek to illustrate the pervasive sicknesses that exist beneath the surface of the colonial societies they depict. The contrast of the illness within the Church (expressed in both the emergent doctrinal disputes of the 1870s and Kingston's tuberculosis) and the fallibility of Pankot's secular authorities (illustrated in Mildred Layton's affair and Susan's deteriorating mental state) is part of Scott and Farrell's attempts to illustrate how physical and spiritual sickness abound in colonial society, penetrating and damaging the institutions, classes and spaces that are its very foundations and essence. By illustrating the extent of this corporeal and psychological malaise, Scott and Farrell seek to refute the tendency towards nostalgia for the world of Empire and the risks that it represents to the body and soul of contemporary Britain.

Interiors: a sickroom of one's own

'Bricks are undoubtedly an essential ingredient of civilization; one gets nowhere at all without them.'

J. G. Farrell, *The Siege of Krishnapur*[48]

Alongside the broader thematic significance and perils of plains and hills within Anglo-Indian fiction, the genre, and these novels, are concerned with the importance of the built environment, composed of the interior spaces of hospital, home and the sickroom. As well as their effects on plot, narrative and characterisation, these spaces act as extensions of the metaphorical and practical hierarchies, beliefs and attitudes widespread within Anglo-Indian society and its representation in fiction found in the exterior spaces of the hill station. Moreover, expressions of British advancement in science and medicine, exemplified by buildings such as the modern Ripon Hospital at Simla, are themselves representative of a longer-standing British interest in healthcare spaces and their optimisation as a means of securing and supporting the actions and goals of Empire. For instance, as Jharna Gourlay writes, despite never personally setting foot there, Florence Nightingale's interest in Anglo-Indian hospitals and her effect on their management was notable, and with her interest in India piqued by the Rebellion of 1857, she would spend the next forty years advocating for change in the sanitary conditions of British and Indian soldiers and civilians alike.[49] As Gourlay illustrates, although she was philanthropic in many of her ideals and allegedly non-partisan in her personal outlook and ambitions, Nightingale's efforts must be viewed as inherently political, since they supported the continued maintenance of colonial power and the aims of the 'civilising mission' both in the provision of care to all Indians, thus demonstrating the Empire's benevolence, and through European medical education, which acts to supplant existing Indian practice. By extension, then, the care individuals received within these spaces reflects and sustains the same ideals and ills of the colonial society to which they belong.

In the same way as the preceding chapters explored the relationship between social perception or construction of illness and the practicality of its treatment by doctors and nurses, the relationship between the broader spatial understanding of where and how illness is contracted and the specificity of where it is experienced, treated and endured must also be examined. Scott, Farrell, Rushdie and Jhabvala all ground their representations of illness within the significance of spaces both social and personal. They do so partly in illustration of those experiential narratives of illness or treatment considered above, but also as a means of exploring how spaces of healthcare are governed and qualified by the exclusionary nature of colonialism and are those in which the good intentions of healthcare and the prejudices of Empire collide. Representing these spaces and how they replicate the inequalities of colonialism is inherent to their engagement with medicine as a component of imperial power, but also as part of its legacy in their contemporary present.

As Biswamoy Pati and Mark Harrison observe, in its most immediate form this exclusion is notable throughout the history of medical institutions in colonial India from the early nineteenth century onwards, either in the establishment of separate hospitals to treat European and Indian patients, both in relation to the general populace and in a military context, or the racial divisions that kept Indians at the margins of medical policy and practice.[50] In Scott's work we see traces of this prejudice in attitudes towards Indian medical staff, alongside that of patients, as well as towards particular hospitals themselves, further suggesting that colonial society's institutions mirror its more widely held values whilst also helping to construct and propagate them.[51] As well as indicating the continuation of colonial prejudice towards Indians, Scott's work is revealing of how the hospital space embodies the divisions between Anglo-Indians. Scott's Sister Prior from *The Day of the Scorpion* is again relevant here, especially since the space of the military hospital in Calcutta is vital to the creation and exercise of the authority she enjoys within her role as a nurse. In the brief episode in which Prior appears, she uses the environment of the hospital to inflict her slights on Sarah Layton by such means as forcing her to remain in the communal waiting area and only allowing her access to Merrick's room under escort, for a duration of her choosing. Whilst in one sense this scene appears to indicate how nursing and medical authority act as a social leveller, or act to empower those individuals otherwise lower on the social class scale than the upper ranks of Raj society, it just as much illustrates the toxic effect of Colonial India's obsession with status and how healthcare spaces serve to reflect the norms and ordering principles of the wider society to which they belong.

Prior's interactions with Sarah should not simply be read as corrective or an expression of social equity, but rather viewed instead as an imitative reflection of existing social behaviours of colonial India. Anglo-Indian society was one composed of privileged access to, or unambiguous exclusion from, particular spaces; institutions such as clubs and hotels best exemplify this practice, with many clubs still observing an official or unofficial 'colour bar' even as late as 1947.[52] Prior's brusque treatment of Sarah is not motivated necessarily by social justice or in pursuit of class equity, but rather in reflection of the spatially emplaced social relations of the Raj; essentially, the manner in which an individual is empowered through the act of dis-empowering others, with space integral to the process. Prior demonstrates that the exclusion she herself might experience in wider colonial society can, in the microcosm of the hospital, be turned against someone like Sarah Layton, who would usually expect and experience privileged treatment. It is thus telling that their meeting ends with Prior forcibly shutting a gate on Sarah as she escorts her from the hospital grounds, firmly emplacing a physical boundary as if to underline the metaphorical one that separates them and returning each woman to her sphere of influence.

Scott returns to and develops his use of healthcare spaces as insight into the British colonial mentality in *A Division of the Spoils* (1975). As the British presence in India moves towards its inevitable dissolution, Scott uses the space of the Royal Army Medical Corps (R. A. M. C.) hospital at Pankot to illustrate the fractious state of the British community behind the façade of national and colonial unity. Told in retrospect, and seemingly tangential to the main narrative, the section concerns Perron's time billeted in the R. A. M. C. annexe whilst under Merrick's command. Rather than acting as one of Scott's subplots that serves primarily to flesh out his representation of the Raj, Perron's experience at the Pankot Hospital functions instead as far more vital a part of Scott's post-imperial reflection on the attitudes and hierarchies of colonial India and Empire. On a surface level, and in terms of its projection of British values, the hospital appears as a place of recuperation, respite and care, both for the patients and the nurses that staff it, many of whom are veterans of the Burmese campaigns. However, as a result of Merrick's actions, the hospital is swiftly revealed as a space in which division, exploitation and suspicion of others' motives is rife. In a complex process of blackmail involving a homosexual affair and the threat of a charge of 'gross immorality', Merrick coerces Lance Corporal Pinker, one of the junior R. A. M. C. staff, to give him access to Susan Bingham's patient file so that he can check her medical and psychological health ahead of their forthcoming marriage.[53] The space of the hospital, described as 'halfway between Area Headquarters and the lines of the Pankot Rifles depot', thus sits uneasily at the centre of a conflict between the social ideal, namely the care of patients, and the personal reality, the satisfaction of Merrick's own agenda, illustrating a conflict between the altruistic exterior and the self-serving interior of the Raj.[54] Perron notes of Merrick the 'extraordinary care he took to manipulate things, people and objects, into some kind of significant objective/subjective order with himself at the dominant and controlling centre'.[55] Scott once again uses Merrick as the Raj's omphalos, making him the embodiment of the self-interest and abuse of status at the heart of Anglo-Indian society just as he did with its racism in relation to Merrick's mistreatment of Hari Kumar.

As critical as they are of the inequities of Anglo-Indian society throughout the life of the Raj, these novels do not present a teleology with regard to colonialism's conclusion. Instead they illustrate how one of the legacies of Empire is the continued association of the hospital with the exclusionary values of colonial society and the preservation of the privileged access to space at its centre. In another illustration of how Jhabvala's *Heat and Dust* offers a critical approach to post-imperial, independent India, when Jhabvala's narrator visits Dr Gopal in *Heat and Dust*, she notes that it is 'an old, grim stone building – the same one Dr Saunders was in charge of – and it is too small for the town's needs'.[56] On meeting Gopal, the narrator finds the same sense of personal entitlement enacted by Saunders a generation earlier; instead of expanded access for all, '[i]n-patients and out-patients overflowed onto the verandahs and corridors and the patch of grass outside', whilst Gopal sits in a 'large, airy, and tidy' office replete with 'solid, old pieces of English furniture' that likely belonged to Saunders himself.[57] Jhabvala suggests that the space of the hospital again features a doctor, Gopal, who is invested more greatly in projecting his own prestige and protecting his position than in correcting the inadequacy of medical provision offered in Satipur. Like Merrick in Scott's work and Saunders before him, Gopal positions himself as the dominant centre of the space, and whilst his attitude is revealed as more resigned indifference than the malice of Merrick, he nonetheless preserves the same import of social hierarchy within space, impatiently dismissing the two outpatients with their 'simple faces under big turbans', whilst detaining the narrator seemingly to take advantage of an opportunity to practice his English. Gopal indicates that a further legacy of colonial society is the continuation of this tendency towards empowerment through the act of disempowering others, inherited in full along with the hospital, the office and Saunders' furniture.

In addition to the shared space of the hospital and its mimicry of social values, the other significant interior space of the Anglo-Indian novel is that of the home and the domestic environment. Given the itinerant nature of Anglo-Indian life, domestic space and the stability it offered was a prized commodity within colonial society, especially since it was only ever a temporary prospect for many administrators, soldiers and civilians alike.[58] Similarly, inevitably even, domestic space was used as a further form of social display. As Anthony D. King has noted, the bungalow, an appropriated form of Indian dwelling that became synonymous with Anglo-Indian domestic life, stood as a symbol of British orderliness and a further form of cultural colonisation as increasing numbers were built in an 'Indo-European' style during the heyday of the late Victorian Raj.[59] In recognition of their imitative functions, these constructions of home within Anglo-India are, as Kim Dovey has argued of domestic space more broadly, 'a product of homelessness and the unhomely', acting as a response to cultural dislocation and the physical, geographical isolation of colonialism itself.[60] To support the vision of domestic order such products sought to project, it was necessary for the resident sahib to be visible, and so the bungalow verandah or garden offered a semi-private, semi-public space for social display to take place. As such, Anglo-Indian domestic space was not only hybrid in origin but also hybrid in nature, effectively acting as a third space that combined both public and private spheres of existence.[61]

Alongside their function of social display, bungalows and domestic spaces were thought to be related directly to health, and so a living space that was conducive to good health in particular was vital. Whilst numerous Anglo-Indian residents complained of a distinct lack of 'mod cons' such as electricity and indoor plumbing as late as the 1940s, these houses remained, in the words of Julian Downing of the ICS, 'pleasant and large', and had a 'spacious' quality that is 'seldom found anywhere today'.[62] In an echo of wider attitudes towards climate, as well as many of Nightingale's reforms around hospitals in both Britain and India, the emphasis on coolness and airiness found in Anglo-Indian bungalows was designed to alleviate the discomforts of the heat and guard against the concerns over India's various 'bad airs', such as miasma or malaria.[63] Their detached status likewise emphasised the divide between the colonial British and their Indian subjects, one that reinforced the same social distinctions expressed within the professional sphere as well as keeping Britons separate from those spaces perceived as 'unhealthy', such as bazaars and slums. Similarly, healthy domestic spaces such as the bungalow served to reinforce the hill station's function as a site of recuperation, one that offered rest and retreat from the otherwise arduous demands of colonial life.[64]

Given their significance within Anglo-Indian society, domestic spaces abound within Anglo-Indian fiction too. The Dak bungalow, recurring repeatedly from Kipling's stories through to Farrell's *The Siege of Krishnapur*, is an evident staple of the genre, whilst the social commentary of Jhabvala's novels is so often situated within the domestic sphere and the changing environs of the home within colonial or postcolonial India. All of the novels under study here contain a host of significant domestic spaces that intersect with illness and its treatment, as well as the wider consideration of the history and legacy of Empire. For example, Scott includes various domestic spaces from the beginning of *The Raj Quartet*, which continue to grow in significance as the British control of India diminishes, ending in *Staying On* (1977) with Tusker and Lucy Smalley's lives shrunk largely to the confines of their bungalow in Pankot as the town modernises around them, both they and their domain now anachronistic where once they conferred prestige.

Of these examples, Rose Cottage at Pankot – the home of Mabel Layton, memsahib and matriarch of the family, and Barbie Batchelor's residence during her tenure as a paying guest – is the site of much of Scott's exploration of the importance of domestic space in relation to health and to the legacy of British rule. Described in terms of its 'essential *soundness*', Rose Cottage is the encapsulation of the Layton family's efforts at effecting a legacy as well as evoking the spatial character of England within the context of Pankot, and Scott writes that the cottage, built in 1890 at the high-water mark of Empire, 'belonged to a time when the British built in a proper colonial fashion with their version of India aggressively in mind and with a view to permanence'.[65] As well as its attempts to replicate the temperate conditions of home through European architecture and in particular its garden, such ambition towards permanence via the built environment here acts as a counterpart to the recurrent infirmity and impermanence of health in colonial space; instead of the frail and fragile British bodies that come and go, the house endures, and becomes, as Gaston Bachelard argues, 'body and soul'.[66] Again Scott engages with the idea of the colonial legacy, including the desire to indicate a 'claim on history through long connexion' via the house, likewise recalled through the similarly enduring gravestones of various Laytons within the Pankot cemetery.[67] However, the function of Rose Cottage is not only to act as testament to that legacy, but also to convey the detail of the lived experience of it, coming to indicate 'the quality of survival and the idea behind it – that survival meant change'.[68] Scott's terms are once again evocative of health and illness, and speak to the desire for healthy domestic space as well as its intended effects; survival, consisting of and including illness, treatment and recovery, creates change and new awareness within the ill subject, and domestic space becomes the site of that process of survival as well as a contributing factor to it.

Scott's novels indicate how domestic spaces are intended to be prophylactic and preventative, creating conditions that are conducive to health and allowing residents to avoid the dangers that lurk elsewhere in the supposedly 'pathogenic' environment of India. However, his description of Rose Cottage also alludes to the fact that alongside this intention, houses, bungalows and domestic spaces are often foremost in the experience of being ill and as sites of care. For example, in Scott's own work, Daphne Manners' examination by Doctor Klaus and the birth of her daughter Parvati both take place at home. Similarly, in Rushdie's *Midnight's Children*, Aadam Aziz's treatment of Naseem through the perforated sheet takes place within 'a spacious bedchamber' within her family home and comes to highlight the simultaneously exceptional and familiar experience of ill health within domestic space. At first, her treatment and Aadam himself are, like Western medicine, seen as invaders and placed on the same level as the 'many good-for-nothings' who have tried to climb into Naseem's room, and from whom she requires protection in the form of the three lady wrestlers that hold the sheet and stand guard.[69] Over time, though, Naseem's various illnesses and Aadam's regular visits become part of the rhythm of the house, and medical practice is absorbed within the quotidian practice of domestic space; rather than just being temporarily subject to the medical gaze or the setting for an isolated clinical encounter, the house is revealed as a site of recurrent illness and host to a long list of conditions that purportedly afflict Naseem. Houses are thus not necessarily resistant to illness, as the British bungalows might suggest, but rather anticipate its occurrence and treatment to take place within their walls and seek to effect survival as part of their being.

The predominant environment through which houses seek to accommodate illness is through the space of the sickroom. In reflection of the potentiality of space, and in contrast to the efforts at permanence otherwise expressed through the bungalow, the sickroom is typically borne out of temporary necessity rather than specific designation, with houses becoming sites of care and convalescence as and when required. Seeing the sickroom as a particular trope of Victorian fiction, Miriam Bailin recognises how it acts as a unifying experience within society, a means of bringing together all social classes through their shared susceptibility to illness, but it is also a site of spatial paradox; Bailin argues that whilst the experience of recovery and receiving treatment might result in spiritual growth and a bond between caregiver and patient, it is simultaneously a source of existential threat, resulting in a conflicted emotional state.[70] The same benefit of care as expressed in the nurturing environment of the home also brings with it feelings of physical, mental and spiritual anxiety, as well as having the potential to transform living space into a site of death, loss and bereavement. Given the currents of neo-Victorianism that affect Anglo-Indian fiction, especially expressed in the work of Farrell, John Masters and G. M. Fraser, Bailin's consideration of the sickroom is relevant to Anglo-Indian fiction too. Similarly, the distance between many communities and permanent medical facilities or hospitals in colonial India, and the expense of prolonged treatment, meant that most people received care and experienced ill health within the domestic sphere.

The use of the home as a location for prolonged recuperation and a site of sickness is particularly apparent in Jhabvala's *Heat and Dust*. Despite not being neo-Victorian in terms of its temporal setting, it is nonetheless significant that it is the embodiment of the colonial Victorian memsahib, Mrs Saunders, the wife of the medical superintendent, who is most firmly associated with domestic space and the sickroom. Jhabvala writes initially of Mrs Saunders as being confined to bed and unable to attend a party, before later revealing more details about her condition when Olivia visits her. Mrs Saunders is bedridden after the death of her infant child and the resultant illness, which was 'something to do with her womb' that had 'never got right' after the baby's death.[71] Motivated by her fears for her own health and anxieties over becoming pregnant, Olivia arrives with 'flowers, fruit and a heart full of tender pity for her'; however, her meeting with Mrs Saunders runs counter to Bailin's assertion of the levelling effects of illness, and Olivia discovers that although her 'feelings towards Mrs Saunders had changed, Mrs. Saunders herself had not. She was still the same unattractive woman lying in bed in a bleak, gloomy house. Olivia, always susceptible to atmosphere, had to struggle against a feeling of distaste.'[72] Jhabvala describes Olivia's struggle with the ideal and reality of the intimate encounter with illness and how its place within the home disrupts the constitutive elements of domestic space, bringing sickness and mortality to the heart of everyday life.

Aside from the metaphorical resonances of Mrs Saunders' condition with regard to the health and vitality of the imperial ruling classes, Jhabvala's association of domestic space and prolonged sickness can be seen as her destabilisation of the Victorian trope of the 'Angel of the House' as well as a key narrative driver. Indeed, it is in part Olivia's fear of becoming like Mrs Saunders and the other station ladies that leads her to reject her otherwise comfortable but suffocating domestic life with Douglas, and that is responsible for the fear that drives her decision to have an abortion towards the end of the novel. Similarly, Jhabvala rejects the typical depiction of grace found in (female) suffering that Scott evokes through characters such as Meg Reid or Barbie Batchelor, describing Olivia's boredom at hearing details of her condition and showing how Mrs Saunders shouts at her servants in frustration and, it is implied, racially abuses them. Jhabvala thus subverts the expected conventions of both illness narrative and domestic space in relation to gender. Domestic space is often historically and culturally considered a female domain, especially in colonial society, where women were thought to be responsible for keeping the domestic sphere clean, harmonious and healthy.[73] Such a portrait appears, initially, to be the case in these novels, with the usual situation being that women are left to manage the domestic sphere due to a general absence of men; Scott's novels are filled with men absent from the home as a result of military service, imprisonment or death. In one of the few instances of complete households in Scott's books, the Smalleys' bungalow in *Staying On*, domestic space is shown to be riven by dysfunction.

Rather than the house acting as the health-giving centre of domestic life in Jhabvala's work, it becomes a source of tension and a liminal space in which the individual is subject to unwelcome and undesirable change. Whilst the sickroom represents a threshold, a staging post between Sontag's kingdoms of the well and the sick where the individual is identified as a traveller but has yet to embark fully on their journey, the house itself comes to represent imprisonment, threatening to change Olivia into one of the colonial caricatures she observes in Sitapur society.[74] In a link between the exteriors and interiors of Indian society, Olivia fears that pregnancy, illness or some other effect of the climate might result in her confinement within the bungalow, suggesting how the same spiritual sickness that pervades the wider context of colonial space also influences the domestic.[75] The house is again associated with 'body and soul' as in Bachelard's analysis, but as a cause of their potential harm and not their enrichment.

The representation of domestic spaces, interiors and the built environment in the novels of Scott, Farrell and Jhabvala can thus be viewed as a further extension of their approach to the history of colonial India and the legacies of Empire more broadly. In much the same manner as they explore the disorder, division and danger in plains and hill stations, their work calls attention to how the values of those institutions on which people base their identity, or that are constitutive of being, become debilitating, and how spaces of healthcare can engender spiritual sickness. Their novels suggest that colonialism itself, with its conditions of power, an inherent tendency towards exclusion, and the production of various hierarchies, acts as a chronic condition that moves physically through the body of a nation, namely India, as well as remains figuratively in the soul of postcolonial Britain. Their work, then, can be viewed as a curative space itself in which to isolate and attempt to purge the lasting legacy of the colonial Empire on the British body politic.

Notes

1. Rediker, *Outlaws of the Atlantic*, 2. The focus on land has been corrected by a growing body of work on the significance of sea voyages, and the ships in which British colonists would travel, within the history

of colonial space, with a range of works seeking to re-centre the sea 'as a site of history, geography and cultural activity'. See Mathieson (ed.), *Sea Narratives*; Bose, *A Hundred Horizons*.

2. See Cresswell, *Place: A Short Introduction*.

3. Harrison, *Climates and Constitutions*, 19–20.

4. As Douglas Ivison argues: 'the genre of travel writing . . . was the cultural by-product of imperialism, often written by those actively engaged in the expansion or maintenance of empire (explorers, soldiers, administrators, missionaries, journalists) and dependent upon the support of the institutions of imperialism in order to facilitate the writers' travels'. Ivison, 'Travel Writing and the End of Empire', 200–1.

5. *Forbes's East India and Colonial Guide*, primarily a gentleman's outfitters, reminded potential customers that the distance to Bombay was 6,570 miles by way of the Red Sea from London, and would likely take three to four months aboard ship; 15. The opening of the Suez Canal reduced this voyage to a mere 35–45 days. Likewise, Wolfgang Schivelbusch's work on the Victorian railway illustrates a more general change in understanding space, time and travel in the industrial age; Schivelbusch, *The Railway Journey*.

6. Margery Hall's recollection was thus: 'It was the East's first assault on my senses, and my memories are of heat, flies, noise, people, and horror of horrors the quayside, scarlet with blood so I thought. This turned out to be only millions of spits, mingled with betel nut'; BL, Hall, 'And the Nights', chapter 1, 2.

7. Wald, *Vice in the Barracks*, 132.

8. BL, Symons, Memoir, Mss Eur F180/82, 4. The vast majority of the memoirists in the BL's collection note that U. P. and the Punjab were considered the best postings, with Bengal the worst.

9. Nasir Faruqui (ICS Bombay) notes that an Assistant Collector was expected to spend 210 days of the year on tour. Faruqui, Mss Eur F180/27, 6.

10. As well as his early links to the hill station of Simla discussed below, Kipling's publications were all inherently reliant on the production of imperial spaces, from *The City of Dreadful Night* (1885), *The Jungle Book* (1894) and *Kim* (1899).

11. Moretti, *Atlas of the European Novel*, 3.

12. There are multiple examples of this practice of using Kipling as a point of reference within the British Library ICS archive, including the memoirs of: Sidney William Cecil Dunlop, Mss Eur F180/51, 1; William Francis Grahame Le Bailly, Mss Eur F180/65, 1; Archibald Ian Bowman, Mss Eur F180/73, 67–8.

13. See Goodman, *British Spy Fiction and the End of Empire*.

14. This engagement with space is not always consistent across these genres, however. For instance, beyond one short yet revealing scene in John le Carré's *Tinker, Tailor, Soldier, Spy* (1974) where George Smiley

finally meets his nemesis, Karla, in a Delhi jail cell, most British spy fiction of the period ignores India (a colony 'lost') in favour of Europe and East Asia, where the nation's influence might yet be preserved.

15. Crane, *Inventing India*, 1. Of the nineteen primary novels that comprise this study, fourteen begin, as Crane observes, with descriptions of topography, landscape or social context.

16. Crane, *Inventing India*, 2. Similarly significant is the choice by some authors, such as G. M. Fraser in *Flashman in the Great Game* (1975), to preface their novels with maps, either of India to better locate the events of the narrative, or of towns, to embed the actions and emplacement of characters.

17. Melvin Maddocks, reviewing *The Siege of Krishnapur* for *Time* magazine in September 1974, stated: 'When an American novelist wishes to demonstrate the naiveté of Americans, he packs his characters off to Europe. This is known as the Henry James gambit. When a British novelist wishes to display the naiveté of Englishmen, he ships his characters out to India. This is known as the E. M. Forster Ploy.' Farrell (Trinity), Box 9159–60, 'Miscellaneous papers', n.p. Again, such decisions find precedent in Kipling, specifically the titular character from 'The Conversion of Aurelian McGoggin' (1887). For Farrell, it is a ploy he repeats throughout nearly all of his Empire novels, with a similar figure visible in the Major from *Troubles* (1970) and Matthew Webb in *The Singapore Grip* (1978). Scott twists the process somewhat through Hari Kumar, an Indian who knows nothing of India, having been raised in England; without the ethnic safety net afforded to the white British characters, Kumar's lack of knowledge results in his brutal treatment by Merrick, and imprisonment.

18. See Coverley, *Psychogeography*.

19. See Frank, *The Wounded Storyteller*.

20. Scott, *TDotS*, 143.

21. Harrison, *Climates and Constitutions*, 2. Similarly relevant here is the practice of 'seasoning', in which new recruits to India would first be sent to more 'temperate' areas of the country in order to gradually acclimatise to the conditions of the subcontinent. See Wald, *Vice in the Barracks*, 127.

22. Scott, *TDotS*, 171.

23. Scott, *SO*, 93. This sense of new life is visible in the various novelists under study here. For example, Jhabvala's novels are full of these kinds of changes, from the shift in Prem's social world alongside his wife's pregnancy in *The Householder* (1960) to the narrator in *Heat and Dust* (1975), whose story concludes with her remaining in India and about to give birth, literally on the cusp of new life.

24. De Courcy, *The Fishing Fleet*, 187–8. The effort was presumably reduced once the government moved to New Delhi in 1911, a mere 250 miles' distance from Shimla.

25. Farrell's papers relating to *The Hill Station* refer extensively to his reliance on *Twenty-One Days in India* (1896) by George Aberigh-Mackay, from which he takes the information about the Ripon Hospital, amongst other details; Farrell (Trinity), Box 9153: *The Hill Station*, 'Notes and Index Cards'. Further information on the Ripon hospital can be found in the *Gazetteer of the Simla District*, 116.
26. Jhabvala, *HaD*, 39.
27. Russell, *The Indian Mutiny*, 322–3.
28. Dennis Kincaid's *British Social Life in India* notes how Kipling's writing caused some irritation for its confirmation of loose living at Simla, though acknowledges it contained more than a grain of truth, stating: 'The joke that you cannot sleep at night at Simla for the noise of the grinding of axes must be almost as old as the hill-station itself'; Kincaid, *British Social Life in India 1608–1937*, 248–50.
29. Dix, *Postmodern Fiction*, 23.
30. Farrell (Trinity), Box 9153: *The Hill Station*, 'Notes and Index Cards'. Rabies, or hydrophobia, is alluded to in Rudyard Kipling's *The Mark of the Beast* (1890), and also appears as one of the common hazards of 'murderous, torturing India' in John Masters' *Nightrunners of Bengal*; 103–4.
31. Fittingly, the centre of treatment for rabies during colonial India was the Pasteur Institute at Kasauli, forty-five miles away from Simla.
32. McLeod, *J. G. Farrell*, 76.
33. Farrell, *THS*, 66–7.
34. Harrison, *Climates and Constitutions*, 19.
35. Farrell, *THS*, 113.
36. McLeod, *J. G. Farrell*, 76–7.
37. Harrison, *Climates and Constitutions*, 20.
38. See also Spurling, 'As Does the Bishop'; Farrell, *THS*, 155.
39. Scott, *TDotS*, 70.
40. Ibid. 70.
41. Ibid. 256–7.
42. Ibid. 74.
43. Ibid. 87. Hilary Spurling writes of Pankot as a predominantly female space, home to the left-behind wives and mothers of Anglo-Indian society. Spurling, *Paul Scott*, 346.
44. Scott, *TToS*, 343.
45. Ibid. 346.
46. Ibid. 363.
47. Ibid. 464.
48. Farrell, *SoK*, 9–10.
49. Gourlay, *Florence Nightingale and the Health of the Raj*, 1.
50. Pati and Harrison, *The Social History of Health and Medicine in Colonial India*, 7.

51. Barbie Batchelor's actions at the morgue, where she falsely claims to be part of the Layton family, has only personal repercussions for her, whilst the Indian doctor on duty, Dr Lal, suffers the professional consequences. Scott, *TToS*, 277–8.
52. BL, Rahmatullah, 'Unpublished Memoir', 76.
53. The episode involving Pinker is one of Scott's more self-reflexive subplots, making passing reference to Graham Greene's *Brighton Rock* (1938) in the character's name, and Greene's particular taste for colonial morality tales such as *The Heart of the Matter* (1948) and *The Quiet American* (1955). Moreover, Scott also implies that despite its reflection of dominant colonial ideology, the hospital also offers a space for resistance and non-heteronormative identities through the character of Corporal Dixon, a male nurse and Burma veteran who is 'known affectionately as Sophie, or Miss Dixon, or Mum', and refers to herself in the third person as 'she'; Scott, *ADotS*, 275. Spurling suggests that the Pinker episode is autobiographical, and refers to Scott's own experiences as a young soldier in 1941; see Spurling, *Paul Scott*, 95.
54. Scott, *ADotS*, 274.
55. Ibid. 281.
56. Jhabvala, *HaD*, 110.
57. Ibid. 110–11.
58. The cost of maintaining a large house with a full complement of servants was prohibitively expensive for most, and many Anglo-Indians would share accommodation in 'chummeries' (for unmarried men), stay in the guest accommodation at the station Club or rent semi-furnished properties; BL, Hall, 'And the Nights', chapter 3, 2; Hobbs, *Indian Dust Devils*, 6.
59. King, *The Bungalow*, 47.
60. Dovey, *Framing Places*, 175.
61. Third Space in this context recalls Homi K. Bhabha's use of the term to denote those liminal encounters between coloniser and colonised; he argues that when these are coupled with global inequalities and non-synchronous temporality, the resultant 'incommensurable differences create a tension peculiar to borderline existences'. Bhabha, *Location of Culture*, 312.
62. BL, Downing, memoir, Mss Eur F180/50, 11.
63. Howell, *Malaria and Victorian Fictions of Empire*, 155.
64. Such understandings of domestic environments within colonial space are not exclusive to India, and are likewise reflected in the Irish 'big house', itself the focus of Farrell's *Troubles* (1970), where the Major retreats to Kilnalough to recover from his experiences in the First World War.
65. Scott, *ADotS*, 167.
66. Bachelard, *The Poetics of Space*, 7.
67. See Chapter 5 for further consideration of memorials and mortality.

68. Scott, *ADotS*, 168.
69. Rushdie, *MC*, 23.
70. Bailin, *The Sickroom in Victorian Fiction*, 5.
71. Jhabvala, *HaD*, 27.
72. Ibid. 26–7.
73. Sara Mills, Philippa Levine and others have argued to the contrary, highlighting how women enjoyed a rich social life in colonial space but were often accused of 'intruding' in male colonial affairs, and how men would inevitably be required to manage the domestic economy. See Levine (ed.), *Gender and Empire*, and Mills, 'Gender and Colonial Space', 130.
74. Sontag, *Illness as Metaphor*, 52.
75. The same is the case in Farrell's *The Hill Station*, where McNab examines Reverend Kingston and all his instincts combine 'to tell him that this was a house where illness would flourish'. Farrell, *THS*, 67.

Chapter 4

Death by the Bottle or the Spoon: Diet, Health and Well-Being

As the contents of the previous chapters have indicated, concerns of illness and health within Anglo-Indian fiction tend to appear in more dramatic forms of disease and sickness. Such approaches are, in many ways, understandable; for instance, it is hard to deny the severity, recurrence and widespread extent of cholera within the history of the British experience of India, its inherent association with the events of the Indian Rebellion of 1857, or the thematic significance of its representation in the work of J. G. Farrell, John Masters, M. M. Kaye, G. M. Fraser and others. From a narrative perspective, too, the inclusion of disease adds an additional peril to the events that unfold within the pages of the Anglo-Indian novel and reflect the widely acknowledged understanding of India as a place where ill health and death were known to move with 'indecent haste'.[1] However, the connection between literature and medicine, and indeed medicine and Anglo-Indian fiction, is not simply to do with how specific conditions affect characters, plotting or theme, but rather extends to all aspects of general physical and psychological health through preventative means.

One of the most significant dimensions of general health in colonial India was the medical and social preoccupation with diet, either in maintaining a healthy body through eating and drinking the right things, the specific use of dietary articles in the course of treatment, or the response to those illnesses supposedly provoked by the consumption of harmful food and drink.[2] Under the ever-present threat of epidemic disease and of the physical maladies likely to befall a European body in the spaces of the subcontinent, the preservation of life in British India depended, as E. M. Collingham argues, on quotidian 'bodily practices' such as grooming, dressing correctly, sufficient washing and appropriate eating and drinking.[3] As a result, the association between food and the maintenance of health was a concern of

Anglo-Indian doctors, dieticians and the British authorities through-out the duration of colonial rule, and dietary advice is a recurrent subject in vade-mecums, medical handbooks and travel guides from throughout the nineteenth and twentieth centuries, offering descriptions and summaries of cuisine likely to be encountered once in India and likely prices visitors could expect to pay for certain items, along-side information on the remedial properties of particular foodstuffs.[4] Such works variously extol the benefits of nourishing and whole-some food in response to the demands of the Indian climate, stress the importance of routine by cautioning readers against consuming too much during the hottest part of the day or late at night, and warn them away from food available at Indian bazaars.

Aside from published works such as these, written for profit and with a specific audience in mind, food and drink are especially prevalent in diaries and travelogues kept throughout the period. Given the physicality inherent to the British experience of India, as illustrated in Chapter 1, narrative accounts and diaries from across the colonial period are invariably sensory documents, a testament to what their authors felt, consumed, contracted and suffered. Food and drink in particular sit alongside climate, smell and sound (including language and wildlife) as aspects of India that diarists remark upon, noting the distinct difference and otherness of these stimuli in India as opposed to in Britain. Beyond the potential shock to the system of this change in diet, food and drink also fulfil various narrative functions in these texts. A description of food and drink consumed, alongside other practical details such as dining companions or prices paid, is for the author's own records or accounts and is a practice of routine. Alternately, recording outlandish or unusual meals conformed to a tendency to exoticise India and its culture, or formed the basis for complaint over its various unsanitary conditions.[5] Occasionally, diarists would report details of food and drink out of boredom. On long journeys, during bouts of long illness, or throughout isolated postings, various authors noted how they came to obsess over meals. In William Russell's memoir, *The Indian Mutiny: A Diary of the Sepoy Rebellion* (1860), he apologises for the excessive space given to describing his eating habits and those of others, but states that given the insular nature of travel aboard ship, passengers would take amusement where they could.[6] Diary records of food also show how eating and drinking were seen as key to maintaining health while overseas. In light of the fact that they would often write for the benefit of family and acquaintances at home, diarists would wish to signal that they were not only eating well, but that they were eating and drinking the 'right' things to maintain their health.

The Anglo-Indian novel acknowledges this dietary focus throughout its pages, with Jhabvala, Farrell, Rushdie, Scott and others all including multiple instances of eating, drinking and (over)consumption.[7] The literary prevalence of food and drink is an example of how the historical fiction of the Raj reflects the textual reality of colonial experience and the long tradition of dietary focus found in memoir, travelogue and other connected forms of writing. However, the inclusion of such subjects and details is not simply in pursuit of verisimilitude or literary realism, but rather is often as significant as those major plot points or themes involving specific medical conditions.[8] Indeed, just as they do with disease, Rushdie, Scott and others seek to explore the history of colonial India by using food, lifestyle and diet as lenses through which to explore the cultural, political and medical legacies of Empire. In particular, as this chapter will illustrate, these texts draw focus on that most perennially British of dietary habits: the use and abuse of alcohol.

As a growing field of historical research has noted, alcohol was a perpetually contentious and paradoxical substance in colonial India: at once a fixture of social life at all levels and in all contexts, from everyday drinking as part of military rations to the lavish nature of viceregal dinners, as well as an established part of medical practice, drink was also a source of recurrent scandal, disorder, medical incapacity and general anxiety for civil and military authorities throughout the duration of the British presence on the subcontinent.[9] Alcohol and medicine are thus two distinct but connected means of gaining insight into British colonial Indian society and its popular representation. In fiction, both from the height of the Raj and its popular representation after 1947, drink often comes with a moral warning or consequence, especially in the nineteenth century and notably in the works of authors like Rudyard Kipling.[10] This moral dimension reflected the medical history of alcoholism. Though historians such as Roy Porter have argued that knowledge of 'drinking-man's disease' and identification of its bodily markers existed as early as the eighteenth century, it was not until the mid-nineteenth century that studies by Magnus Huss gave alcoholism its name, and the condition (more often as 'inebriety') began to be considered and treated in a more clinical sense.[11] Even so, despite this gradual pathology, addiction to alcohol was still generally perceived as a moral deficiency (a perception strengthened greatly by the temperance campaigns of the nineteenth century) and thus as much a spiritual issue as a medical one.[12] As Mariana Valverde argues, though the term 'alcoholism' was in more widespread circulation in medical and public contexts from the 1920s, it would not be until the mid-twentieth century and the development of Elvin Morton Jellinek's Disease Concept of Alcoholism that the condition would become accepted into the *Diagnostic and Statistical Manual of Mental Disorders* and be supported by research at the World Health Organization.[13]

As a result of these connections across medical practice, memoir, historical narrative and literary fiction, the history of alcohol in India is a rich field of enquiry and offers insight into the everyday practices of colonial society as well as acting as a repeated 'contact zone' between British and Indian culture. Recognising and reflecting the extent of colonial drinking culture, Anglo-Indian fiction includes repeated instances of alcohol consumption and consequently, through analysis of Rushdie's *Midnight's Children* (1981) and Scott's *The Raj Quartet* (1966–75) as well as a range of medical sources related to diet, alcohol and inebriation, this chapter will illustrate how drinking is central to literary approaches to satirising, subverting and undermining the supposed benefit that Empire, and the model of British lifestyle that comprised the so-called 'civilising mission', presented to India and Indians.

In order to explore the role of alcohol within these texts, the chapter is split into two sections. The first focuses on Scott's depiction of Anglo-Indian drinking culture in the Second World War and the latter days of the Raj, with particular attention to the alcoholism and addiction experienced by characters such as Mildred Layton and Ahmed Kasim. The chapter argues that alcohol and the condition of alcoholism are presented as a means of addressing thematic, narrative and metaphorical aspects of colonial experience, as well as the legacy of Empire itself expressed through social hegemony. It considers the effects of drinking on European characters at a time of imperial crisis, and analyses Scott's efforts to draw parallels between the personal and the political across various classes and strata of colonial society through the recurrent factor of alcohol consumption.

In the second section, the chapter turns to *Midnight's Children* to explore how the use and abuse of alcohol within the narrative acts as a key metaphor through which to read the transition from a colonial to an independent India and the difficulties of Partition, as well as the legacies of British social, legal and medical habits on the Indian body. Through analysis of the published text of *Midnight's Children* as well as Rushdie's original manuscripts, it shows how Rushdie's decision to employ alcohol and alcoholism so prominently is a means through which to undermine the general contemporary belief in the widespread benefits that British colonialism brought to India. Instead, the novel reveals the British presence as having had a debilitating effect on the physical, psychological and social health of newly independent Indian individuals and the wider nation alike. Rushdie thus not only portrays such legacies of British rule as destructive, but also seeks to criticise the illusory ideals of the 'New' India itself, drawing parallels between the fictional self-images in which both states indulge. The British may have introduced Rushdie's Indian drinkers to alcohol, but they remain enthusiastically complicit in the habit despite the British departure.

All-consuming India: alcohol in the novels of Paul Scott

'I think a clear head might be advisable this evening'
'. . . In this country?'

Paul Scott, *A Division of the Spoils*[14]

Just as it did in the Raj itself, alcohol occupies a significant role in Scott's *The Raj Quartet*. As the novels progress, it is evident that alcohol is a key ingredient in his efforts to depict the fullness of British social life within colonial India. Before the reader comes to know the dinners, parties, weddings and other gatherings all kept afloat with drinking, however, alcohol is shown to be integral to the main thematic events of the first novel, *The Jewel in the Crown* (1966), and the shadow that the rape at the Bibighar casts over the lives of those connected with the events of its aftermath. When we meet Hari Kumar he is in the garden of the Sanctuary Mission, having been found lying in a ditch by Sister Ludmilla, who first thought him hurt or ill but discovered instead that he was drunk. We learn later, or are invited to infer, that Hari's hangover is not the result of an evening with Colin Lindsay, a childhood friend from England, as the text (and Hari) initially leads us to believe, but rather as a consequence of his shame at having been unable to prevent the assault on Daphne Manners, in combination with Colin's indifference to him when they meet at Mayapore, having chosen to observe the racial prejudices of Empire over their friendship.

Off the page, too, alcohol is important to an assessment of Scott's writing. Scott not only experienced the hard-drinking social scene of colonial India first-hand, but also, like some of his characters, struggled to control his drinking throughout his life. As Spurling records,

Scott alleged that he was 'taught to drink at age six . . . whisky, port, gin, wine – the lot, anything the adults drank, I drank too – diluted, I grant you, but who knows?'[15] By the early 1960s his drinking had become routine and accompanied his writing throughout the day; towards the end of his life in 1977, he would consume a quart of vodka on a daily basis and had developed cirrhosis of the liver.[16] Scott's tendency towards drink, however, was as much a result of the change in his social circumstances through conscription and posting to India as it was of any inherent propensity towards addiction, or of his childhood 'tuition'. In his pre-war suburban and artistic circle, Scott apparently had little appetite for drinking; the world in which he found himself in India, though, was one in which drinking was a regular occurrence, supported not just by the habitual routine of Anglo-India but by a rigidity of expectation compounded by the homosociality of military life.[17]

As Thomas B. Gilmore argues, it is necessary to acknowledge Scott's own difficulties with alcoholism, but they should not overshadow or overdetermine his depiction of the condition and other illnesses in his writing. For Gilmore, such biographical analyses tend to dominate criticism whilst the literary importance, metaphorical connotations and narrative effects of drinking within a text go overlooked.[18] Unlike Rushdie, whose depiction of alcoholism evidently facilitates developments of plot and character and possesses a tangible allegorical function within the text in the absence of any biographical relationship to the condition, the temptation with Scott is to assume, in the characterisation of various hard-drinking figures that appear across his series of novels, a distillation of real experience as a means of working through his own personal issue. Given his engagement with amoebiasis elsewhere in his novels, we might infer that such an approach is again part of Woods and Whitehead's construction of 'first wave' narrative medicine; by depicting his alcoholism within *The Raj Quartet*, Scott is able to bring some measure of control and order to his experience through narrative and writing and thus reflect, record or alter his own behaviour.[19] However, on closer examination of Scott's inclusion of alcohol and alcoholism within his series of novels, it is evident that, as in Rushdie's work also, drink and drinking problems are indicative of a deeper social, spiritual and physical malaise amongst his characters and the decaying imperial world they inhabit, and thus possess a greater metaphorical resonance than biographical criticism might suggest.

Alcohol is a consistent presence throughout *The Raj Quartet* and spans the social and professional lives of various characters across the divides of class, race and gender. Scott presents alcohol, and indeed the condition of alcoholism, as a means of addressing thematic, narrative and metaphorical aspects of colonial experience as well as the legacy of Empire itself, expressed through social hegemony. In the case of Britons such as Teddie Bingham and Ronald Merrick, at this point both members of the Muzzafirabad Guides (a fictional regiment engaged in the Burmese campaign) but of different class backgrounds, alcohol becomes part of the expected social ritual, giving structure to their relationship as it develops initially through conversation in the Mess and providing a focal point for the expected camaraderie of military, and also White European, life whilst on station. Similarly, when Guy Perron reports to the Maharanee's house in Bombay in the opening chapters of *A Division of the Spoils* (1975), ostensibly as a guest but actually to gather intelligence, he does so with a bottle of rare Scotch whisky as a gift, in an indication of how alcohol opens all doors, as well as his letter of introduction – thus providing a means of facilitating his mission.[20]

The narrative significance of alcohol is evident across the series, too, and is seen as not only a catalyst to events in its own right but also key to the manner of their telling. In the series' treatment of Merrick, for example, alcohol is a consistent factor, present during his abuse of Hari Kumar during interrogation and in evidence at points of dialogue and conversation where Merrick's actions become more widely known. For example, when interviewed in *The Day of the Scorpion* (1968), Kumar relates how:

> When I was stripped the two constables held me with my arms behind my back, in front of Merrick's desk. Merrick sat on the desk and poured himself a glass of whisky. Then he just sat and smiled at me until he'd drunk it.[21]

Merrick fortifies his intentions through drinking whisky and in the resulting interrogation and humiliation of Kumar that follows, Scott's suggestion is that the emboldening effect of the drink enables not just the egregiousness of his abuse of Kumar, but for Merrick to accept the truth of his own racism and his role as the colonial oppressor, something he otherwise represses in favour of his adherence to the traditional narrative of bringing order to India through the rule of British law. Though Merrick is not drunk, the place of alcohol in this scene and his loss of his usual control resonates more broadly with notions of the loss of British control over Mayapore in the context of the Quit India riots that occur in near parallel to the so-called

Manners Affair, as well as implying a relationship to a much longer history of British colonial excess through drink, violence and the abuse of power.[22] In conversations Merrick has with Sarah Layton and Dmitri Bronowsky (the Nawab of Mirat's White Russian wazir), though the actual content of each exchange is often oblique, alcohol affords a degree of intimacy that becomes confessional and potentially incriminating, respectively:

> 'What will you have, Ronald?' she asked, using his given name because for the first time it seemed natural to do so.
> 'Whisky if I may.'
> 'Whisky soda, Sahib *ke waste*, Abdur. *Burra peg hona chahie. Aur* Tom Collins *meri lie.*'
> 'Memsahib.'
> When Abdur Rahman had gone Merrick said, 'You think I need a *burra peg* then?'
> 'I don't know about need. Deserve.'
> 'I used hardly to drink at all.'[23]

Merrick's acknowledgement of the fact that he 'used hardly to drink at all' here is at once a tacit admission of his guilt and a suggestion of how the implications of his actions at Mayapore have begun to become clear to him, both as a result of the stone-throwing episode that mars the wedding day of Susan Layton and Teddie Bingham, and in terms of how his behaviour has altered under the strain of guilt and shame of his treatment of Kumar. Whilst never able to be openly remorseful – because of his belief in preserving the façade of British infallibility which he feels is vital to the security of Empire, as well as the possible criminal charges and resultant scandal such actions might provoke – the change in his behaviour suggests that he recognises his wrongdoing. Scott is not asking the reader to feel any sympathy for Merrick, since he never finds the courage to atone fully for his abuse of his power; however, he is, through Merrick's changed relationship to alcohol, able to convey the psychological strain he has caused himself and the remorseful legacy of his excess. Merrick's changing relationship with alcohol is Scott's way of illustrating how alcohol functions in terms of its role as cause, effect and remedy for a host of situations in the context of colonial India. As Merrick begins to lose control of events after his abuse of Kumar, resulting in the spoiling of Bingham's wedding party, the repeated appearances of bicycles on his property (suggesting he is being watched – it is implied that Merrick had planted Hari Kumar's bicycle at the

Bibighar to incriminate him), and, ultimately, his murder, he loses his previously ascetic degree of self-control when it comes to alcohol. Where previously he is shown to use conviviality around alcohol as a form of intelligence-gathering at the club, here his consumption is far more personal than professional.[24] Although never becoming an addiction in its strictest sense, as events wear on, this relationship becomes akin to a dependency; the more Merrick loses his control over events, the more he seeks the release of drink.

As well as its centrality to the main narrative and its role as bed-rock for social relations in the novels, alcohol is also depicted as a tonic or prophylactic for various conditions in reflection of its restor-ative reputation in medical practice. Despite warnings against over-indulgence, vade-mecums emphasise alcohol's beneficial stimulant effect on the digestive system and recommend its use in quotidian circumstances for combating lassitude and other more specific condi-tions, or supporting recovery in more exceptional cases.[25] Such prac-tices and common belief in alcohol's tonic properties for both body and mind remained in place in British India for decades, and are visible in Scott's experience of India, which he pours into his novels. For example, on returning to barracks after a three-day field exercise in *The Towers of Silence* (1971), Teddie Bingham's first thoughts are of a bath and 'three fingers of whisky'; and in echo of Merrick's own use of alcohol in response to stress, when unsettled by learning of Indian deserters to the Japanese, undoing his faith in *Man-Bap* (the traditional notion of Empire as mother and father to Indians), Bing-ham resolves to 'get mildly drunk. Or even quite drunk' as a means of shoring up his mental state.[26]

Aside from moments of acute need, alcohol features in regular medicinal practice, both physical and psychological. Captain Nigel Rowan of the Civil Service, key to the events of *A Division of the Spoils* and Kumar's eventual release, acknowledges the daily role of alcohol in his diet with his 'second routine whisky-soda, the one he used to wash down the evening dose of pills'.[27] Further, at Perron's first meeting with his commanding officer in Bombay, Leonard Pur-vis, he is offered his choice from Purvis' drinks tray, containing 'a generous selection: gin, whisky, rum, several bottles of Murree beer and various squashes and cordials'.[28] It becomes evident during their interview that Purvis' dedication to drinking is motivated by more than social habit. As noted in Chapter 1, Perron surmises that Purvis has amoebic dysentery. On being asked whether he has seen any doc-tors, Purvis replies that he has not sought medical advice and that the 'only thing that really helps is the liquor. No wonder the sahibs have always gone around half-cut.'[29] Purvis' character and behaviour speaks to the long-standing use of alcohol as self-medication in treating various conditions amongst the Anglo-Indian community, but also its role in alleviating the general psychological hardship of India, especially in cases of unwanted or unwelcome postings.[30]

Scott uses Purvis to illustrate his cognisance of the contradictory position of alcohol in colonial society, namely that whilst drinking affords some physical or mental relief, largely unchecked consumption (especially amongst the officer classes) results in just as much harm. Purvis is a reluctant servant of Empire, describing himself as an economist by trade and revealing to Perron over a number of drinks the circumstances through which his rival (using Purvis' economic theories on the long-term deleterious effect of imperial possessions on British finances) has been able to rise within the Treasury back in Britain whilst Purvis has been posted to languish in India, conveniently out of the way. As a consequence of his amoebic condition and his mental state revealed by their conversation, Perron observes in Purvis the symptoms of paranoia exacerbated by dependence on alcohol.[31] When Purvis' efforts to engineer a posting to Delhi fail and he is instead attached to the upcoming Operation Zipper (the British attempt to recapture Port Swettenham in Malaya), he experiences a psychotic episode in which he drinks to excess, destroys much of the furniture in his apartment in an alcoholic rage, and then attempts suicide by slashing his forearms with a broken whisky bottle, in fact a second bottle of the rare vintage he gives to Perron for the Maharanee.[32] Returning early from the party to give back the unfinished whisky, Perron is able to find Purvis in time and prevent his death on this occasion through the application of first aid and the assistance of an IMS doctor billeted within the same building. It is with a degree of grim humour that Scott writes of how the doctor, full of the bonhomie of Empire and without irony, instructs that Perron had 'better go next door and have a bloody strong drink'.[33]

Alcohol is a fixture of the novels and appears in nearly all of its contexts and in the lives of nearly all of its characters. However, it is through the thematic comparison of two main families in the series – the Laytons, in particular Mildred Layton, and the Kasims through focus on Ahmed Kasim – that Scott's use of alcohol takes on its most significant metaphorical resonances. Introduced in the second novel of the series, *The Day of the Scorpion*, the Laytons are an old Anglo-Indian family whose history and position are near-synonymous with Pankot, the main setting for much of the narrative. Their pedigree is further emphasised by their long history of intermarriage with another notable Pankot family, the Muirs. Scott's point is to employ the various generations and branches of Laytons as a mirror through which to reflect the change in these old families of British India, the upheaval wrought by the war, and the slow diminuendo of Empire in general. For example, Colonel John Layton, commander of the Pankot Rifles captured in the Desert War of 1941 (along with, we are told, the majority of his men), is the embodiment of the old guard of the Indian military whose prestige has been damaged by the war and the indignity of surrender; his daughter Susan belongs to the superficial and psychologically fragile generation set to inherit the responsibility of governing India and woefully incapable of meeting it; Uncle Arthur and Aunt Fenny are cast as the tedious colonial socialites with no knowledge of India beyond the confines of their dinner parties and limited social sphere; and Mabel Layton, John's mother, is a Victorian memsahib dying away as Empire follows suit. Sarah Layton, meanwhile, the elder daughter, is one of Scott's more hopeful characters. Sarah undergoes a sexual and philosophical awakening that gives credence to her existing moral feelings on India and Indians; whilst such a development is itself a cliché of Anglo-Indian fiction (satirised in Farrell's Fleury, who in old age becomes a conservative reactionary despite his youthful radicalism), Sarah represents a possible analogue for a postcolonial or post-imperial Britain. Her failure to take the pretence of imperial India seriously, as noted by another of Pankot's minor memsahibs, Lucy Smalley, is not the failing it is perceived to be within the narrative world, but rather a virtue when read in the historical context of the novel's publication after the end of Empire.[34]

The character of Mildred represents Scott's more ambiguous and therefore more nuanced engagement with the roles of Anglo-Indian society through drinking. Like Scott's own alcohol consumption, Mildred Layton's drinking is enabled and encouraged by her place within Anglo-Indian society. As the matriarch of the influential Layton family, Mildred exists in a world of entertaining, organising lunches and dinners throughout which alcohol is a constant presence. Though these functions appear to be indicative of a leisurely existence (taking place far from the fighting on the Burmese border that is the backdrop of much of the series), they are not simply representative of the frivolity of civilian life. Rather, as the 'burra mem' and wife of the Colonel, Mildred's commitment to keeping up the social calendar can be viewed as part of her essential war work and contribution to wartime morale, as well as some form of compensation for John Layton's implied loss of face. Drink, therefore, in a reflection and intensification of its peacetime use, plays a significant part in maintaining the psychological stability of the Anglo-Indian community in a time of crisis.

Peter Morey argues that Mildred Layton's drinking is 'symptomatic of imperial dissolution'; however, to assume such a direct correlation between apparently destructive drinking and the decline of the Raj is too straightforward.[35] As is made clear throughout *The Raj Quartet*, Mildred, unlike Rushdie's Ahmed Sinai, remains in control and physically unaffected by her excessive drinking. She does not develop the kinds of corporeal symptoms associated with alcoholism, such as those demonstrated in Ahmed Sinai's deterioration, and the apparent moral laxity expressed in her affair with Kevin Coley is neither a direct result of her drinking (in that their affair is not spurred by the spontaneous abandon of drunkenness), nor has it only occurred as Mildred's drinking increases during the early years of the war, having begun some time ago and long before John Layton became a prisoner of war.

Instead, and in light of Collingham's analysis of the bodily practices of Anglo-India, Mildred's drinking might be thought of in the same way as other quotidian practices such as the eating of British food and keeping up with European fashions, namely as a means of keeping the British body safely European whilst in India. Other than in certain contexts, such as Hindu or Sikh members of the Indian middle classes, drink is a mark of distinction between the European and the Indian, and was common to men and women in Anglo-Indian society; to consume alcohol in the fashion that Mildred does might be thought of as a means of ensuring this crucial division, vital to British prestige. Indeed, the increase in Mildred's drinking after John Layton's capture and amidst the changes wrought on Anglo-Indian society as part of the war is not representative of imperial dissolution, the falling apart of Empire from within, but rather may be read instead as an attempt to combat it. Mildred drinks not to destroy herself or the Raj but to preserve the integrity of both; her drinking is a means of dealing with crises both personal and political and an effort to continue the same kind of outward control, if not projection of carefree hedonism, inherent to the Raj at its height.

Scott writes of how Mildred's drinking ironically offers a point of continuity and stability in the disordered circumstances of Pankot, and India, at war:

In a curious way it sharpened her distinction. In her, drink released none of the vulgar or embarrassing traits disguised by soberness in people of softer grain; it gave extra keenness to those edges in her personality that made her a woman that no one in their right mind would want to cross ... there were occasions when her fortitude was felt by those who knew her well to be a fortitude shown not just for her own benefit but for theirs as well, so the drinking was for them too; a resistance to pressures they were too conscious of not to acknowledge as collective and likely to increase.[36]

Mildred's drinking is shown not as a selfish act through which she is allowed to give licence to her personal failings and infidelities, but rather representative of the collective spirit of Anglo-Indian society alluded to throughout the series: one of a community whose strength comes from bearing the collective hardships of India together, and presenting a united front to the Indian community that surrounds and outnumbers them. Drinking affords Mildred a little of the 'authority of the old order' and preserves her primacy as the 'burra mem' by sharpening her attitude. Rather than a problem which gives an individual licence to commit actions recognised as out of the norm and that require apology or excuse, drinking here makes Mildred more formidable; as with 'Dutch courage', it exacerbates her existing combativeness and makes her, perhaps perversely, more greatly admired by the circle of women that gravitate around her. Far from being aberrant to her gender, Mildred's drinking is key to the performance of her identity at the head of the colonial social hierarchy. Although, to acknowledge Morey's suggestion, there is a relationship between Mildred's drinking and the end of Empire, it is one of compensation and intensification as opposed to loosening or laxity. Scott writes that because the splendour of pre-war colonial life and the British power that was concomitant with it, 'the game that had never been a game', was now 'very likely up', Mildred's drinking is a message that demonstrates to the other Britons in Pankot that she will embody its responsibilities until the bitter end. Newcomers like Purvis might go to pieces as a result of drink, but for Anglo-Indians like Mildred it simply hardens their resolve. In a brief moment of reflection after Teddie Bingham's death, we are told that Mildred's 'drinking habit had been less frequently indulged', but then resumed 'as if she had decided that giving anything up was a sign of weakness'.[37] Indeed, rather than losing herself to the bottle, it appears alcohol helps Mildred find herself. In the context of the series' underlying political themes, particularly the Quit India riots, the suggestion of Mildred's embodiment of the British character is apparent; any change in habit or action would be compromise, and compromise would imply a decline in the traditional authority of the Raj and an acknowledgement of fault. The steadfastness and reliability of Mildred's alcoholism is thus a little of the 'Old India', now only glimpsed fleetingly in the silver plate of the Pankot Rifles' mess or the facets of a Carews gin bottle.[38]

Scott's depiction of Mildred as the embodiment of the British Empire is itself reflective of the history and development of colonial Indian society. Though traditionally masculine in character as a result of the East India Company's presence there, the role of the military, and the significance of male-dominated industries like textiles and tea or jute plantations in developing Anglo-Indian society, it was a consequence of the Indian Rebellion and the gradual dominance of colonial domestic life through which the memsahib came to prominence.[39] The image of the 'redoubtable Mem' is one Scott continues throughout his Indian novels, onto the final pages of *Staying On* (1977), with Lucy Smalley continuing to make the best of what life in India presents her with. However, as well as this consistency, his novels recognise that they are dealing with a time of transition, and his decision to cast Mildred as an alcoholic deepens her thematic parallels with a character who is ostensibly her social opposite: Ahmed Kasim. Like Mildred, Ahmed is part of a prominent colonial family. His father is Mohammed Ali Kasim, known as MAK, a minister in the Indian National Congress who is imprisoned under the provisions of the Defence of India Act.

Ahmed serves as personal secretary to 'Count' Dmitri Bronowsky, Wazir to the Nawab of Mirat. Ahmed's role is presumably in part, at least ostensibly, to prepare him for a potential future position in the government of India. However, as the narrative makes clear, his role is as much again a means of keeping him occupied and out of the way, lest he damage his father's political credibility amongst his Muslim League counterparts. As a result of his fairly lax responsibilities, it is revealed in Ahmed's first appearance that his chief preoccupation is his dedication to drinking. The reader's first introduction to Ahmed comes over drinks between him and Bronowsky early in the second novel of Scott's series, in parallel with Mildred Layton's own introduction to the narrative. Mildred is also the subject of their conversation, with Ahmed revealing how he had noticed her tendency towards excessive drinking at recent parties and functions. However, as much as the conversation is about Mildred, it becomes just as revealing of Ahmed's character and social position as it does hers, and it also offers a suggestion of how Scott sees alcohol in relation to the Indian middle classes.

> Having handed young Kasim a glass of the forbidden whisky Count Bronowsky said, 'So Mrs Layton drinks, you say. Do you mean in secret?'
>
> Ahmed, taking the glass, held it well away from his nose. He disliked the smell of alcohol. In the palace there wasn't a drop to be had except what his servant or he himself managed to smuggle into his room there. He smuggled it on principle and had trained himself to drink a certain amount every day. It disappointed him that regular tippling hadn't yet given him a real taste for it let alone made him a slave of habit. A serious drinker, and finally an alcoholic, struck him sometimes as the only thing really open to him to become in his own right.[40]

The suggestion that becoming a serious drinker is the only role Ahmed can call truly his own is also true of Mildred, and the parallels between the two characters become apparent here. For instance, Mildred has been led to the life of the dutiful memsahib, expected to always play her part as Mrs John Layton, in the same way she was the daughter of General Muir, enjoying a degree of social elevation and distinction as a result. Ahmed, meanwhile, is conspicuous by being related to MAK, and his position with the Nawab is not based on merit, but rather his father's connections and the political convenience of the arrangement. Drinking, then, becomes a way for both of these characters to express some personal choice within the constraints and expectations of their social circumstances and family ties, later referred to as the '*received* life' by Sarah Layton, one that is as restrictive as it is materially privileged.[41] Ironically enough, as Ahmed's internal reflections here suggest, aspiring to a loss of control through alcohol is one of the few things in his life over which he has control, a feeling of frustration also expressed in Mildred's drinking and her affair with Kevin Coley, and both characters can be seen to push at the constraints of colonial society.[42] Similarly, the semi-secrecy of their drinking is another link between them; we are told that Ahmed eats raw garlic, partly because it is 'good for the constitution', but also because 'garlic is stronger on the breath than the smell of whisky. So you see it has its religious and social uses too.'[43] Mildred, meanwhile, uses her position to defer open scandal too, but still their habits are well known by some and at least rumoured by others. However, in the same way as Mildred's drinking becomes preservative and not dissolutive of her status, Ahmed's drinking is not self-destructive either. Despite his efforts with the garlic, or even perhaps because of it (and his willingness to 'play the game'), his consumption is tacitly forgiven for reasons that are not very different to those applied to Mildred's. Ahmed's drinking, whilst criticised by his family and his father's political rivals, is condoned because it allows him to fit into and thus preserve the existing structures of the Raj. Drinking makes Ahmed someone that the British think they understand and recognise; alcohol, to follow Collingham's suggestion, Europeanises him.[44]

Alcohol's role in transforming Ahmed Kasim, at least to some extent, in the eyes of the British again evokes the ambition of Thomas Babington Macaulay, and his efforts to develop an Indian middle class to act as intermediaries between Britain and the general population of India. Neil Ten Kortenaar details the influence of Macaulay's 'Minute on Indian Education' from 1835, and his stated attempt to create 'a class of persons Indian in blood and colour, but English in tastes, in opinions, in morals and in intellect'.[45] Drinking was integral to this process of transformation. Gina Hames states in *Alcohol in World History* (2012) that alcohol was both a mark of Westernisation and a status symbol, noting that alcohol imports to India increased 900 per cent between 1875 and 1928, meeting the demands of a newly Anglicised Indian middle class made up of men such as Ahmed Kasim.[46] It is, of course, ironic that the tastes and habits British social education evokes in Ahmed are womanising and a particular predilection for whisky, and not the high-minded ideals that Macaulay's tract originally intended.

In a period of transition at the end of Empire, however, Scott's series suggests that Ahmed's liminal role as racial intermediary leaves him not wholly part of either side that develops in the weeks before Partition. Indeed, the events of *A Division of the Spoils* reveal Scott's uncertainty with what to do with the Macaulay Indian after independence. Ahmed's habits and the change wrought upon him by British society – by this point in the narrative he has become more the dedicated drinker of his introduction in book two – suggest a conflicted future in Pakistan, where alcohol is prohibited, but as a Muslim he also has no future in a Hindu/Sikh majority India. Scott's depiction of the disorder and bloodshed of Partition is brief, and usually alludes to events happening off the page rather than dealing with them directly. Ahmed's death, at the hands of a group of Sikhs who drag him from a train, is one moment when the book explores the intimate experience of violence that is the consequence of British withdrawal from India. Indeed, Scott appears critical of the values of Macaulayism that Ahmed has imbibed and which lead him to his death; Kasim sacrifices himself to save the British in his carriage and goes willingly in the hope that the rest of the party will live. His sacrifice is made all the more bitter by Sarah Layton's later reflection that the British were never really in danger and were not targeted in any of the attacks across India, implying a degree of futility to Ahmed's selflessness in the moment of his death. At the same time, Scott's approach is too neat a way of dealing with the conflicts that the Europeanisation of Ahmed Kasim produces, and is representative of the failure, inability or deliberate avoidance of his narrative in exploring the longer legacy of British effects on India from a non-British perspective. Instead, the work of showing how that class of Indian would have to change, or be changed, as a consequence of independence would be done by novelists for whom the experience of an identity disordered by the adoption of British social and dietary habits was altogether much more familiar.

Empire of the sundowner: legacies of drinking in *Midnight's Children*

For all the breadth of *The Raj Quartet*, and its efforts at representing a cross-section of colonial society as Scott had experienced it, its viewpoint remained deliberately Eurocentric. Salman Rushdie's criticism of Scott in his essay 'Outside the Whale' (1984) was famously that '[t]he *Quartet*'s form tells us, in effect, that the history of the end of the Raj was largely composed of the doings of the officer class and its wife. Indians get walk-ons, but remain, for the most part, bit-players in their own history.'[47] Many of Rushdie's criticisms of Scott's writing are valid, especially on the dubious quality of some of his metaphor and characterisation. However, as the literary and historical context of the period suggest, the idea of writing an account of the Raj that represented faithfully all sides of the situation was not Scott's intention, nor would it even have been feasible for him to attempt; moreover, it is arguable that Scott could not have hoped to represent the interiority of Indian characters as effectively as his British ones, even had he tried. As Rushdie's own work would suggest, though, the other shortcoming of *The Raj Quartet*'s effort to fathom the life and death of the Raj was that it stopped all too short. Although *Staying On* endeavoured to explore the genteel decline of Tusker and Lucy Smalley as India modernised around them, its farcical tone belied the real questions of existential change that lay at the core of Indian independence and the legacies of British rule that lingered afterwards. Instead, it would be Rushdie's *Midnight's Children* (1981) that sought to engage fully with many of the themes that Scott acknowledged, particularly the conflict within Indian identities as a result of British rule. Described by Abdulrazak Gurnah as a 'grand' book both in ambition and scope of its subject, *Midnight's Children* takes in nearly sixty years of Indian life and death on an epic scale, but crucially, on a human one too.[48]

Rushdie's novel has garnered a great deal of academic criticism since its publication. The bulk of this analysis has understandably explored the postcolonial complexity of the novel's main narrative, but has often overlooked the extent of the medical themes, and significant subplots that contribute to, develop and intersect with Saleem Sinai's story, as well as Indian history itself.[49] One example is the handful of chapters that concern the circumstances of Saleem's family's move to Bombay and Saleem's birth. Ahmed Sinai, Saleem's father, and his wife are told by a friend that property is going cheap as the British leave ahead of the declaration of independence, at this point only seventy days away. Ahmed meets and enters into a bargain to purchase a house on the estate of William Methwold, a British resident and descendent of the William Methwold of the East India Company, who lobbied for the acquisition of Bombay as a British territorial possession in the seventeenth century. The modern Methwold sells the four identical villas that comprise his estate on the condition that they come with all the contents, and that the new owners do not remove or alter any of the contents until after independence is declared.[50] Along with 'talking budgies . . . moth-eaten dresses . . . used brassieres' and 'half-empty jars of Bovril' come 'cocktail cabinets full of good whisky', which propel Ahmed on his journey towards the alcoholism that defines his character for the remainder of the novel.[51]

Alcohol, and Ahmed Sinai's addiction to it, is one of the most prominent medicalised themes of the novel, revealing of Anglo-Indian relations, colonial history and culture.[52] However, unlike Scott and his decision to erase Ahmed Kasim from the narrative without dealing with the implications of his drinking and his altered identity, Rushdie goes further and uses alcohol as a means of interrogating not only British history and experience, but also the power of British cultural hegemony during and after colonialism and the state of Indian selfhood in the newly independent nation. Rushdie's portrayal of Ahmed's condition corresponds to a simplified version of Jellinek's concept of alcoholism, developed and refined between the 1940s and the publication of his book *The Disease Concept of Alcoholism* (1960). Initially categorising alcoholism into four stages, beginning with a pre-alcoholic stage through to full dependency, Jellinek's later work would expand this into five stages (Alpha to Epsilon alcoholism), only some of which he considered to constitute 'disease' pathologically.[53] Rushdie depicts three identifiable stages in Ahmed Sinai's decline into alcoholism in *Midnight's Children*: a pre-alcoholic stage of intoxication, a Beta phase of inebriation through daily consumption which leads to social and physical problems, and finally a Delta/Gamma addiction involving inability to abstain and a loss of control. However, despite the correspondences between Rushdie's portrayal and these clinical stages, the novel also reflects Gilmore's assertion that alcoholism must be conceived of not only in medicalised terms but as a 'total illness, with far-reaching effects that are not only physical but also psychological and spiritual'.[54] Rushdie's concern, expressed through alcohol, would be both for the body and the soul of the new Indian subject.

The first of these stages, intoxication, is prompted by social interaction at the Methwold estate. In what he believes is a bid to secure the purchase of the estate, but, as the reader discerns, is as much to do with Methwold's manipulation of him and delight in allegorical game-playing, Ahmed begins to spend more time with Methwold, who introduces him to the 'cocktail hour', something we are told has 'never varied in twenty years'.[55] Alcohol, and this episode, invite consideration in relation to Homi Bhabha's formulation of mimicry in *The Location of Culture* (1994), a book that ties itself to *Midnight's Children* from its own opening sentence. Bhabha argues that 'mimicry emerges as one of the most elusive and effective strategies of colonial power and knowledge', representing an 'ironic compromise' between the demand for identity and the counter-pressure of historical change.[56] Mimicry of the coloniser offers, in Bhabha's view, the pretence of visibility and identity at the cost of authenticity to the colonised subject; they are rendered visible, but sacrifice their original selfhood in the process. As Ahmed Kasim accomplishes with his falconry, for Ahmed Sinai alcohol becomes a means of obtaining visibility in the eyes of the coloniser (Methwold), but renders him, in Bhabha's words, virtual, 'almost the same *but not quite*'.[57]

There are two forms of mimicry going on in Rushdie's text at this point: the cordial, homosocial surface mimicry of how Ahmed mirrors Methwold's behaviour, but also that of a much more deeply ingrained mimicry within Anglo-Indian or Anglicised Indian class structures that his turn towards the bottle reflects. In relation to the former, Rushdie writes that 'in the presence of the Englishman' Ahmed's voice had changed; 'it had become a hideous mockery of an Oxford drawl', and he begins to invent stories of apocryphal Mughal ancestry along with that of a family curse that would come to fruition, remaking his past (as Rushdie would later note of the colonised subject in *Imaginary Homelands*) to suit his present purpose.[58] Mimicry thus becomes the realisation of power; the Estate, we are told, alters its inhabitants in both action and identity:

> [E]very evening at six sharp they all came out into their gardens or onto their verandahs because that was the cocktail hour, and though they were all Hindus or Muslims and Parsees and forbidden the juice of the fermented grape or any other hard stuff, they drank it anyway, and waved to one-another across their hedges, View-Halloo, they cried, Ain't it a ripping night.[59]

Such behaviour conforms, at least initially, to Bhabha's notion that mimicry displaces power, here by showing up the ridiculousness of the colonial routine, the affected accents, habits and forced conviviality. However, at the same time, it embodies the idea of hegemony in the very public conformity of Ahmed, his family and their friends to expected and recognisable social roles, especially within what is still British domestic space. They become not only intoxicated by drink, but by the heady lifestyle of the sahib, with the semi-public space of the verandah in which to demonstrate their ascendency. This spatiality, too, is again significant – in studies of space and place, the domestic sphere is considered the 'first space', constitutive of individual being, of the true self away from the second space of the workplace.[60] For Ahmed's alcoholism to begin here demonstrates how the colonial project worked through domestic colonisation, as well as territorial. Alcohol reinforces this process, acting as a catalyst in breaking down the rules, religious or caste-based, by which they live and through which they determine their racial, social and political identities. Ahmed and the other residents are still socially and spatially othered, but their Indianness is further eroded through drink, resulting in the mutability of the self. This mutability extends through time and space, and the negotiation of selfhood occurs in what is itself a transitional site between the public and private, outside and inside, and, at six p.m., the moment at which day fades into night. As such, their sundowners become a toast to Empire at the threshold of imperial twilight, as the sun that never set finally goes down on colonial

British India. Such resonances mean the episode also echoes the divisions in Indian identity that are exacerbated by Partition. Beyond the barriers of the hedges denoting the separation between the families and their religions, the 'ripping night' becomes an allusion to the 15th of August that entwines the personal and political in its reference not only to the tearing of the existing social and political fabric that occurred with independence and Partition, but also to the torn sheet that was responsible for the Sinai family dynasty. Ahmed and the other residents are figuratively torn between their origins and their new-found distinction, their Indianness and their Anglicisation.

The notion of domestic colonisation extends to the other layer of mimicry taking place in this section of the novel. Just as Scott did with the character of Ahmed Kasim, Rushdie's text speaks to the legacy of 'cultured' British society on India in the trace of the so-called 'Macaulay Indian' that Methwold and his actions attempt to embody in Ahmed Sinai. Whilst, as Neil Ten Kortenaar argues, the objects that clog the villas influence the behaviour of their occupants alongside the cocktail hour, the significance of drinking in relation to mimicry in the novel and Macaulayism goes much further.[61] Methwold's interactions with Ahmed are framed around instruction and its long-lasting effects, with Saleem stating that Methwold 'would come round to teach my father to hate all full bottles of scotch and to dedicate himself to the emptying of these monsters which imprisoned the fluid object of his love'.[62] Moreover, Methwold's act of leaving the cocktail cabinets full of good whisky, Saleem believes, '[introduced] my father to what was to be the greatest and truest love of his life, the onlie [sic] begetter of our ensuing family atmosphere'.[63] Alcohol becomes integral to Ahmed's mimicry, and is another reflection of how vital drinking, and more specifically drinking whisky, was to denoting the Indian middle classes. Unlike Ahmed Kasim and his relation to Pakistan, however, Ahmed Sinai's mimicry is still acceptable in post-independence India; D. C. R. A. Goonetilleke notes that the transfer of power on Methwold's departure passes to those Indians already predisposed toward the culture of the West.[64]

The mutability of the Indian in the face of British influence is acknowledged by Rushdie, who writes of how Methwold 'presided over this blending of superior western civilisation with good honest native stock! A glorious age, he must have felt, was being given a glorious end,' in so much as his efforts leave behind a lasting legacy embodied in the habits impressed upon Ahmed.[65] Rushdie's choice of diction is significant here; the action is one of 'blending', suggestive of hybridity, even of passing and 'blending in', but also of whisky terminology. A blend is substandard, inferior, yet at the same time the act of mixing makes its base ingredients more palatable. The kind of abasement that alcohol engenders within Ahmed does much to undermine the notions of resistance that Bhabha argues are inherent to mimicry. Alcohol erodes Indianness in a way that other forms of Anglicisation, such as education or language, do not. Education and language can be turned back against the oppressor, as indeed they were by the Indian nationalist movement from the early twentieth century onwards, whereas the tide of alcohol that begins to wash Ahmed's identity away is irresistible. Of course, mimicry still works in two directions, and Methwold himself is held up for ridicule with his pronunciation of 'Sabuckuck theek-thaak hai' (an Indianised saying meaning, ironically, 'everything's just fine', but also evocative of the countdown to independence and the section's title) and vanishes, never to be seen again; however, as the book progresses it emerges that the effects of his 'little game', like those of Mountbatten's, have long-lasting implications.[66]

Rushdie's decision to begin his Ahmed's decline into alcoholic dependency at the point of political and national emancipation illustrates his own complex relationship to Indian identity and Indian history. On the surface, it appears as a straightforward criticism of the decadent and disempowering influence of the British; the fact that Methwold introduces Ahmed to the whisky that then precipitates his decline is a pointed reference to the negative influence of the British presence on Indian culture, seeing as it damages his personal health and his marital and professional relationships, induces him to break his religious vows, and dilutes his Indian identity. However, given the repeated statements on the importance of allegory throughout the novel, Ahmed himself and the class and generation of Indians he represents and belongs to are also the subject of Rushdie's criticisms. Ahmed, like Nehru and Gandhi, strikes a bargain with the British that, whilst seemingly empowering, has destructive and unforeseen consequences. Just as Gurnah observes of Nehru that his 'ambition for post-independence India begins to disintegrate almost as soon as India is founded, in the Partition violence and the language marches', Ahmed's decline and disintegration begins at exactly the same point.[67] It is an example of how, as in the Anglo-Indian fictions of Scott, Farrell and Jhabvala, the relationship between the individual and the nation is so often read through the prism of medicine and health, supporting Jeffrey Meyers' observation that the sickness of the hero is often analogous to the sickness of the state.[68]

The second stage of Ahmed Sinai's alcoholism begins after the formal declaration of Indian independence. As Saleem explains:

> cocktail cabinets had whetted his appetites, but it was my arrival that drove him to it . . . In those days, Bombay had been declared a dry state. The only way to get yourself a drink was to get yourself certified as an alcoholic; and so a new breed of doctors sprang up . . . whisky Doctors.[69]

Saleem goes on to detail how Ahmed and most of the 'respectable' men of the neighbourhood would queue up each month at Dr Sharabi's surgery and emerge with the 'little pink chitties of alcoholism'; however, the ration soon proves inadequate for Ahmed's needs and he begins to send his servants along to the doctor too, and the gardener, before resorting to paying for further supplies, with Rushdie writing that '[t]he poor, having little else to peddle, sold their identities on little pieces of pink paper; and my father turned them into liquid and drank them down.'[70] With his reliance on whisky becoming more acute, Ahmed further assumes the habits of the now departed Methwold, turning to philandering and making a series of ill-advised business decisions.

Again, the change wrought upon Ahmed in this section can be read initially through the productive context of mimicry. In introducing his concept of mimicry, Bhabha draws on the work of Jacques Lacan, beginning his chapter with an epigram that reads: 'The effect of mimicry is camouflage . . . it is not a question of harmonizing with the background, but against a mottled background, of becoming mottled.'[71] The linguistic and associative resonances with Rushdie's description of Ahmed's alcoholism are evident. The notion of his becoming 'mottled' in his mimicry evokes not only the mottled complexion of the habitual drinker, but also the dimpled bottles he draws from Methwold's cabinets, with the confluence between the drinker and the drink another way in which he is 'blurred at the edges' by his burgeoning dependency.[72] We are told too of the 'whisky doctor' 'Dr Sharabi's mottled-glass surgery door', itself suggestive of opacity, of hidden practices such as the black market trade that drives the selling of ration chits, and of secret drinking behind closed doors in the newly dry state of Bombay.[73]

Moreover, the mottled background Lacan refers to is reflected in the diffusion of Ahmed's identity as a result of the methods he employs to obtain his alcohol ration. Rushdie writes of how Ahmed is known at:

six different stores under six different names. He was a Hindu, a Muslim, a Sikh, a Jain and two Parsees for the sake of a drink. For whisky's sake he became a teacher, an ice-cream salesman, a monk, a keeper-of-a-Tower-of-Silence and a swimming-bath-attendant as well as a property-owner-and-entrepreneur.[74]

In this stage, Ahmed's drinking becomes a form of erasure leading on from his mimicry, in which he begins to lose control and loses his grip on his identity. Whereas in the first stage and during his interactions with Methwold, Ahmed alternated between public and private states – the Macaulay Indian with Methwold, and 'Janum' with his wife Amina – here his identity becomes less stable, becoming refracted through the facets of the whisky bottle and into these various illusory roles. Ahmed's mimicry then becomes paradoxical. He is credible enough to pass as these different individuals, to 'blend in' in these different contexts, but in so doing becomes less distinct at the same time – as Rushdie writes: 'Ahmed Sinai blurred the edges of himself by drinking.'[75] He becomes all and none of those other identities at once, never truly any of them, and the act of trying to become other renders his own stable self diluted, watered down. Yet there is still stability present in his clinical identity; he is officially (if ironically not in the clinical definition, yet) 'an alcoholic', and his identity as such has been diagnosed, certified and negotiated by a combination, or another blending, or even a mixture, of Bombay's medical, legal and social practices. There is a contradictory play of control and power going on here, in so much as Ahmed is able both to replicate other identities but also become the subject of replication himself.

In his description of Ahmed's 'sickness' and of his multiplicity, Rushdie again draws comparisons between the state of the individual and the state of India. Ahmed takes on these different guises, and in doing so becomes all India, suggesting how the desire for alcohol, and indeed addiction and its medical definitions, all act as unifiers, cutting across boundaries and divisions of religion, occupation and caste. However, again class and social rank complicate Rushdie's depiction of Indian unity. Ahmed, as a middle-class entrepreneur and 'Macaulay Indian', of course has the freedom to do this, and his economic status enables his drinking through the exploitation of the poor; ironically, his adoption of 'low class' identities is at odds with the middle-class habit of whisky drinking. Such exploitation of the lower classes again puts drinking in the realms of bankruptcy, both in the figurative moral sense that Ahmed courts through exploiting those below him in social standing and through his philandering, but also in the literal sense of where his drinking takes him; by the end of this section, he has been ostracised from the business community, his assets frozen, with only the option of further erasure, to declare himself bankrupt, as a means of escaping his predicament.

Beyond the secular, social aspect of Ahmed's alcoholism, this section of the novel also introduces a spiritual dimension to drinking; an element that Rushdie's archive suggests went through a process of gradual refinement. In the 'First Draught', Rushdie writes of Ahmed's dependency with reference simply to 'whisky'. However, in a successive version he introduces the term 'djinn', an Arabic word that has a range of interpretations including genie, demon, or, more suggestively, a malevolent or 'bad spirit'.[76] Such a choice of diction has multiple metaphorical associations. To free a genie from a bottle often brings unintended consequences as well as initial riches; the term evokes ideas of the 'demon drink'; and it is also homophonous with that famed colonial beverage and quasi-medical indulgence, gin and tonic. Following on from Methwold's playfulness around independence, ironically undercut through tying Indians to an English way of life, the novel preserves its prevailing allegory in relation to the djinns. Saleem recounts how Ahmed tells him a story of a fisherman who found a djinn in a bottle washed up on the shore, warning him, 'let them out of the bottle and they'll eat you up', whilst all the while clutching a 'green bottle with a white label'. In telling his classmates of his father's actions the next day, Saleem is met with ridicule: 'My father fights with djinns; he beats them . . . and it was true. Ahmed Sinai . . . began, soon after my birth, a life-long struggle with djinn bottles. But I was mistaken about one thing: he didn't win.'[77]

This section of the novel can be read, in light of Gilmore, as a point of spiritual and political crisis for the new Indian state; a battle for the 'soul' or 'spirit' of the Indian subject embodied in Ahmed, just as much as it is in Saleem as a midnight's child. Medicine, too, is transformed, and the 'whisky doctors' of the first draught become 'djinn-doctors', responsible for the soul as well as the pathologised body. Through Ahmed, his drinking and the wider context of state-enabled alcoholism, Rushdie criticises the notion that the 'birth' of a new nation does away with the compromise and the weakness of old. The 'new' India, for all its patriotic zeal and moralising, is shown by Rushdie to be as complicit in the behaviour it formerly condemned. The new legislation that turned Bombay into a dry state, itself a rejection of Macaulayism and part of a constitutional promise to prohibit intoxicating drink and drugs (except 'for medicinal purposes'), is shown to be impossible to enact and undermined by those who supposedly desire its implementation.[78] Alcohol becomes another means of criticising the gulf between the impossible and illusory ideals of the new India and its reality, just as Rushdie does elsewhere in the novel with nationalism and propaganda through Jamila Singer's role in Pakistan and later government, and the clearance of the slums in which hundreds die. Moreover, it is not the British that push Ahmed into alcoholism, but rather the actions of his fellow Indians. As a Muslim and a vulnerable minority, Ahmed faces financial persecution by Bombay's Hindu businessmen, including having his assets frozen and pushing the family into considerable financial difficulty, which exacerbates his drink dependency. Rushdie's point, again, is that the idea of unified India as one state, as declared by the nationalists, is fallacious.

The final stage of Ahmed Sinai's alcoholism is clinical addiction. Progressing beyond the pre-alcoholism of the earlier sections, Ahmed's behaviour begins to advance through the various phases of Jellinek's scale, shifting from the Alpha and Beta categories, where drinking occurs first as a response to social or emotional problems and then involves heavy drinking on a daily basis, and then into the more advanced Gamma and Delta phases. In Ahmed's case, many of these symptoms begin to appear in the years following the seizure of his assets, particularly in the form of his increasingly erratic behaviour in the home and at work. However, again corresponding to Jellinek's phases, Saleem recounts how, at this stage, although 'djinn-sodden', Ahmed's drink problem is manageable enough for him to still function.[79] In fact, his drinking gives him the confidence to sell what property he has left and use the money to play the stock market to some success, with Saleem noting how it was 'a feat made more remarkable by Ahmed Sinai's constantly-worsening drinking habits'.[80]

Unlike the first two states, the grip of Ahmed's addiction tightens at a much faster pace in this section of the novel, and Rushdie writes that 'his financial coups obscured his steady divorce from reality . . . under cover of his growing riches, his condition was getting steadily worse', to the point where 'by July, Ahmed Sinai had entered an almost permanent state of intoxication'.[81] This permanent state puts Ahmed on the path towards the more advanced stages of the disease concept, those phases which Jellinek considered constitutive of full-blown addiction. The earlier stages, in his opinion, constituted a state of physical dependency but not, crucially, a loss of control. However, despite the nuances of Jellinek's diagnoses, Ahmed reaches a point where the dilution of his identity and the indistinct self of the previous sections are replaced by an intensity of emotion, and he experiences extremes of despair, despondency, malice, anger, romance and manic activity, alongside his financial success.[82] Gilmore's assertion that alcoholism is 'total illness, with far-reaching effects that are not only physical but also psychological and spiritual' can again be observed in Ahmed's swift decline. He begins to believe in the family curse he invented as part of his mimicry, and at one point is found trying to transfer his misfortune to the family dog: 'This was that same fictional curse which he'd dreamed up to impress William Methwold, but now in the liquescent chambers of his mind, the djinns persuaded him that it was no fiction.'[83] Whereas before the fluidity and confluence between drink and drinker extended to Ahmed's legal and social identity, alcohol now begins to affect his psychological stability.

Such developments signify progression into the Gamma phase of the Jellinek scale. In the Gamma phase, according to Valverde, the alcoholic begins to develop tissue tolerance, dependency, and suffer from a loss of control.[84] The most significant shift in this section of Ahmed's alcoholism is in how the effects of drinking are portrayed. Rather than a change to his mannerisms, his company, identity or behaviour, in the Gamma phase the alteration is writ large in bodily signs of decline and damage. For instance, Saleem notes for the first time that 'Ahmed Sinai's face [was now] ravaged by whisky' and that his 'battles with djinns' had left him dusty, unwashed and with blood-rimmed eyes.[85] Ahmed's self-inflicted 'mottling' shifts from the social to the physical. Ironically enough, this shift in Ahmed's status towards full-blown disease concept alcoholism occurs after the system of medicalised alcohol rationing had ended and the certification of alcoholics was no longer necessary. Prohibition in Bombay was enacted between 1948 and 1950, and then again after 1958, being repealed each time to combat the increase in criminality that it produced.[86] This shifting political and legal landscape renders Ahmed an officially certified alcoholic when clinically he is not, and then leaves him clinically an alcoholic when such certification no longer matters. Despite the ironic tone to this diagnosis, Rushdie makes a significant point regarding medicine and its effects on the individual. If we are to read Ahmed in terms of the allegory with which we encounter him throughout the novel, then his condition is a reflection of how medicine can be manipulated by those with influence or power but has severe shortcomings when it comes to improving the quality of provision and treatment.

The final part of Ahmed's role in the novel involves a further legacy of alcohol. Saleem receives a telegram whilst in Pakistan urging him to return to Bombay as soon as possible because his father has been diagnosed with a 'heartboot', something later explained as a swollen lower left ventricle, causing the heart to look, quite literally, like a boot.[87] This condition, also known as cardiomegaly, has multiple causes, one of which is long-term alcohol abuse.[88] The shock of the 'heartboot' sends Ahmed into recovery and, tended by his wife, Saleem explains how:

> not only did Ahmed Sinai make a recovery so complete as to astound Breach Candy's European doctors, but also an altogether more wonderful change occurred . . . under Amina's care, he returned not to the self which had practised curses and wrestled djinns, but to the self he might always have been, filled with contrition and forgiveness and laughter and generosity and . . . love.[89]

However, despite this near miraculous recovery and the swing back from addiction to a comparative state of rejuvenation, Ahmed cannot escape the legacy of his past. Having re-established their relationship, Ahmed and Amina move, again using a spatial metaphor, to another dry state, Pakistan, and begin a successful towelling business (another allusive means of becoming dry). Not long afterwards, though, Ahmed suffers a debilitating stroke – again as a result of the long-term physical strain of his drinking – and is rendered near insensible as a consequence, before then being killed by bombing in the Indo-Pakistan war of 1965–7.

In considering Ahmed's narrative arc, *Midnight's Children* is again both aware of and deeply concerned with reflecting history, especially in terms of generic convention and the writing of embodied experience found in Anglo-Indian print cultures. For instance, Rushdie's novel echoes the kinds of stern warnings when it comes to drink of the literature that precedes him. However, his approach does differ in that the moral dimension is largely absent here; although Ahmed has many failings as a result of his drinking, Saleem, and by extension Rushdie, do not frame Ahmed's addiction in terms of moral weakness, nor do they pass judgement on his character and his flaws. However, the consequences, ranging from the social to the professional, familial and medical, are repeatedly made apparent all the same. Ahmed's story could be framed tragically, especially with so much of his life affected by substance abuse as well as the later pathological hangover from his drinking, but the novel does not seek to do so. Rushdie resists the common oversimplification of addiction narratives in that there is no 'miraculous recovery' for Ahmed, but nor is this a narrative of a tragic or wasted life.

Taken in its totality, Ahmed's relationship with alcohol can be seen to mimic and imitate the narrative structure of the kinds of sources employed by Collingham and other historians in their explorations of embodied experience of India. Ahmed's decline begins with surprise and transformation, moving to acclimatisation, before eventual ruin and near dissolution forces him to leave India to achieve some degree of rehabilitation. Echoing such a structure and embodying it in a character whose unstable national identity fluctuates as a result of the force of history and his own personal mimicry, Rushdie applies the tropes of literary postmodernism to the genre of Anglo-Indian writing. The reuse of form, theme and imagery are recurrent tropes of the postmodern project and conform to Rushdie's satirical and ironical commentary on the British and Indian past, and the means of communicating any kind of personal and historical narrative, here demonstrated in Saleem's retelling. Alcohol becomes integral to such an account, as well as a central ingredient of the history of Empire.

Notes

1. Hervey, *The European in India*, 304.
2. A continual preoccupation with bowel movements is also visible throughout the Anglo-Indian society of Scott's novels, from the amoebiasis of *A Division of the Spoils* (1975) to Tusker and Lucy Smalley's two adjacent toilets in *Staying On* (1977).
3. Collingham, *Imperial Bodies*, 3.
4. Examples of such works include: Hull, *The European in India: or Anglo-Indian's Vade-Mecum* (1874); Duke, *Queries at a Mess Table* (1908); Menkel, *Healthful Diet for India* (1927); Forbes's *East India and Colonial Guide* (1841); Roberts, *The East India Voyager, or Ten Minutes' Advice* (1839); Kenny and Leigh Hunt, *On Duty Under a Tropical Sun* (1882) and *Tropical Trials: A Handbook for Women in the Tropics* (1883).
5. Graham Huggan calls such literary techniques the 'exoticist production of otherness' used to support a solipsistic vision of the 'orient' within European literature and culture; Huggan, 13.
6. Russell, *The Indian Mutiny*, 3.
7. In Farrell's archives he notes that 'the British past lies like a heavy meal on the stomach of educated India', an opinion derived from his own visit to India, where he noted a prevalence still for the treacle and bread-and-butter puddings of the colonial past; Farrell (Trinity), Box 9155: 'Unpublished diary', 72.
8. See Vlitos, *Eating and Identity in Postcolonial Fiction*.

9. See Wald, *Vice in the Barracks*; Goodman, 'Spaces of Intemperance'.

10. An example lies in the air of dissipation that surrounds Hummil, the British engineer stuck in a remote station in Rudyard Kipling's *At the End of the Passage* (1891); Hummil's drinking habits exacerbate his unhappiness to the point where Spurstow, the station doctor, unloads his gun lest Hummil do himself harm.

11. Porter, 'Drinking Man's Disease', 385–96.

12. Valverde, *Diseases of the Will*, 66. See also Herring et al., *Intoxication and Society*.

13. Valverde, *Diseases of the Will*, 99; 111; 114.

14. Scott, *ADotS*, 34.

15. Spurling, *Paul Scott*, 30.

16. Ibid. 406.

17. Ibid. 72. Scott's mentor, Clive Sansom, had 'a horror of alcohol', and so Scott never drank whilst under his tutelage.

18. Gilmore, *Equivocal Spirits*, 12.

19. Whitehead and Woods, *Edinburgh Companion to the Critical Medical Humanities*, 3–4.

20. Scott, *ADotS*, 48. Merrick later uses the same whisky to curry favour with John Layton, and further ingratiate himself with the family.

21. Scott, *TDotS*, 337.

22. See Fischer-Tiné, 'The drinking habits of our countrymen', 393.

23. Scott, *TDotS*, 253. A 'burra peg' was the Anglo-Indian name for essentially a double-measure, and is quite literally a 'big drink'.

24. Scott, *JitC*, 107.

25. Hull, *The European in India*, 236; Duke, *Queries at a Mess Table*, 40.

26. Scott, *TToS*, 145; 181. It eventually leads to Teddie's undoing too; fearful of what Merrick might do to captured Indian deserters and having redoubled his belief in Man-Bap, he walks into an ambush, where he is killed.

27. Scott, *ADotS*, 213. The whisky is actually a gift from Merrick, and a further example of how alcohol is used to build social bonds within the Raj.

28. Scott, *ADotS*, 31.

29. Ibid. 44.

30. In *Heat and Dust*, Douglas reflects on the death of John Nicholson at Delhi as '[b]etter than to drink yourself to death . . . Some of them did that too. It can get very tedious if you're stuck out in a district all on your own'; Jhabvala, *HaD*, 154.

31. Scott, *ADotS*, 43. As noted in Chapter 1, Scott imbues Purvis with some of his own traits and habits, although again, these are exaggerated and not enacted as a means of writing a pathography.

32. Ibid. 99.

33. Ibid. 103. Later in the novel, it is revealed that Purvis tried again not long after his admission to hospital, where, having been placed in a ward on an upper floor, he fell from his window to his death.

34. Scott, *TDotS*, 156. Though only minor characters in *The Raj Quartet*, the Smalleys would go on to be the main characters of Scott's Booker-winning *Staying On* (1977). It is important to note here too that Scott does not, unlike other Anglo-Indian authors, try for too much out of Sarah Layton; he curtails her potential romance with Ahmed Kasim, likely out of recognition of Forster's influence on the representation of Anglo-Indian relations. Her pregnancy too, unlike that of Jhabvala's narrator in *Heat and Dust*, is aborted, Scott having explored the trope of birth at the death of the Raj in the first novel through Daphne Manners.
35. Morey, *Fictions of India*, 140.
36. Scott, *TToS*, 48–9.
37. Ibid. 309.
38. In *Staying On*, Tusker Smalley is described as the last member of the 'old school' of British and 'needed his liquor'; see Scott, *SO*, 8.
39. Robinson, *Angels of Albion*, 20–1.
40. Scott, *TDotS*, 107.
41. Scott, *ADotS*, 712.
42. It is likewise noted that the Nawab in Jhabvala's *Heat and Dust* drinks his own 'special concoction'; restricted by the British and the ICS, the Nawab instead brings control to those small things within his purview such as his drinking, and his control of Harry.
43. Scott, *TDotS*, 108.
44. In Jhabvala's *A Backwards Place* (1965), whisky does likewise for Kishan Kumar, actor, playboy and Bombay socialite. Protagonist Bal becomes intoxicated by Kumar and attempts to mimic him; Jhabvala, *A Backwards Place*, 22.
45. Kortenaar, *Self, Nation, Text*, 168.
46. Hames, *Alcohol in World History*, 91. Goonetilleke notes that the transfer of power on Methwold's departure passes to those Indians already predisposed toward the culture of the West. However, again the cross-section of religions and occupations of the group suggest that such a predisposition can exist in any Indian, and not just a particular group; Goonetilleke, *Salman Rushdie*, 26.
47. Rushdie, 'Outside the Whale'.
48. Gurnah, *Cambridge Companion to Salman Rushdie*, 91.
49. It is debatable as to whether a main narrative exists in the novel; despite the presence of a protagonist and the bildungsroman-esque nature of the book, its form and preoccupation with how the past intrudes on the present precludes a sense of linear narrative. However, Ralph J. Crane argues that such framing is a consistent trope of Anglo-Indian fiction, noting that novels by Paul Scott and Ruth Prawer Jhabvala, and Richard Attenborough's *Ghandi* (1982), all begin in the present before going backwards within narrative time. See Crane, *Inventing India*, 88.
50. Rushdie, MARBL, Fiction, *MC* MSS 'First Draught', 103–6.

51. Rushdie, *MC*, 98; Rushdie, MARBL, Fiction, *MC* MSS 'First Draught', 106.
52. Alcohol is present throughout the novel, as well as in the sections under discussion here. Even the book's arch-villain, Reginald Dyer, the man responsible for giving the order that led to the massacre of unarmed civilians at Amritsar in 1919, has an association with alcohol. Dyer was an Anglo-Indian, born in Muree in the Punjab (now Pakistan), where his father worked as a brewer; see BL, Collection 233/2 Beer supply, Madras and lower Burma.
53. Valverde, *Diseases of the Will*, 111–12.
54. Gilmore, *Equivocal Spirits*, 5.
55. Rushdie, *MC*, 95.
56. Bhabha, *Location of Culture*, 122.
57. Ibid. 123. Italics in original.
58. Rushdie, *Imaginary Homelands*, 33.
59. Rushdie, MARBL, Fiction, *MC* MSS 'First Draught', 106.
60. Martin, 'Drinking: An Apprentice's Diary'. Martin goes on to argue that the pub or alehouse is the 'third place', and constitutive of social identity.
61. Kortenaar, *Self, Nation, Text*, 168.
62. Rushdie, MARBL, Fiction, *MC* MSS 'First Draught', 106. Originally called 'Westmead' in the 'First Draught', Rushdie alters the character's name to the more historically resonant 'Methwold' swiftly in the course of his revisions. Presumably the increased closeness to historical fact suited the novel's approach to historiographic metafiction and magical realism.
63. Rushdie, MARBL, Fiction, *MC* MSS 'First Draught', 106.
64. Goonetilleke, *Salman Rushdie*, 26.
65. Rushdie, MARBL, Fiction, *MC* MSS 'First Draught', 107. Sarah Upstone draws on Bhabha to note that the colonised body is 'paradoxically a site of attraction and abjection, a location 'always simultaneously inscribed in both the economy of pleasure and desire and the economy of discourse, domination and power'; indeed, in Methwold's games, as well as his affair with Vanita, the colonised body becomes this site of inscribed domination and desire, tempered with the knowledge of impending loss of power. See Upstone, *Spatial Politics in the Postcolonial Novel*, 150.
66. Methwold reappears in self-reflexive, postmodern fashion in *The Ground Beneath Her Feet* (1999). Chronologically earlier than *Midnight's Children* and presumably in the same fictional universe, Methwold appears as a scholar of comparative mythology, for approximately ten pages (41–51). Though much changed from his portrayal in *MC*, he is still associated with alcohol, drinking whisky with Sir Darius Xerxes Cama, and the novel has Sir Darius succumb to drink and addiction like Ahmed Sinai does.

67. Gurnah, *Cambridge Companion to Salman Rushdie*, 95.
68. Meyers, *Disease and the Novel*, 4–5.
69. Rushdie, *MC*, Box 16/1, 149.
70. Rushdie, *MC*, 131–2.
71. Bhabha, *Location of Culture*, 121.
72. Rushdie, *MC*, Box 16/1, 150.
73. Rushdie, *Midnight's Children*, TS: Box 17/3, 139.
74. Rushdie, *MC*, Box 16/5, 150.
75. Rushdie, *MC*, 132.
76. The Quran (55, 14–15) states that djinns are made from a 'smokeless fire' much like that which alcohol gives off when burnt, as Ahmed does in the novel; *MC*, 131. In 'On the Best Means of Preserving Health in India: Alcohol', Surgeon General C. R. Francis states that the term 'jin' shares no etymological root with alcohol, however, 'its demoniacal character may render it deserving of such'; 3.
77. Rushdie, *MC*, 131.
78. Hames, *Alcohol in World History*, 92.
79. Valverde, *Diseases of the Will*, 111. Rushdie, *MC*, 202.
80. Rushdie, *MC*, 202.
81. Ibid. 203.
82. In the 'First Draught', Homi Catrack explains that he is not keen on liquids because they mean dilution whereas he believes in concentration and intensity. However, he is persuaded to drink neat whisky and finds it 'a wonderfully intense experience'. MARBL, Fiction, *MC* MSS 'First Draught', 106–7.
83. Rushdie, *MC*, 203–4.
84. Valverde, *Diseases of the Will*, 112.
85. Rushdie, *MC*, 236; 283. Ahmed's decline and alcoholism corresponds to colonial assessments of the Indian capacity for drink; Francis states that the Indian physique is incapable of managing alcohol consumption, and doing so results in 'the worst passions of human nature being let loose'; Francis, 'On the Best Means of Preserving Health in India: Alcohol', 47–8.
86. There were earlier attempts at prohibition, including during British rule in Madras in 1937. See Phillips, *Alcohol: A History*, 276; Sharma et al., 'The Evolution of Alcohol Use in India', 8–17. It is mentioned in Scott's *Staying On* that Tusker Smalley once ran afoul of the Bombay prohibition laws, causing a minor scandal and a good degree of personal and professional embarrassment, though the matter is never directly explained. See Scott, *SO*, 89.
87. Rushdie, *MC*, 294.
88. Baskin, *Principles of Cardiac Toxicology*, 212.
89. Rushdie, *MC*, 297.

Chapter 5

No Such Thing as History Nowadays: Medicine, Health and the Legacy of Empire

'India, as everyone knows, is divided equally between jungle, tigers, cobras, cholera, and sepoys.'

Rudyard Kipling, *Plain Tales from the Hills*[1]

Anglo-Indian fiction is full of recurrent threats to the health, and lives, of its characters. In its inclusion of these hazards, the genre records and reflects the prejudices and beliefs of its subjects, characterising and repeatedly rearticulating the understanding of India as potentially deadly to British bodies. As such, the counterpart to the glamour and splendour of the Raj in these novels is the persistent representation of India as fraught with prospective danger, with harm lurking around every corner. This risk, and high incidence, of mortality is not only a legacy expressed within Anglo-Indian fictions on page and screen alike, but also one that informs the broader structures of the memorial culture that exists around colonial India and the British Empire in general. Despite the irony behind Kipling's words above and his disdain of those who characterised India in such a reductive fashion, he and his own writing served to entrench such sentiments as much as they dismissed them. Rushdie himself argued that Kipling 'made India a bestseller' by turning it 'into a real place, a place which neatly fitted the British prejudices of the time', especially in relation to its racial stereotypes and its dangers.[2] In Kipling's own refrain within the 'White Man's Burden' (1899), the possibility, if not probability, of death in the service of the ideals of colonialism is laudatory.[3] Moreover, Kipling's exhortation to any budding imperialists on their way to far-flung colonial spaces to 'make them with your living/And mark them with your dead!' illustrates how alongside the social, political and medical changes wrought by the colonial project, mortality too is a defining aspect of its presence and an occurrence that leaves material traces, legacies and memorials of its own.[4]

Farrell, Scott, Jhabvala and Rushdie all sought to engage with the memorialisation of the Raj and its various physical, political and cultural legacies that lingered in their contemporary present. They did so in part based on their own experience or else through use and re-use of historical sources, events or contexts, and their Indian novels are largely retrospective in their framing and narration. Many of their works draw directly from Kipling's array of tropes, with all of them, sometimes multiple at once, appearing across the course of their books. For example, Farrell and his contemporaries G. M. Fraser and Norman Partington acknowledge the lingering fear and fascination with the 'Mutiny' narrative through novels that directly represent the Indian Rebellion. Unlike Partington, Farrell and Fraser sought to parody this story, but they nonetheless retell it too, and indeed use its continued currency within the British cultural imaginary to drive interest in their own work. However, many of Kipling's dangers do not appear in the narrative present of the Anglo-Indian novels under discussion here, but rather haunt its characters and their societies instead, with the spectres of illness and diseases such as cholera lurking within the landscape such as in *The Hill Station* (1981), or the allusions to the lingering memories of 1857 that are encountered in Jhabvala's *Heat and Dust* (1975).[5] Even snakes make an oblique appearance in *Midnight's Children* (1981) through the inclusion of the 'old snake doctor' and anti-venom expert Dr Schaapsteker, who moves into the upper floor of the Sinais' bungalow and whose rent sees the family through the worst of Ahmed's alcoholism.[6]

In part, such references to these established tropes are an expression of these authors' literary moment; their inclusion is a form of indirect intertextuality, noting and repeating without replicating the hallmarks of a genre that enables more searching critique through parody and irony, or which complements the more specific instances of reference to earlier works of imperial and Anglo-Indian fiction.[7] However, they also indicate how much the society of the Raj prized and perpetuated particular forms of cultural production, how dependent it was on the representation of inherited metaphor and narrative form, and how vital the prominence of cultural memory was within its literary and artistic output. The repeated return (and re-run) of events such as the Rebellion of 1857, or the recurrent presence of illness, creates a cultural perspective that is always looking over its shoulder and which is indebted to its past either as the basis for its essential understanding of the world, or as a guide to future action. The emphasis on such terms of reference, even with all of Kipling's facetiousness taken into account, creates a culture of memorialisation in which the past is made continually present, and which places the spectre of mortality at the heart of the British Raj. Colonial society is represented as one that above all valued its traditions, either in ways of governance, social ritual or a general predisposition towards respect for the actions, authority and sacrifice of its forebears. Again, as Kipling recognises, the possibility of death in the service and preservation of colonial society was characterised as an ever-present part of life.

Acknowledging this cultural impetus and following on from the preceding chapters and their consideration of health, medicine and treatment, this chapter explores the recurrence and meaning, of mortality and death that accompanies the representation of illness throughout Anglo-Indian fiction. Across its two connected sections, the chapter argues that at the same time as illness and death are narrated as a part of past experience within these novels, the past itself is narrated through illness and mortality. In doing so, it draws focus on the instances of endings, memory, hauntings and nostalgia that intersect with mortality to create the culture of memorialisation that exists within Anglo-Indian fiction. It also shows how this memorialisation structures and sustains the genre of post-imperial historical fiction to which the novels of Scott, Farrell, Jhabvala and Rushdie belong. The chapter thus analyses a further complexity inherent to colonial legacies with regard to postmodern and post-imperial writing, namely the paradox that by seeking to engage with, critique or parody Anglo-Indian literature these authors give life to the very genre and tradition they seek to criticise. Indeed, their choice of historical fiction is a symptom of memorial culture itself, with the use of history in service of narrative prolonging the life of that history, and the British Empire, into the present of their contemporary moment. The chapter therefore explores the notion of the imperial legacy with a particular emphasis on narrative and literary form and how these works utilise retrospective accounts, or are concerned overtly with temporality and the act of looking back.

Savage endings: John Masters and the experience of aftermath

The Raj Revival did not spring into being fully formed in the early 1970s but was instead the product of a gradual accumulation of time, memory, cultural currency and developing public interest in the vanished world of the British Empire in the decades following the end of the Second World War. While the emergent and pervasive geopolitics of the Cold War would come to dominate the literature, culture and society of the 1950s and 60s, such interests did not mean that the Empire went entirely neglected in the pages of British fiction, of course. Indeed, all British fiction in this period is arguably possessed of a relationship to Empire, and even those novels set far from former imperial or colonial territory reflect, on a latent level, the ongoing struggle within British political and cultural life to come to terms with the new reality of a post-imperial, postcolonial world and the national efforts to stay relevant within it.[8] Others, meanwhile, did not sublimate the loss of Empire in the importance of elsewhere, but rather continued to write in the tradition of the imperial novel, either as a result of seeking comfort in familiarity or because they perceived that literary fiction was the only medium through which the urgent, difficult, necessary questions of British identity could be explored sufficiently.

The decade after independence in India, then, is neither void nor vacuum for fictions about Empire, but rather a period in which the challenges of the immediate aftermath of British colonialism were met by those novelists who saw that its legacies could be more productively explored through literature than politics. Whilst the trickle of novels would take time to swell into the flood it later became, the existence of such works is an important precedent that establishes the various narrative and thematic foundations of the Raj Revival and represents a literary legacy that Scott, Farrell, Jhabvala and Rushdie themselves would later inherit and seek to develop.[9] For instance, until this point in this book the novels of John Masters have been a latent presence instead of an active one, providing corroborating or extenuating detail to support the interventions of his more widely recognised literary successors who came to prominence a decade later. Masters, with his rather fusty image as the archetypal old colonialist – all sunburn, stern demeanour and imperial moustache – seems representative of the kind of mid-century novelist that literary history is content to forget. To read Masters, though, is to recognise that in amongst the undeniable tendency toward colonial swashbuckling is an awareness of the restrictive nature of the growing nostalgia for the British Empire, an appreciation of the human experience of the Raj and a reflective approach to the representation of Anglo-Indian society that did not seek to hide its pettiness as it esteemed its virtues. Masters' novels would thus shape the genre of post-imperial writing ahead of the Raj Revival, and his Savage saga acts as a foundational series on which rests the later blossoming of the historical novel of Empire in the 1970s. Given this impact, his works invite the same scrutiny as the others that comprise this volume, especially in terms of the precedent they set with regard to the themes of illness and memorialisation explored elsewhere in this chapter.

Like the novelists who come after him, Masters is another writer who remains difficult to pinpoint within a defined literary movement or context. Spurred to write initially not out of literary ambition but rather a need to earn a living at the end of his military service, Masters' first book, *The Nightrunners of Bengal* (1951), was a then unfashionable historical novel concerning the Indian Rebellion, intended as a potboiler.[10] Although there is only a distance of four years between the publication of Masters' *To the Coral Strand* (1962) and Scott's *The Jewel in the Crown* (1966), by the time of the high-water mark of the Raj Revival's first wave (arguably the ten years between the publication of Farrell's *The Siege of Krishnapur* in 1973 and ITV's adaptation of *The Jewel in the Crown* in 1984) Masters had seemingly laid his own ghosts to rest, having moved away from writing about the British experience of the Raj, and was instead exploring Indian identities through books such as *The Ravi Lancers* (1972) or Cold War themes with an Indian twist in *The Himalayan Concerto* (1976).

Partly as a consequence of this lack of neat fit, and partly through a mistaken tendency to equate his opinions on Empire with those of his characters, Masters has a chequered reputation and, like Scott, if he is not neglected entirely, often comes in for generally disdainful criticism for his romanticised depiction of the Raj or the occasionally crude nature of the symbolism and themes of his fiction. In relation to exploring the immediate aftermath of Empire and its representation, however, Masters is a significant voice, and his novels represent a vital transition within the genre of Anglo-Indian writing between that of Kipling's realism, Forster's modernism and the resurrection of historical fiction in its later, more playful, postmodern format. Peter Morey and Richard Steadman-Jones, for example, have argued for a reappraisal of Masters' work, especially considering its contemporary popularity across the political spectrum of its time, Masters' debt to and development of Anglo-Indian fiction, and his rare ambitions to explore the conflicted perspective of India's Eurasian community at the end of Empire.[11] Whilst never feted with the kinds of acknowledgement inherent to a prize such as the Booker, Masters' work was nonetheless a popular success, especially in the USA, where he lived for the rest of his life after leaving India and the British Army in the late 1940s.[12] Steadman-Jones notes that this favour with an audience 'who at the very least were unsympathetic to Britain's status as an Imperial power' suggests that his fiction sought to provide something more complex than the 'illicit sensualities of Imperialism'.[13] The additional (post)colonial remove of being a Briton in America influenced Masters' fiction in that the exploration of independence and liberty from aloof and oppressive colonial rule would have taken on new and charged meaning, especially in the context of the burgeoning US–Soviet rivalry of the 1950s and the growing 'informal empire' headed by the USA.[14] Critical without condemnation of Empire, then, and sympathetic without being sycophantic to its servants, Masters' fiction exhibits some considerable overlap in intent with the writers who would follow him; whilst not a Booker winner, Masters writes about Empire in a manner recognisable in the fictions of Scott, Farrell, Jhabvala and, in his echoes of Kipling, even Rushdie.

Master's major novel of the 1950s is *Bhowani Junction* (1954). Set over the span of a few weeks in the summer of 1946, Masters' temporal co-ordinates are specifically and carefully chosen, with the threat from the Second World War safely over and Indian independence still comfortably far off. Independence is, by this point, an inevitability, but not to the extent that it has yet to entirely undermine or alter the tenor of British rule. Masters gives his reader a portrait of Anglo-Indian society in the slow lull of transition as opposed to preparing for, or recovering from, Partition. The novel's title refers not just to the railway town in which it is set, nor to the importance that the train (itself a major instrument of colonial rule and a perennial legacy of the Raj) plays in its plotting, but rather reflects the metaphorical crossroads at which the narrative and its characters stand. For Eurasians such as Victoria Jones and Patrick Taylor, the junction is ontological. It concerns their choice between adhering to the system of colonial rule (in which they achieved status through the denigration of the Indians below them in the social hierarchy, just as they in turn were denigrated by the Britons above them) or pledging themselves to the oncoming new India as Indians.[15] For Rodney Savage, a British officer and career soldier, the junction is geographical, concerning whether he stays on in India or returns to England, but also temporal. For Savage, as the inheritor of the 300-year-old legacy of his family history in India, the junction is a meeting of past and present, of tradition and change and of the colonial and postcolonial.[16] The novel evokes these historical and temporal echoes, for example in its recollection of the Indian Rebellion of 1857 and the fear that accompanies the Indian Naval 'Mutiny' that takes place in the course of the narrative, or the bearing that various characters' family members both immediate and ancestral have on their actions and selfhood in the present.

Beyond its substantiation of such backwards-looking perspectives, the significance of *Bhowani Junction* for this study lies in its status as the first instalment of Masters' depiction of Rodney Savage as the embodiment of the British post-imperial paralysis that would lead eventually to the Raj Revival. Whereas *Bhowani Junction* dealt with what was then comparatively recent history, Masters' return to the story of Rodney Savage in *To the Coral Strand* would come after an interval of nearly a decade. Chronologically, the plot follows on from the events of *Bhowani Junction* with the interruption of only a few months, with Savage making reference to the recent resolution of his and Jones' affair. However, thematically, *To the Coral Strand* takes place in a different world altogether. Set between Independence Day in 1947 and 1950, the novel's framing narrative deals with the new India's development towards nationhood and its efforts to incorporate the princely state of Chambal under its control. These events are essentially only convenient background for the novel's true interest, though, namely the disintegration of Rodney Savage's selfhood and of the world of the Raj that afforded and sustained his identity.

The difference between the two novels as filtered through the character of Savage is palpable, although also contradictory. In one sense, *To the Coral Strand* is a far coarser portrait of Savage and the genre of Anglo-Indian fiction, one that seems uninterested in shying away from or masking its stereotypes, and in the course of the narrative the reader follows Savage through a checklist of the various staples of the colonial novel, including a dramatic tiger hunt, numerous alcoholic benders, and dubious episodes of sexual encounter with the 'wide-mouthed', mostly naked and suggestively named Gond tribeswomen Devi and Kunthi.[17] As such, the novel reiterates and reinforces those colonial tropes of Empire as a space of leisure, treasure and (sexual) pleasure for the British imperialist, corroborating the assessment of Masters' work as the 'pornography' of imperialism referenced by Steadman-Jones, as well as further linking him with the later novels of his contemporary, Ian Fleming.[18]

At the same time, *To the Coral Strand* leaves behind the racism of Patrick Taylor that appeared throughout *Bhowani Junction* and contains the suggestion that Masters' writing had become far more self-reflexive in nature, implying that the inclusion of the excesses of colonialist fiction were, in part, more self-aware and satirical than might first appear. Masters appears to explore the interplay between the role of fiction and the creation of identity through the character of H. Huntingdon Blauvelt, famous novelist turned sportswriter, hunting enthusiast and alcoholic, who appears to be a caricature of Ernest Hemingway. With Blauvelt having cried off a third day of hunting due to a succession of illnesses including fever, dysentery and neuralgia (in reality, all a cover for his alcoholism), Savage confronts him and in conversation is told the truth behind his persona: 'once a certain image of you has been created, you have to conform to it'.[19] Whilst such advice is relevant to Savage's performance as a 'pukka sahib' in the context of the plot, Masters goes a step further and, in what appears to be a reference to his own place and reputation within the history and lineage of Anglo-Indian fiction, has Blauvelt state: 'everyone thought it was autobiographical. Jesus, it wasn't even wish fulfilment.'[20] Acknowledging his own Indian Army background and criticising the assumption that his characters' thoughts and desires are also his own, Masters does essentially the opposite to contemporaries like Fleming, who always embellished their association with the subject of their fiction where possible.[21]

Such elements of *To the Coral Strand* suggest that Masters is attempting to move beyond the themes of *Bhowani Junction*, which are essentially Forster's, and instead present a far more considered meditation on the past of Empire that recognises the legacy of Britain's colonial history and explores its restrictive effect on post-imperial identity in microcosm through the disintegration and decline of Rodney Savage. His novel thus anticipates and acts as the blueprint for the Raj Revival writers that would follow him just a few years later. Indeed, Masters' inclusion here is because to read *To the Coral Strand* is to observe the themes of Farrell, Scott, Jhabvala and Rushdie in protean form, especially the frequency, utility and significance of illness and medicine, and the acknowledgement of the power inherent to memorialisation, history and looking back. Masters is significant not only for his influence, though, but also for his own literary engagement with these themes. Instances of illness and medical treatment abound from the opening pages of *To the Coral Strand*, from the character of Margaret Wood, a trained nurse and medical missionary recently widowed as a result of her husband's cancer; detailed descriptions of paratyphoid, medical procedures and various injuries and wounds; reflection on the status and expertise of Indian practitioners of Western medicine in independent India; and Rodney's rather self-justificatory explanation that aside from simply enjoying Devi and Kunthi's sexual favours, he has been teaching them 'hygiene, sanitation, and elementary first aid' in fulfilment of his role as the benevolent sahib, and the identification of medicine with progress.[22] Medicine and illness are interwoven into the fabric of colonial and postcolonial life throughout the novel as incidental occurrences of plot and characterisation, but they also act as defining themes in their own right, particularly in service of Masters' pursuit of ideas of decline and recovery and his embodiment of the history and legacy of colonialism in Rodney himself.

Beyond the surface details of the plot in which Rodney attempts, and mostly fails, to find a suitable role for himself within post-independence India, *To the Coral Strand* is as much a long narrative of decline, with the use of the body as a central element of Masters' chosen metaphor. In addition to the novel's recurrent concern with the body of the state, as Morey and Mehmet Fikret Arargüç have noted, in the form of the Leviathanesque fashioning of India as a single country 'from a hundred countries' and the incorporation of Chambal, the novel links each of Rodney's various schemes and the corresponding part of the narrative to the body, either in their expression or their ending, in three distinct phases.[23] In the opening section of the novel, when Rodney works for the construction and development company McFadden Pulley and as a *shikar*, or hunting guide, he is preoccupied with sensory and corporeal pleasures, particularly sex. In addition to his orchestration of an orgy at an Indian temple, Masters describes Rodney's being in relation to his physicality, either in his repeated drunkenness, lingering descriptions of his 'lean, well-muscled' body and relationship with Frances Clayton, or in his enthusiastic participation in the carnivalesque crowds of both the Independence Day celebrations and the fertility festival of Holi.[24] In this section of the novel, Rodney, and the figure of the sahib, is still depicted as vigorous, potent and hyper-virile, conforming to his self-styled persona of 'cold, cruel, efficient, ice-blue eyes, all steel and sex', first revealed in *Bhowani Junction* and seemingly still relevant despite the end of Empire.[25] Masters also calls attention to the psychosomatic effects of Rodney's experience, expressed both in the interplay between his physical and mental state and in his efforts to address or correct his situation. Like Mildred Layton in Scott's *The Raj Quartet*, Rodney's excessive drinking is a physical remedy to address a mental condition; he repeatedly seeks to shore up his resolve through drink, noting that he drinks not to forget but 'only to remember'.[26]

Masters depicts Rodney's actions as taking place in the 'present tense of . . . immediate aftermath', in which the political situation of

India has yet to stabilise following Partition and independence, and various characters attempt the resolution of the terms of the new reality.[27] Rodney's sahib mentality remains possible because the shift between Empire and independent India is not complete; the newly independent India is not yet whole and the sum of its being not yet fixed, so neither is Rodney's identity, which leads to psychological disruption. Indeed, his self-destructive behaviour, his drinking and his intensifying mood swings are indicative of a trauma response, bringing out a destructive disregard for his own well-being that informs his actions in the novel's second phase, the battle for Chambal. Here, Masters repeatedly calls back to the ghosts of the Indian Rebellion, illustrating how Rodney's mental state is becoming increasingly unstable, dominated by the rhetoric of imperial history and its long litany of violence. Having captured some prisoners on the border of Chambal, he considers how '[t]hese bloody people had betrayed me' and that he needs to show them 'that the day of the pukka sahib was over. The day of Hodson and Edwardes and Nicholson was coming back, the day of the hard men of total power, instant decision and no remorse.'[28] Rodney's references to Kipling and his association between the end of the Roman Empire and that of the British Empire further suggest how, in a time of political uncertainty and existential threat, he too retreats towards the comforting securities of the imagined and narrative past as a means of informing his contemporary actions.[29] Rodney's involvement with Chambal is not motivated simply by his professed desire to preserve the autonomy of the princely states, but because it is a way he, and by extension the Empire, can strike back at a decolonised India he views as insufficiently appreciative of Britain's colonial legacy.[30]

His efforts, though, are unsuccessful, and, undermined by supposed allies, Chambal's defences are swiftly overrun. Rodney's failure to defend Chambal both affirms his narrative of betrayal, evoking the Rebellion of 1857 as well as the British view of Indian nationalism during the Second World War, and illustrates to him the reality of the end of Empire through the combination of the political and the personal.[31] He discovers that his anachronistic identity as a sahib no longer makes him invincible, and in his attempt to reach the front in his Bentley he is intercepted by advancing Indian tanks. In case it was necessary to further underline the sea change in geopolitics that this section of the novel reflects and represents, Masters describes how Rodney's British-made Bentley is utterly destroyed by the US-supplied Sherman tanks of the Indian Army. Managing to evade the shell, Rodney is instead shot, tellingly, in the back, and left bleeding from the bullet's exit wound in his stomach.[32] Beyond the leaden symbolism here, Rodney's wound is again relevant within the novel's use of temporality and the process of change as a result of recovery. He suffers the kind of wound that does not kill outright, but instead affords the individual time to reflect on the prospect of their mortality in the aftermath of injury. Given first aid and stabilised by Indian medics, he escapes custody, only to end up taking refuge with Margaret Wood in her clinic.

The short but detailed episode in which Margaret treats Rodney marks the beginning of his steep decline into a form of post-imperial melancholia and paralysis after the disillusionment of his efforts in Chambal. Masters continues his emphasis on the interrelation of Rodney's physical and mental state through extended description of Margaret's attention to the dressing, cleaning and bandaging of his wound and a surfeit of detail on his pulse rate and temperature, alongside Rodney's subsequent delirium and fever. Recognising that in his near-death state she is 'eavesdropping on his soul', Margaret expects him to express himself in the terms of an idealised England, namely 'school . . . green fields and cricket'.[33] Instead, Rodney produces a monologue composed of snatches of Hindi, memories of his lovers, Janaki and Victoria Jones, commands and orders from his military service, and a hundred different Indian and English names, in 'sentences [that] fell disconnected from the fluttering lips, but formed a single world, a single life'.[34] Masters suggests a correlation between the physical wound of his gunshot and the inner turmoil of nostalgia, the open wound of memory. Whilst the scene resembles a near-death experience in so much as Rodney revisits his strongest emotional attachments, this brush with mortality does not result in the conversion and repudiation of the world of Empire that might be expected through the use of such a trope. Instead, in the event that he lives whilst the world of the Raj slips finally into memory, Rodney becomes fixated on the past, his consciousness arrested in the act of looking back: 'all was of the past. *This* had been. For the future – nothing.'[35] Arargüç argues that the instances of long-term memory, reminiscence and daydreaming in Masters' novel are an attempt to discursively evade responsibility for the exploitation of imperialism through the reconstruction of identity, as well as to lament its ending.[36] However, the nostalgia that Rodney embodies is shown to be profoundly negative, resulting only in vulnerability, his increasing belligerence, violence or self-defeating actions. His nostalgia is evocative of grief and a remembrance without which he cannot imagine his own existence; as Leslie Jamison argues, 'the cause of injury is in the past, but the healing isn't done'.[37] Masters implies that for a British readership to identify with such nostalgia positively would be equally self-destructive, and the novel's overriding message in its final third is to emphasise the necessity with which such imperial baggage must be left behind.

The dominant medical thread of the novel's final section is the familiar trope of pregnancy and (re)birth, once again signifying Masters' earlier exploration of the kinds of themes that would go on to define the novels of Scott and Jhabvala at the height of the Raj Revival. Betrayed by Sumitra, the Rani of Kishanpur, during the sub-Great Game skulduggery of the war in Chambal, Rodney is pardoned by the Indian government, having served his purpose in enabling Chambal's absorption, and takes a job as a night watchman at a warehouse in Bombay.[38] Margaret tracks him down and finds him at the nadir of his post-imperial decline, unconcerned with the squalor of his lodgings, dressed in dirty clothes, stooped and stubbly: 'a middle-aged Anglo-Indian down on his luck'; when she persuades him to permit her to examine his gunshot wound, Margaret discovers he has crabs, is 'covered with bug bites' and 'must have lice, too'.[39] Though lacking in subtlety, Masters' description of Rodney's physical and mental decline here is an appropriate counterpart to the priapic 'lady's man'[40] and thrusting Rod of the book's first third, and of *Bhowani Junction*. Indeed, the further time elapses since the end of Empire, the greater Rodney's sexual and mental deterioration. Masters describes how Rodney becomes paralysed in his despair, suggesting that his refusal to accept the change in his fortunes and the end of Empire shifts over time from first admirable and a sign of his fidelity and dedication, to frustration in that he cannot see how he is manipulated, before finally becoming tragic in his broken-down state. Resolving to help him in return for how he had cared for her during her bout of paratyphoid, Margaret explains how whilst Sumitra and India may have nearly killed him, she, and by extension England, must revive him.[41]

What truly revives and resurrects Rodney, who is largely indifferent to Margaret's constant and selfless care, is that he learns of Sumitra's pregnancy and the prospect that he will be a father. Masters' plotting is once again contradictory and double-edged. It is notable that Sumitra's pregnancy and her and Rodney's affair is largely free of the scandal that accompanies Olivia's relationship with the Nawab in Jhabvala's *Heat and Dust*, illustrating a difference in expectations across genders, but also the irrelevance of the racial division and colonial propriety of the Raj of the 1920s when compared with a postcolonial and independent India. However, the terms of that pregnancy, and what it represents, remain firmly in the realm of history and the stifling context of personal and colonial legacies. For Sumitra, her relationship with Rodney is steeped in the conflict that connects them and is an affirmation, as another of Rodney's lovers acknowledges, that such conquest would always reflect the inequalities of the colonial encounter: 'he overwhelmed me, the same way his people overwhelmed my country'.[42] Similarly, despite his single-minded pursuit of Sumitra and their child, Rodney recognises that to continue his family tree would be to perpetuate the Savage legacy and pass on 'that damned albatross, which had been hanging round my family's neck for about a hundred and fifty years now' to a further generation, only one without the security of the colonial hierarchy with which to mitigate it.[43]

In its tumultuous and somewhat macabre denouement, however, *To the Coral Strand* offers some hope for the reconciliation of the colonial legacy with the reality of the postcolonial present. Unable to resist the temptation of 'what a baby really is – our projected selves, our dreams, our hopes, our future', Rodney forces Margaret to reveal Sumitra's whereabouts, and the two of them attempt to reach her as she goes into labour just as a hurricane hits Bombay.[44] Finding that the baby is a breech birth, and lacking the necessary training, equipment or recourse to a hospital to deliver it safely by caesarean section, Margaret is forced to dismember the baby or allow both it and Sumitra to die. Masters depicts this painfully slow process in a scene as detailed and precise as his earlier description of Margaret's care of Rodney's stomach wound, again using medical procedure tonally, applying its restrained, deliberate register amidst the drama of the surrounding scenario. It is a scene of unexpected bodily horror and personal tragedy for the characters, with an ambiguous implication. Unlike the birth metaphor of Scott, in which Daphne Manners and Hari Kumar's daughter Parvati never knows her parents but grows up secure and loved by the Chatterjee family, or that of Jhabvala, in which the narrator prepares herself for the hopeful future her Anglo-Indian child will bring as a corrective to Olivia's past, here Masters forces the reader to witness the bloody partition of Rodney and Sumitra's child and the death of the united Anglo-Indian identity it might have embodied.

Yet Masters does include within this experience of loss the prospect of future personal and spiritual growth and healing. The novel's final exchange is notable for the destiny that Rodney's ordeal has revealed to him and the new purpose he has found as a result of his suffering. Having been pushed back to the sea by the vicissitudes of (post-)imperial history, the coral strand of the novel's title, and, fittingly, the place at which his ancestor Jason Savage first came ashore in the 1620s, Rodney experiences an epiphany:

> 'What I saw and did tonight turned from an ending into a beginning . . . from a final terrible experience into a command for the future. Look, my hands are strong, my eyes steady. I can learn.'
> 'What?' she asked dully.
> 'To be a surgeon.'
> She turned and stared at him. 'You? A surgeon? It takes a long time . . . Yes. You could be a surgeon. You have the nerve . . .'[45]

Rather than the finality suggested by the ending of his hopes for a child, and resisting his initial urge toward suicide, Rodney breaks the historical cycle of the Savages, having returned it full circle to its point of origin. Recognising that India no longer has use for his talents as a soldier or a place for him as a sahib, Rodney instead imagines a future helping to heal the wounds of others, and, by implication, the open wound of nostalgia that had driven his refusal to accept reality. In doing so he resembles the characters later found in Farrell, Scott and Rushdie, using the prospect of this future path into medicine as a means of remedying his previous adherence to the values of the British Empire. Masters employs the prospect of Rodney's training as a surgeon both as an example of 'physician, heal thyself', acting as a corrective to his loss of purpose and position with the end of colonialism (just as it would later do for Scott's Sarah Layton), but also in ironic echo of medicine's civilising intent; in spite of his own earlier efforts to bring medical knowledge to the Gond tribespeople as a means of preparing them for the future, it transpires that he is the Savage for whom medicine becomes transformative. The qualities of the pukka sahib – his strength, steadiness and nerve – are shown to still possess value, despite the ending of the empire that produced them. In being denied his 'projected self' and the prospect of extending the Anglo-Indian connections of the Savages ever further, Rodney nonetheless finds new purpose. Masters' suggestion is that the same process must happen for postcolonial Britain; that same 'projected self' of national identity, buttressed by imperial history, must also be sacrificed in order to find a future.

The Retrospective Raj: memorialisation and legacy in Anglo-Indian fiction

Although Masters lies outside of the group of novelists that make up the core of this volume, exploring the significance of *To the Coral Strand* is instructive in light of the thematic precedent his works set for Anglo-Indian writing after Empire. While the novelists of the Raj Revival would see themselves as pursuing fiction that was critically, ideologically and intellectually distinct from Masters and the jingoistic mode of production he was often (erroneously) thought to represent, the objectives of their writing are not nearly as dissimilar as generally perceived. Instead, and linked by the circumstances, context and shifting political climate in which they were written, both Masters and the Raj Revival share the recognition that continued adherence to the ideals of Empire offered no future and would instead affix only looking back. However, this is not to say that there is no distinction between them; Masters' novel was published when belief in Empire was still, in part, possible, while Farrell, Jhabvala, Rushdie and Scott wrote at a time when such a belief was untenable.

Given this sea change in context, it is arguable that for all the specificity and individual character of their individual plots, the Anglo-Indian novels that comprise this volume are all as much about the circumstances of their production as they are the Indian subcontinent and the colonial society they represent. As well as the various conditions, terms of enquiry and use of metaphor derived from medicine, what unites these novels is the engagement with the actions, attitudes, myths, stories and histories of Empire and the attendant belief in British exceptionalism they produce. Peter Morey argues that 'every reading is above all an indicator of its own historical moment', and the same conditions are true of this volume too.[46] The novelists of the Raj Revival wrote about Empire as a means of understanding its ending and the effect it had on their contemporary context; this book explores their writing on Empire because the same post-imperial melancholia that drove them likewise lingers in modern Britain's return to nostalgic neo-nationalism.

Of course, the literary turn towards Empire and Britishness in the twentieth century was not unique nor limited to these authors, but instead became an increasingly prominent part of the post-war literary zeitgeist as time continued. A range of complementary media and genres sought to examine the process by which the historical shift in Britain's global status that came with the end of Empire was translated first into geopolitical reality, and then subsequently into myth. This process reached its critical point in the aftermath of Suez in 1957–8 and Harold Macmillan's 'Winds of Change' speech in 1960, encouraging a host of authors, filmmakers and artists to respond to the nation's shifting circumstances. In part, these texts worked to buttress and encourage national cohesion, seeking to assert or create the perception of a united Britain in the face of rapid political and social change, and offer a vision of Britishness that was both comforting in its existence and corrective in its action.[47] By the time the Raj Revival emerged as a recognisable genre in the 1970s, the prospect of halting or reversing British decline had itself become a distant memory, though the desire for comfort remained as strong as ever. As noted in the Introduction, the Raj Revival thus satisfied a growing mood of post-imperial nostalgia, connecting directly with the experiences of those who were there and who bore the Raj in liv- ing memory, their children, or those who despite having no personal knowledge of British India first-hand were nonetheless captivated by the romance inherent in its representation.[48]

To some extent, the Raj Revival was an inevitable development within a culture that had always sought to bolster its image through the generation of national myth.[49] As the gulf between the real and the imagined state of Britain grew in the course of the overlapping shifts across the post-war, Cold War and postcolonial periods, the emphasis on the act of looking back became greater. Raphael Sam- uel, writing in the 1990s, notes that 'the last thirty years have wit- nessed an extraordinary and, it seems, ever-growing enthusiasm for the recovery of the national past', and he identifies the growth in membership of the National Trust as well as the social currency and value of the concept and term 'heritage' as telling indicators of this interest in 'both the real past of recorded history, and the timeless one of tradition'.[50] However, for Rushdie, writing in the wake of the Revival's first rush of popularity, it was instead an intensifying effect of the nation's continued decline, a form of 'cultural psychosis' causing 'many Britons to turn their eyes nostalgically to the lost hour of their precedence'.[51] Whereas Samuel's analysis suggests an almost logical and largely benign process through which such swift decline in international standing might produce an introspective culture of memorialisation, for Rushdie such actions are a pathology, a psycho- somatic trick of the mind in which 'the recrudescence of imperialist ideology and the popularity of Raj fictions . . . [are] the phantom twitchings of an amputated limb' which, although the source of such feeling may no longer exist, is felt no less keenly for its absence.[52]

Rushdie's choice of medical metaphor is indicative of the manner through which the colonial Empire returns to British literary consciousness in this period. The resurgence of interest in the history and memory of British India returns at first not in any tangible, physical form, but as a phantom, with the spectre of the nation's former prominence and influence haunting a diminished and divided post-imperial Britain. Indeed, the exponential growth of historical imaginings of Britain in the post-war period indicates, as Katy Shaw argues, the beginnings of turn towards an 'English culture more interested in co-opting the past than embracing the future', which has only intensified over the course of subsequent decades.[53] Drawing on the connected but distinct emotion of nostalgia, in which the individual undergoes a simultaneously painful and pleasurable longing for times past, Shaw considers this historical interest as an example of hauntology, or the 'science of ghosts, a science of what returns', covering those emotions, feelings and memories that are deliberately recalled as well as those phenomena that return unwillingly or that are unanticipated.[54] Whilst Scott, Rushdie, Jhabvala and Farrell were not necessarily themselves motivated by a desire to generate nostalgic yearnings within the collective body of post-imperial Britain, their novels, and more specifically their adaptations, provoked them all the same through their reuse of and return to the locations, narratives, signifiers and spirit of colonial India and its modes of cultural production.[55] Moreover, the Booker Prize that unites them is itself an expression of nostalgic discourses designed to encourage, realise and recognise the legacy of Empire within contemporary writing in English.[56]

Ayo A. Coly identifies such nostalgic returns as an inevitability of hauntology, especially in reference to its original definition in the work of Jacques Derrida; Coly argues that Derrida's acknowledgement of how certain cultural inheritances repeatedly replicate and express themselves is how the 'colonial spectralizes itself in the postcolonial'.[57] For Coly, such texts can never escape the spectre of colonialism, even if it seeks to turn those cultural inheritances back on their origin through parody or pastiche, as 'a radicalisation is always indebted to the very thing it radicalises'.[58] Coly argues that instead of a way of recognising and revealing the inheritances and legacies of colonialism in the present, hauntology is instead a tragedy; it suggests a process of arrested development, and one that remains always myopic as it glosses over the victims of colonial oppression, and how their own post-imperial hauntology is one of traumatic return and not the pleasurable nostalgia or ironic revisitation enjoyed in the post-imperial metropole.[59] When read in relation to these willed and unwilled returns, the British Empire as realised in the pages of Anglo-Indian fiction and wider culture of post-imperial nostalgia thus becomes a cultural and political revenant, returning to haunt the consciousness of a nation that had never, in Dean Acheson's infamous words, found a role after colonialism. The return of the Raj in this period then might be thought of not simply as a revival but more aptly a resuscitation or a resurrection, not of the Empire itself, although that particular fantasy would be performed in microcosm in the course of the Falklands conflict, but rather in the structures of feeling and of value that the Empire was thought to represent.

As a consequence of the retrospective nature of Anglo-Indian fiction as a genre and the elegiac, memorial effect of historical fiction as its predominant mode of expression, there is a general context of remembrance within the textual representation of colonial India, just as there is *for* colonial India in the contemporary present responsible for the production of these novels. In particular, Scott and Jhabvala most readily adopt the tropes, perspectives and spaces of memorialisation throughout their narratives, including the use of traumatic contexts or settings, such as the changing colonial India of the Second World War, as well as locative examples, such as cemeteries and memorial statues. Significantly, both Scott and Jhabvala seek a temporal correspondence between the Raj and its memory in the present day, with both *Heat and Dust* (1975) and *The Jewel in the Crown* (1966) using letters as narrative and structural devices, as well as including other examples of retrospective textual production and material culture such as diaries, memoirs and the generation of (fictional) interviews. Such stylistic decisions around memorialisation and mortality mirror the authors' own concerns, especially in relation to Scott and his declining health and failing marriage. As Spurling notes, in addition to his long-term ill health as a result of amoebic dysentery, Scott's chronic alcoholism had intensified during the period after the publication of *A Division of the Spoils* (1975) and during the writing of *Staying On* (1977), affecting his relationship with his wife Penny and irreparably damaging his health. Although he could not have been certain of his condition whilst writing it, not long after the publication of *Staying On* in March of 1977, Scott was diagnosed with cirrhosis of the liver and colon cancer.[60] Despite hospital treatment and an immediate change in his lifestyle, his condition worsened rapidly and he was too unwell to attend the Booker Prize ceremony in November of that same year, dying shortly afterwards in March 1978 at the age of fifty-seven. It is therefore inviting to read *Staying On* as an expression of Scott's own physical decline and an as a work driven by, and about, the awareness of an imminent ending.

Although memorialisation and mortality are present throughout the entirety of *The Raj Quartet*, from Daphne Manners' death in childbirth to the simmering feud over Mabel Layton's final resting place and through to Sister Ludmilla's palliative care and her efforts to preserve the dignity of even the most impoverished members of colonial society, themes of ending and memorialisation structure and inform Scott's final novel, *Staying On*, to a far greater extent.[61] The preceding chapters have thus predominantly considered *The Raj Quartet* as Scott's attempt to engage with the culture and society of the Raj as it was lived, and how illness was experienced as part of life, through the lens of historical fiction. *Staying On*, meanwhile, takes place long after Indian independence and instead represents the afterlife of the Empire as Scott saw it, in the contemporary present of the late 1970s.

Like *The Raj Quartet*, to which it forms a far lighter and more openly tragicomic coda, the novel takes place in Pankot, focusing on the minor characters of Tusker and Lucy Smalley, both of whom appear briefly in the earlier novels as somewhat lower-ranking members of the British community. The novel describes how, in the gradually modernising hill station, Tusker and Lucy struggle to belong and argue over where their future may lie. Driven to a fit of apoplexy by a note of eviction from the proprietors of the new Shiraz Hotel (which has replaced the old colonial Smith's Hotel, in whose annexe Tusker and Lucy still live), Tusker suffers a heart attack, and the novel ends with Lucy contemplating an uncertain but hopeful future back in Britain. In its combination of the personal and the political effects of a modernising India, *Staying On* is, as Peter Morey suggests, Scott's attempt to deal with various competing legacies, both in terms of fiction in his inability to leave the world of *The Raj Quartet*, and of history in his return to India and the last remnants of colonial society. Furthermore, to read *Staying On* in light of *To the Coral Strand* is to recognise how indebted Scott is to Masters, picking up in particular on the themes of sexuality and impotence, legacy, and the changing nature of the new India in comparison to the old world of Empire, and exploring them in the altered context of the late 1970s as opposed to Masters' early 1960s. As a consequence, Morey asserts that both *The Raj Quartet* and Scott's work more generally are more complex than Rushdie's criticism of them suggests, but that in trying to engage and dismantle these legacies, Scott is ultimately ensnared by them.[62]

Staying On begins, appropriately, with its ending, describing Tusker's fatal heart attack and conforming to Crane's analysis of how so many Raj Revival texts seek to situate their plotting in the present before inducing the reader or viewer to look back through the use of narrative point of view.[63] This 'teleogenic' approach, in Lennard Davis' terms, again reflects the genre of post-imperial fiction to which the novel belongs, as well as the specifics of its subject matter and setting in India, serving to effect 'the transformation of past events by subsequent ones'; by ending Tusker's life only to resurrect him shortly afterwards, Scott invites us to examine the circumstances of his demise but also that of the Empire's death and revival, acknowledging the inextricable connections of the personal and political with regard to his characters' lives and his own.[64] Indeed, what makes Tusker's death striking is not its effect in creating the non-linear narrative form of the novel, but that it soon becomes apparent that it is just the first (and last) of a series of various figurative, social and professional deaths that Tusker experiences in India that the reader encounters, and which introduces and foregrounds the themes of death, memory, change and resurrection from the outset. As the course of the novel unfolds, Scott describes how Tusker's life is marked by moments of demise and rebirth, from his nicknaming as 'Tusker' by some 'young punk' of a lieutenant before the war that supplants his former self (indeed, we are never told his first name), his short-lived stint as a 'box-wallah' in Bombay after trouble with alcohol, and then latterly, his final 'massive coronary', which Scott in fact includes twice, bookending the novel.[65]

It is in the midst of these experiences, however, that Scott places the most emotionally resonant point of ending: Tusker and Lucy's memories of the independence ceremony of 14 August 1947, a moment that haunts not just the characters within the text, but the entire Raj Revival genre itself. Lucy recalls the ceremony as one of the few instances of emotional connection she and Tusker ever share, being otherwise able to only express their emotions obliquely, reaching for each other within the context of that 'terrible, lovely moment' when the Union Jack was 'hauled down inch by inch in utter, utter silence'.[66] As the Raj ends and India's independence begins, Tusker and Lucy stand wordlessly, hand in hand, suspended at the tipping point of power before the cheering crowd returns them to reality. The scene is characteristic of Scott's text, a temporal intersection of memory, history and trauma, signifying that a process of arrest as much as change has occurred between the narratives of *The Raj Quartet* and that of *Staying On*. Whilst for India this moment is a rebirth and represents the coming to life of hopes and ambitions for the future, for the Smalleys and other Britons like them who stay on it is the moment of psychic wounding beyond which there is only afterlife, nostalgia and looking back. All of Tusker's subsequent 'deaths' occur in the shadow of this one, where he is transformed from the colonial to the postcolonial, and, rather than the bodily death that opens and closes the novel, it is instead this point of ending beyond which Lucy's uncertain future looks to move.

Read in conjunction with this description of trauma at the end of Empire, *Staying On*'s preoccupation with mortality, remembrance and haunting becomes a quest narrative in which Tusker and Lucy search for meaning in their own memories, in the broader history of the Raj, and amongst the physical remnants of the Old India that remain – just as Scott does in the process of writing the novel itself. The narrative is filled with examples of memorial culture, particularly in relation to textual production and representation, such as the pictures of Tusker and Lucy in their youth, Tusker's obsession with Edgar Maybrick's history of Pankot (with his efforts to find fault in its narrative suggestive of the ongoing tension between history and memory), and the reconnection with Sarah Layton in the form of the letters Lucy sends, having read John Layton's obituary, and later receives in return.[67] Elsewhere, too, the physical traces of the Raj remain, particularly in the form of Pankot's graveyard, which, now near emptied of its former reverence, is shown to have as much an instrumental as sentimental use. In a chance meeting with Lucy, 'who uttered a little cry like that of a ghost on its way to a haunting', Joseph the Eurasian gardener reveals that he visits the graveyard not primarily out of remembrance but also in an attempt to learn English from the headstones as he tends the graves.[68] Pausing before Mabel Layton's grave for a photograph, Scott compounds the intersections of memorialisation, past and present, with Lucy remarking that 'you'd be surprised how welcome they'll be and how nostalgic people are [in England] . . . pictures of the church and churchyard will be looked and looked at and sighed and sighed over, I assure you'.[69] In doing so, Scott's novel exemplifies Rita Sakr's argument that the representation of monumental space might sometimes appear marginal but can act as an anchor for the politics of a specific novel and its context; in *Staying On*, monumental space both informs the political consciousness of the Raj Revival and provides the means of its realisation.[70]

Such instances of textual and material return are examples of how, as Coly states, the 'colonial spectralizes itself in the postcolonial' with varying effects.[71] For Lucy, the communication with Sarah

Layton is a moment of temporal conjunction as elements of her past, present and possible futurity intersect. Initially, this prompts a feeling of loss, as Lucy weighs the solidity of her place in the Raj's hierarchy against the prospects of a future in which she can only see further decline in Tusker's health and uncertainty in their situation. However, unlike Tusker, and in a link to Sarah Layton's own process of spiritual awakening in *The Raj Quartet*, Scott suggests that through such introspection Lucy can adjust to the reality of postcolonial India and, by extension, that Britain might also assimilate the legacy of its colonial past in its post-imperial present. Lucy realises that by allowing herself to remain one of the 'old-style British', she is just as much a relic as any of the pictures, gravestones and other detritus of the Raj, and remains an object of curiosity rather than truly alive.[72] Finally taking stock of their post-independence life as well as the succession of slights and snubs they experienced during the Raj, she reflects that 'when I look back on it . . . India brought out all my very worst qualities. I don't mean *this* India . . . but our India, British India, which kept me in my place, bottled up and bottled in.'[73] In recognising the Raj as restrictive and emotionally stifling, Lucy realises that the prestige she chased within it did not give her stature but rather diminished her, just as her continued adherence to its values does in the present. The implications of *Staying On*'s Forsterian ending, then, in which Lucy seeks a friendship with Susy, a Eurasian, on equal terms, are, in their own limited way, hopeful, and suggest that death is not just about the end of an individual or a way of life, but as much concerns the way that those who go on living keep and retell the memory of what has passed.

As noted above, many of Scott's themes draw on the precedent set by John Masters. One recurrent theme in the work of both novelists is their use of the body, albeit with a key difference; though Masters' approach to nostalgia can be read through the body of Rodney Savage, his fiction is that of men and women in their prime, and he never engages with the physical decline of old age. Scott, in a continuation of the terms he employed throughout *The Raj Quartet*, focuses on the body, living, aged and dead, to express his post-mortem of Empire in the form of *Staying On*. Indeed, the oscillation between the metaphorical capital of body and corpse is embodied in Tusker himself, who functions as both in simultaneity throughout the narrative, allowing Scott to explore the process of his physical decline having, like the Empire, established his death from the opening pages. *Staying On* is thus, in part, another historical novel of India, even if that history is much more recent than Farrell's or Jhabvala's, and this temporal remove again allows Scott to explore the past of Empire by narrating it through the progression of Tusker's illness and approaching mortality. Scott approaches Tusker's physical decline with typical frankness, describing leaky, faltering, deficient bodies over that of decorous ill health.[74] Scott notes Tusker's 'poor frail body. Not a patch on what it once was ... the face pale, the skin slack. Brown spots blotched his hands and arms,' but also notes that whilst such decline may be recognised as inevitable, the same codes of colonial stoicism remain, stating that '[t]he English, once they began falling physically apart, did so with all their customary attention to detail, as if fitting themselves in advance for their own corpses to make sure they were going to be comfortable in them.'[75] Alongside the dramatic irony in so much as the reader knows Tusker's death is imminent, Scott's suggestion is that Tusker's body is representative of the figurative body of the Empire too; its values and social codes remain despite their physical degeneration over time. Such imagery recalls the myth of the orderly withdrawal from Empire that grew in its wake (itself supported by the neatness of the timetable-like chronology of Tusker's death that structures the opening chapter), which elides the violence and chaos of Partition and again embodies the revenant nature of the Raj and the colonial Briton. Tusker lives on in the pages of the novel, a walking corpse whose actions in the final days and hours of his life will inform the character of his own memorialisation to come.

Again evoking Masters, Scott continues this association between Tusker and the embodiment of the Empire through the emphasis on and recurrence of sex and sexuality through the novel. Given that he retired long ago, Lucy's suggestion to Ibrahim, their butler, that Tusker is a man who has 'always been active' and 'suddenly finds himself inactive' intimates that sexual dysfunction and frustration lie behind his cantankerous behaviour.[76] Tusker's decline, then, is not as a result of his lack of a role in the new India, in echo of Britain's own postcolonial lack of direction for its energies, but rather in response to the fear of dissipating potency and the loss of virility that is a consequence of age. Similarly, such impotence is further mocked by his nickname, Tusker, with Scott implying the irony in its rutting, phallic nature compared to Tusker's present physical state, just as Masters did with Rodney Savage. Such suggestiveness is in part an element of Scott's chosen form; the comic novel format means *Staying On* leans heavily towards the ribald and the bawdy in its pursuit of humour, especially in its deliberate caricaturing of the enthusiastic lovemaking between the skinny, undernourished Mr Bhoolabhoy and his voluptuous, voracious wife, Lila.[77]

However, beyond these superficial comedic aspects, the novel seeks to entwine sexual health, and sex and death, at a far deeper metaphorical and ontological level too. Recalling the myth of the Fisher King that structured T. S. Eliot's *The Waste Land* (1922) and which further links the health of an individual with the health of the land that they allusively represent, Tusker's declining potency and virility come to stand for the collapsed edifice of the British Empire as its last surviving members dwindle in number and in health.[78] Scott inverts the image of the rapacious colonist and undermines the cuckolding rhetoric of imperialism that had been associated with the British takeover of India, showing both to have come to a close in the postcolonial era. Moreover, Tusker's various social deaths take on new meaning when read in relation to sex, from the social embarrassment caused by his enthusiastic semi-drunken participation in Holi, with its symbolism of menstrual blood and fertility, and the scandal that ends his employment with Smith, Brown & McKintosh in Bombay, where he 'had bitten Mrs Poppadoum's ear, spilt his wine and said "**** it"'.[79] In combining these instances of Tusker's sexuality and self-destruction, Scott draws on Sigmund Freud's formulation of the death drive or the link between Eros and Thanatos as expressed in 'Beyond the Pleasure Principle' (1920). Each of Tusker's actions are moments in which his sexual instincts result in social death or ending, or with Lucy's recollection of them likewise expressed in spectral terms: 'the thought had lasted only a moment and the ghost of it, returning to haunt her now, gave her no comfort'.[80]

Such Freudian undercurrents are themselves a haunting drawn from Scott's prior work. Scott's pervasive interest in sex and death is a deliberate recall of the psychiatrist Dr Samuels in *The Towers of Silence* (1971), whose emphasis on matters of sexual health in the preservation of physical and mental health shocked Tusker, and Pankot society at large, back in the 1940s. In the context of that earlier novel, the implications of Samuels' analysis were with regard to Susan Bingham, widowed and with a newborn baby; Sarah Layton, whose sexual awakening had resulted in a secret abortion in Calcutta; and Ronald Merrick, whose frustration, born of repressed homosexuality, Scott suggests is responsible for his abusive behaviour of Hari Kumar.[81] In *Staying On* Scott again links sex and selfhood, and sex and death, through Lucy's interiority and her memory of the various endings and transitions in her and Tusker's marriage, and their unfulfilling, hesitant sex life. In particular, she describes Tusker's retirement from the military in 1949, where, returning home, he 'shook her to the core' by exclaiming 'Right, that's ******* that' and 'later shook her again by making love to her twice between lights out and reveille'.[82] Describing Tusker's orgasm as 'not so much a climax as a sigh, after which he collapsed as if pole-axed', Scott recalls the 'little death' of Roland Barthes' analysis and the metaphorical death of the Empire embodied in Tusker, drawing together the climactic association of the content and the objective of the novel, and offering a finality to his exploration of the Raj and its ending.[83]

Notes

1. Kipling, *Plain Tales from the Hills*, 30.
2. Rushdie, MARBL, Nonfiction, 'The Haunted House: An essay', n.p.
3. Kipling, 'The White Man's Burden', ll. 31–2.
4. The foremost memorial space in the colonial Indian imaginary is the Lucknow Residency and the various forms of statuary recognising the 1857 massacre at the Bibi Gar in Cawnpore; however, there are hundreds of other sites maintained unofficially by the British Association for Cemeteries in South Asia, founded, aptly, in 1977. See <http://www.bacsa.org.uk> (last accessed 14 August 2020).
5. Jhabvala notes that in the Saunders' bungalow the 'prints on the wall had also been there a long time; they were mostly scenes from the Mutiny, as of Sir Henry Lawrence struck by a bullet in the Lucknow Residency' and had been 'handed on through several generations of government issue'; Jhabvala, *HaD*, 119.
6. Rushdie, *MC*, 137. Schaapsteker, or 'Sharpsticker Sahib', becomes a conglomeration of all manner of lore, superstition and characteristics of snakes, down to his tongue that 'flicked constantly in and out between his papery lips'. There is a further link to 1857 here; one of the defenders of Lucknow, Surgeon Joseph Fayrer, would go on in his later career to become the leading authority on the treatment of snakebites in colonial India.
7. Hutcheon, *A Theory of Adaptation*, 7.
8. Adam Piette calls attention to the relationship between Graham Greene's *The Quiet American* (1952), in which an ageing Briton attempts to stay relevant next to a young CIA operative in colonial Vietnam, and the work of Hugh Carleton Green, his brother, in the MI5-backed Information Research Department; Piette, *The Literary Cold War*, 153.
9. Contemporaneously, though different in her focus, Jhabvala herself was concerned with the newly independent India in her novels of the period, beginning with *To Whom She Will* (1955).
10. *The Nightrunners of Bengal* (1951) would mark the beginning of the Savage family saga that would recur throughout his first seven novels in the form of various members and branches at different points in British imperial history.

11. Morey, *Fictions of India*, 88. Steadman-Jones, 'Colonial Fiction', 76, 84.
12. Masters' third novel, *Bhowani Junction* (1954), was adapted for a film of the same name starring Ava Gardner in 1956; greatly changed in plot and by its casting, such commercial cross-platform success again sets a precedent later emulated by subsequent Raj Revival writers.
13. Steadman-Jones, 'Colonial Fiction', 75–6.
14. Clay, *John Masters*, 156.
15. This is particularly embodied in Jones, and Morey notes how her choices are represented by her three suitors and an array of changing costumes and behaviours to accompany each one; Morey, *Fictions of India*, 89.
16. It is important to note too that for Masters and Savage, it is always 'England' and never 'Britain'.
17. Rodney explains how Devi and Kunthi are themselves essentially legacies of imperial history, afforded to him for his personal use in recognition of his great-grandfather's relationship with the Gond tribe and his role as their 'Deliverer': Masters, *TtCS*, 28, 31.
18. Steadman-Jones quotes a 1961 essay by Ronald Brydon in which the two authors are linked, a connection borne out by the diminishing returns of Fleming's fiction in particular; the decline from the efforts towards (if not achievement of) plausibility in *Casino Royale* (1953) to the orientalism, yellowface and downright silliness of *You Only Live Twice* (1964) is precipitous. See Steadman-Jones, 'Colonial Fiction', 76.
19. Masters, *TtCS*, 114. It is notable that all of Blauvelt's 'illnesses' are those which are contracted historically and which haunt him in the present. All of them similarly have colonial or foreign roots, with his fever contracted in Uganda in 1924, dysentery from Greenland in 1938, and neuralgia from Saint Mihiel in 1918.
20. Masters, *TtCS*, 114.
21. See Lycett, *Ian Fleming*, for further detail on Fleming's character.
22. Masters, *TtCS*, 92.
23. Morey, *Fictions of India*, 80; Arargüç, 'Imperialist Nostalgia', 3.
24. Masters, *TtCS*, 69.
25. Masters, *BJ*, 286.
26. Masters, *TtCS*, 44.
27. Jamison, 'Grand Unified Theory', 118. The need to resolve the disruption to established modes of being is redolent of the individual's response to trauma as defined by Vedat Sar and Erdinc Ozturk, who state that the new experience must be incorporated into the individual's internal regulation system, or schemas; if this cognitive map cannot be redrawn then trauma may arise. See Sar and Ozturk, 'What Is Trauma and Dissociation?', 9.
28. Masters, *TtCS*, 201.
29. Ibid. 174.
30. Ibid. 147–8.

31. Masters acknowledges in particular the 'Quit India' protests of 1942 onwards and the courting of Japanese support in the creation of the Indian National Army, both of which also later structure key events within Scott's *The Raj Quartet*.
32. In an additionally symbolic, and slightly preposterous, turn of events, it transpires that the commander of the tank that shot him is not only an old comrade from Burma, but also family; as Rodney explains, he and Rikaldo Purohit are related though their great-great-grandfather, William Savage. Masters, *TtCS*, 245.
33. Ibid. 268.
34. Ibid. 268.
35. Ibid. 269.
36. Arargüç, 'Imperialist Nostalgia', 4–5.
37. Jamison, 'Grand Unified Theory', 118.
38. Sumitra is the direct descendent of Sumitra Rawan, also Rani of Kishanpur, who led Indian forces against the British in the Rebellion of 1857, and who had an affair with the Rodney Savage of that time, twentieth-century Rodney's great-grandfather. She is Masters' representation of Lakshmi Bai, the Rani of Jhansi, who, incidentally turns up in G. M. Fraser's *Flashman in the Great Game* (1975), where she captures, and later resists the advances of, Harry Flashman.
39. Masters, *TtCS*, 319; 321.
40. Masters, *TtCS*, 66.
41. Ibid. 311.
42. Ibid. 333. Janaki, Rodney's first love and the wife of his best friend, who speaks this line, is earlier described by Rodney in the fetishised language of the orientalist: 'her hair [was] flowing like a dark river so that all I could see was hair and all I could feel was flesh, and all I could smell was . . . India'. *TtCS*, 33–4.
43. Masters, *TtCS*, 140–1.
44. Ibid. 349.
45. Ibid. 382.
46. Morey, *Fictions of India*, 156.
47. Bennett and Woollacott, *Bond and Beyond*, 18.
48. Drawing on Maurice Halbwachs' work on collective memory, Rauf Garagazof outlines the manner through which a common sense of folk memory, supported by culture, can be both a radical act and one that softens the sharper, more complex edges of national events; see Garagazof, *Collective Memory*, 2.
49. In particular, the national mythology of this period crystallised around the contemporary representation of the Second World War, a further legacy that Britain continues to deal with today. See Basinger, *The World War II Combat Film*.
50. Samuel, *Theatres of Memory*, 139.
51. Rushdie, 'Outside the Whale'.

52. Ibid.
53. Shaw, *Hauntology*, 2.
54. Ibid. 2. Renato Rosaldo likewise explores nostalgia, and the curious paradox of its post-imperial expression in longing for a thing your own nation's actions destroyed; see Rosaldo, 'Imperialist Nostalgia', 108.
55. Alan Johnson argues that part of Farrell's intention within *SoK* is to deliberately undermine such imperial nostalgia through the shambolic state of the garrison. However, Farrell's anti-nostalgia is itself undermined somewhat by the fact that, though altered and shaken by their experiences, the British at Krishnapur emerge victorious and the myth of British exceptionalism reinscribes itself. See Johnson, 'Ghosts of Irish Famine', 275–92.
56. Strongman, *The Booker Prize*, 4. It is noteworthy too that these authors all haunt each other's works, as if in a loose, continuous dialogue, and also that their earlier works haunt their later ones; aside from Scott and Farrell's continuity in their narratives in *Staying On* and *The Hill Station* respectively, there are additional currents of self-reflexivity and call-backs throughout all the books considered here. Similarly, their association extends to more direct connections, with Farrell reviewing Scott's *A Division of the Spoils* for the *Times Literary Supplement* in 1975, and Rushdie's memorable comments on Scott's work in 'Outside the Whale' (1984).
57. Coly, *Postcolonial Hauntologies*, 13.
58. Ibid. 13.
59. Ibid. 14. For instance, Francis B. Singh's criticism of Farrell's work is again relevant here in so much as the voices and perspectives of Indian characters in *SoK* are limited, or mostly non-existent. See Singh, 'Progress and History in J. G. Farrell's *The Siege of Krishnapur*', 23–9.
60. Spurling, *Paul Scott*, 407.
61. Scott, *JitC*, 166–7. Sister Ludmilla reflects not only on how in its care of the dying the Sanctuary provides a service beyond Merrick's comprehension, but also alludes to how the spectre of cholera continued to haunt British India long after its peak in the nineteenth century.
62. Morey, *Fictions of India*, 151.
63. Crane, *Inventing India*, 88.
64. Davis, *Resisting Novels*, 213. As noted in the introduction, Sara Wasson links Davis' approach directly to narratives about illness and health: see Wasson, 'Before narrative', 106–12.
65. Scott, *SO*, 86; 5.
66. Scott, *SO*, 171.
67. Tusker's objections conform to the tension between history and memory as described by Pierre Nora, in which the orthodoxies of historical narrative erase, omit and marginalise the specificities and differentials found in memory. See Nora, *Realms of Memory*.
68. Scott, *SO*, 147.

69. Ibid. 151.
70. Sakr, *Monumental Space in the Post-Imperial Novel*, 3.
71. Coly, *Postcolonial Hauntologies*, 13.
72. Scott, *SO*, 111.
73. Ibid. 168.
74. Mantel, *Ink in the Blood*, 6.
75. Scott, *SO*, 29. Tusker is explicitly stated to be seventy, and is just a week or two shy of his seventy-first birthday when he dies; though young by modern standards, this is nonetheless a fair age given the reputation of India as a place where death moves with 'indecent haste'.
76. Ibid. 39.
77. The sexual humour is compounded by Scott's attention to toilets, excretion and bodily functions throughout, which acts as a counterpoint to the charge elsewhere expressed in the novel that 'one of the troubles with the British in the days of the *raj* was that they had taken themselves far too seriously'; Scott, *SO*, 117.
78. Fifield, *Modernism and Physical Illness*, 142.
79. Scott, *SO*, 215.
80. Ibid. 214.
81. Rushdie, 'Outside the Whale'.
82. Scott, *SO*, 90. Scott cannot help undercutting this theme of the novel with more humour, however; Lucy reminisces over her sexual awakening and her lust for her family's driver, the suggestively named Toole.
83. Danticat, *The Art of Death*, 129.

Conclusion: Imperial Sunsets

'[J]ust look at the huge, undiminished appetite of white Britons for television series, films, plays and books full of nostalgia for the Great Pink Age.'

Salman Rushdie, 'The New Empire'[1]

The novels of the Raj Revival explored throughout this book are a window into the ongoing British cultural obsession with Empire. They act as a temporally and culturally acute indicator of how British popular culture has remained fixated by the ideas and ideals of Empire long after the end of the colonial era. These novels, their themes, their literary recognition and their general popularity all indicate not only how India was perceived in the immediate decades that followed the end of the British Raj, but also how it has lingered within popular consciousness up to the present day. As such, the book is a contribution to the ongoing critical consideration of the cultural, political and historical legacies of Empire and illustrates how fictions of colonialism were not simply of interest to former colonial Britons, but were also of wider appeal to domestic British audiences who were connected to British India through perceived national kinship. Although aided by the contextual circumstances of their production and the fact that the Raj lingered still in living memory, these novels and other media that sought to represent the world of Empire spoke to the consuming concerns of national self-identity inherent to the post-war and post-imperial period.

In recognition of this contextual and continual impact, this book is in part an effort to further restore critical focus to British writing of the 1970s, and to argue for the longevity of its concerns and the significance of its contribution to contemporary fiction. Whilst the writers examined here have experienced various peaks and troughs of popularity over the last half-century, the Raj Revival remains as culturally prevalent as always and historical fiction more popular than ever. Consequently, *The Retrospective Raj* argues that the 1970s are as significant an era for the development of British national identity and the exploration of its crises through culture as any other period after the Second World War. The historical fictions of J. G. Farrell, Paul Scott, Salman Rushdie and Ruth Prawer Jhabvala emerge at a time of social disintegration and fracture, illustrating a Britain pulled in different directions by the lure of the past and the push-back against it. These novels contribute a further dimension to the long-standing debate over the relationship between Britain and its colonial possessions, and the significance of Empire within the daily life of British society both during and after its end. Whilst critics like Bernard Porter have argued that the effects and legacy of Empire linger in only the most minor of cultural and material borrowings, others, such as David Cannadine and Andrew Thompson, see instead a British national identity structured by the undergirding of colonialism, and whose adjustment to postcolonial reality is only arrested by its memory of Empire.[2] Ralph J. Crane and Bart Moore-Gilbert argue that the cultural relationship between India and Britain is one of deep and abiding inspiration, with India providing 'exotic' literary possibilities in relation to everything from location and style to genre, character and metaphor, but also inviting repeated reflection on British and Anglo-Indian identities in the process.[3] The fictions of the Raj Revival examined here are a further link in this narrative, as well as its inheritors. They act as historical touchstones in their own right, too; as well as a continuation of the relationship Crane and Moore-Gilbert describe, the works of Scott, Farrell, Rushdie, Jhabvala and others are the foundations of a modern genre that remains – like Empire itself, it seems – as appealing as ever, supported equally at the level of cultural taste-making through prize culture and criticism, all the way through to the bottom line of sales.

Like any work of scholarship, this book has not sought, nor would it have been able, to tell the entire story of the 'long inarticulate love' between Britain and India expressed in the literature and culture of the past seventy years.[4] In its focus on the novels of Rushdie, Farrell, Scott and Jhabvala, linked as they are by their themes, their temporal proximity to one another and the particular distinction of their receipt of the Booker Prize, it has inevitably been selective. Whilst seeking to acknowledge their existence and importance, it has not considered novels by Indian writers from the same period and has instead explored the effect of the end of Empire on the British themselves. In so doing, it has sought to answer a question Rushdie himself once posed; as his archives reveal, the thesis behind his pitch for a project called 'The Haunted House' was to explore whether it was possible to consider India 'as seen from Britain?'.[5] *The Retrospective Raj* answers this question in the affirmative and argues that in their efforts to reorient British identity in the aftermath of colonialism, these British writers and their work are as much a response to the end of Empire as those Indian voices heard who explored and fashioned the meaning of independence. Unlike the urgency, optimism and pursuit of equity that accompanied the work of authors from formerly colonised nations, for British writers the demand was to make sense of the nation's changed fortunes and the legacy that colonialism had left in its wake, starting with authors such as John Masters before progressing into the Raj Revival of the 1970s and beyond. The decision to consider such authors, who, Rushdie aside, are not traditionally thought of within the boundaries of postcolonial literary criticism, is to argue for their place within the broader continuum of global postcolonial literatures of the period.

A key and recurrent means through which these authors engaged with the history and legacy of Empire was through the utility of illness, health and medicine. Although the fictional engagement with medical themes in these novels is theoretically and stylistically complex and varies between its component authors, what unites them is the belief in illness as a prime theme of the genre and as a major element of the literary and contextual history on which they draw in the composition of their novels. As argued above, Rushdie, Scott, Farrell and Jhabvala are acutely attuned to the history of colonial India and the regularity with which illness, health and medicine play a role in that history, on both a personal and political scale. These themes, intersecting on occasion with their own personal life experiences, interrelate throughout and across their fiction, offering a coherent means of reading their work through comparative analysis to one another and in conjunction with existing discourses of postmodernism and postcolonialism. As the book has further shown, these authors combine literature, history and medicine to exchange, augment and subvert form, literary and poetic technique, idiom, metaphor, knowledge, opinion and belief, as well as historical record, throughout their novels. This awareness of the history of Empire especially, and the plasticity of their approach to it, is used to interrogate the beliefs and prejudices of their own contemporary present and make a far more incisive contribution to the discourse of post-imperial literatures than typically assumed. Again, with the exception of Rushdie, these novelists are not credited as widely for the complexity, nuance and significance of their works as this analysis demonstrates they should be.

In its engagement with the representation of illness, health and medicine in these novels, this book has addressed a range of themes across the course of its chapters. Chapter 1 examined the literary links between medicine, illness and Anglo-Indian fiction, illustrating not just how specific authors engaged with the history of British India through a medical lens but also, crucially, why they did so. Having established the terms of its analysis, Chapter 2 drew focus on the expression of power and expertise as well as the representation of colonial hierarchies, through consideration of the representation of medical men and women within post-imperial fiction. Its analysis suggested that doctors and nurses are a significant presence within the pages of these novels not simply because of the frequency with which medicine and ill health themselves appear, but in their function as an embodiment of colonial medical authority; their representation within these narratives offers these authors the means of considering how that authority might be affirmed, subverted or resisted. Chapter 3 considered the importance of space, place and environment both within Anglo-Indian fiction and the medical history of colonial India, recognising the connection between literary and physical representations of space and territory. Developing the arguments of earlier chapters, it analysed the spatial emplacement of colonial and medical authority throughout post-imperial fiction, considering the way in which Anglo-Indian writers depict colonial hospitals, clinics, medical schools and public places within their narratives and the way in which these spaces, as well as India itself, are repeatedly pathologised or act as settings for the application of British power.

Chapter 4 reflected the juxtaposition between the political and the personal in Anglo-Indian fiction through an examination of health and well-being in relation to diet. Following on from the spatial context of the previous chapter, it developed the examination of quotidian practices of Anglo-Indian society to argue that these authors use alcohol and alcoholism to satirise, subvert and undermine the supposed benefit that this application of British power presented to India and Indians, as well as the alleged danger with which India threatened the European constitution. Acknowledging this cultural context and following on from the preceding chapters and their consideration of health, medicine and treatment, the final chapter explored the recurrence and meaning of mortality and death that accompanies the representation of illness throughout Anglo-Indian fiction. It argued that at the same time as illness and death are narrated as a part of past experience within these novels, the past itself is narrated through illness and mortality. In doing so, it considered the significance of endings, memory, hauntings and nostalgia that intersect with mortality to create the culture of memorialisation that exists within Anglo-Indian fiction, and the retrospective context of the period in which these novels were produced.

In approaching these subjects, this book has considered a forty-year historical narrative of decline and regeneration in post-war Britain and its expression through Anglo-Indian fiction. Ranging from the immediate aftermath of Indian independence and post-war austerity, the book has explored not only the consistent major themes of the Anglo-Indian engagement with the history of Empire in fiction published over the ensuing four decades, but also the developments and changes over time within the literary genre itself, and how its novelists responded to Britain's shifting fortunes and standing in an era of rapid decolonisation and declining global influence. The decision to conclude the book's analysis in the early 1980s recognises the point at which Margaret Thatcher rearticulated the rhetoric of British nationalism, marking a new era of British national identity that would be reflected in the renewed focus on representing the lost world of Britain's Indian empire. The fiction that came after this point took on a different character and new-found confidence in its representation of Empire and is the subject of a book in its own right. Although indebted to the Raj Revival, the objective of later works was no longer to parody or critique like Farrell and Rushdie or to reflect change over time as Scott and Jhabvala do, but to turn the clock back and indulge in the compensatory pleasures of imperial fictions. The nostalgic qualities of these fictions removed what accountability and self-reflection existed within the British attitude towards Empire at this time, and ultimately paved the way for the kinds of fictions, and the kind of thinking, that have led once more to the resurgence of belief in British exceptionalism.

Neither the historical point at which this volume ends nor the discourses of finality in its last chapter should be seen as an indication that the questions of nostalgia, identity and the psychological sickness or infirmity of the British state are in any way settled. The cultural and political emphasis on multiculturalism in the 1990s made it appear, albeit briefly, as though Britain had found a way to transcend the conflicts over its recent history, accepting that it might no longer (and never again) be the wave-ruling Empire of its traditional mythos and making peace with its place on the post-imperial geopolitical stage. Placated by the exercise in political theatre played out in the Falklands, and content, or so it appeared, to play the enthusiastic sidekick to an increasingly belligerent United States, Britain had found a means of reflecting the legacy of Empire within the newly reordered post-Cold War world: reliant on partnerships and alliances, but as first among equals within them, and with British exceptionalism intact. Seeking similar distinction through cultural hegemony, Britain effected a nostalgic and revisionist nationalism through the retelling and reuse of its past, buoyed by a projection of renewed vigour and clout in the creative arts.[6]

However convincing the major chords of national harmony suggested by 'Cool Britannia' might have seemed at the time, it was only an interlude in this ongoing story, and, as indicated in the Introduction, the self-same divisive questions of identity, history, nostalgia and how to reconcile the weight of the British past with its present continue to exercise authors, historians and writers across various media. Whilst as Robert Saunders, David Thackeray and Richard Toye have argued, the contested cultural and historical relationship to Empire was not the sole motivation behind the British referendum on membership of the European Union, it nevertheless weighed heavy in the atmosphere of debate before and after 2016. Saunders' assertion that the 'Empire 2.0' intentions of a 'buccaneering Britain' might have been eye-catching but had no basis in policy, real or imagined, has to date been borne out.[7] However, the rhetoric of renewed nationalism, including the disdain for 'citizens of nowhere', the hope of a 'red, white and blue Brexit' and the desire to 'take back control', affirm the rejuvenated attitudes to the 'global' nature of Britain's historical presence. In this mindset, to remain a member of a part of a trading relationship is to accept compromise, to recognise the decades of British decline as irrevocable; to 'take back control' is corrective, restorative and a resumption of national destiny.[8]

In much the same way as the British national relationship to Empire and its legacies have intensified over the last half-decade, the cultural politics of illness have also returned to the popular consciousness over the period of this book's development. Given its themes of nationalism and illness, it is fitting that the research and writing of a book that began in the shadow of Brexit concluded in the midst of the global coronavirus pandemic. Although impossible to have anticipated at the outset of my research, the effects of the COVID-19 pandemic are equally impossible to ignore. Just as in the fiction under discussion here, the relationship between disease, medicine and projections of national identity remains inherently intertwined and interdependent. The COVID-19 pandemic has brought the spectre of disease – so prevalent and potent in Farrell's imaginings of the cholera-ravaged garrison at Krishnapur or lurking in the hills of Simla, and part and parcel of colonial society to so many of Scott's characters – back to the forefront of daily life. Many of the same attitudes, behaviours and concerns visible in the novels that constitute this study remain or have resurfaced, spanning from an emphasis on the supposedly redoubtable British spirit in the face of adversity through to social anxiety over the excessive consumption of alcohol. The British media has played an active part in generating and documenting these familiar nationalistic stirrings, from the call for stiff upper lips and bulldog spirit throughout the first wave, championing the social solidarity of doorstep clapping and the effectiveness of a little pomp and circumstance, finding heroes in the selflessness of Captain Tom Moore's efforts to raise funds for NHS charities by walking laps of his garden, through to (ultimately unrealised) plans for Union flag-emblazoned 'Oxford' vaccine vials. Although the AstraZeneca vaccine bottles remain unadorned, it seems that the point has been made with the design of the UK Global Health Insurance Card instead, whose entire fascia is a rippling Union Flag. With a degree of irony that would not be out of place in a satirical novel, the card is now less effective than the one it replaced, offering coverage in fewer countries than under the previous scheme despite the promise of its name.[9]

Members of the British government have sought to project a similar jingoistic tone, again with varying degrees of success. Prime Minister Boris Johnson's efforts at reassuring an uncertain public early in March 2020, when he described with typical bonhomie how he had visited a hospital and continued to shake hands with everyone he met, were undercut by the subsequent deterioration in his health and his eventual hospitalisation with COVID-19. Despite Johnson's mishap, British exceptionalism appears alive and well. With characteristic diplomacy, Conservative MP and education secretary Gavin Williamson made clear how nationalistic instincts continue to guide the response to health, medicine and treatment in the contemporary present. Speaking in December 2020, Williamson expressed a lack of surprise at the swiftness with which the UK regulator had approved the Pfizer vaccine ahead of France, Belgium and the United States, stating that this was to be expected given that the UK was, in his opinion, a 'much better country' than all of them.[10] Although such patriotic statements may comfort some, they will doubtless ring hollow to many. At the time of writing, World Health Organisation figures place the UK as fifth in the world for total deaths attributed to coronavirus, and first for number of deaths per million population.[11] In a piece of neat historical circularity, or relapse if you will, on the eve of the nation's return to life outside the European Union the *Daily Mirror* newspaper saw fit to label Britain once more the 'Sick Man of Europe'.[12]

Such a return to this state of national malaise was not an inevitability, as this book has illustrated, but is nonetheless grimly predictable. The nation's unwillingness, or inability, to accept the reality of its post-imperial status has meant that, like the ghosts and spectres of memory that recur within Anglo-Indian fiction, the same issues have returned to haunt the contemporary present. The existential questions of identity, historical representation and cultural memory with which modern Britain is grappling are still those of the post-war, post-imperial moment for which the nation has never produced a definitive answer. Britain, just as in the 1970s, exists in a liminal and transitional state, albeit one where the trajectory appears reversed; having so recently rejected the means by which it restored itself from economic and social disintegration nearly a half-century ago, it is hard to read such a move as anything other than regressive. Rather than coming in from the cold and joining the European community of nations, Britain has elected to return to its isolation on the edge of the continent. When compounded by the continued disruption of the COVID-19 pandemic, these supposed uplands look dimmer and less sunlit than once they might have.

With another acknowledgement of the circularity of this history and narrative, it seems fitting to conclude this book where it began. As time moves ever closer to the seventy-fifth anniversary of Indian independence in August 2022, there will be a renewed focus on the events of that period in recognition of their historical significance and in celebration of the continued connection between India and Britain. Doubtless there will be further chapters in the ongoing story of Anglo-Indian relations, too, and little let-up in fictions of India past and present within this context of commemoration. Given the comforting reassurance of heritage and nostalgia, and the boom in the popularity of historical fiction that occurred when Britain was last in such a state of national uncertainty, it is likely that the existing enthusiasm for fictions that seek to celebrate, critique or retell its colonial past will only intensify in years to come. Like its geopolitics in general, though, the British relationship to the telling of this (hi) story is in a similar state of flux. Organisations such as the Indian Civil Service Association and the British Association for Cemeteries in South Asia remain popular and continue their important work to preserve both the narrative history and physical remnants of the Raj; however, their membership is now almost entirely second-generation, and there will come a point where recollections of colonial India pass from living memory and into that of historical record.

With change, like the ending of the Raj itself, comes opportunity. Social justice movements such as Black Lives Matter or initiatives such as the National Trust's Colonial Countryside project ask searching questions of Britain's relationship to its history and the way in which its narrative has so far been composed.[13] The questions such efforts ask of history and heritage, of cultural representation, and around equity of inclusion in the national story are vital if that story is to have any meaning to future generations. As Britain's empire recedes further into the past, what remains will exist in the realm of narrative and retelling, all of which, as this volume has shown, are subject to the elision of time and distance and the distortions of heat and dust. By seeking to reframe and reshape this narrative, just as the novels of Scott, Farrell, Rushdie and Jhabvala did, it is possible, hopeful even, that Britain's tendency towards retrospection may take on a little more in the way of introspection too.

Notes

1. Rushdie, MARBL, Nonfiction, 'The New Empire: Notes', 3. This essay would later form the basis of Rushdie's essay of the same name in *Imaginary Homelands* (1992).
2. See Porter, *Absent-Minded Imperialists*; Thompson (ed.), *Britain's Experience of Empire in the Twentieth Century*. Beyond Porter's more notorious critique, various authors explore the connectedness of Britain and its colonial possessions, particularly in the form of commerce, capital and the sale of empire goods; see Magubane, *Bringing the Empire Home*. Likewise, the activities of the Empire Marketing Board between 1926 and 1933 effectively formalised advertising practices prevalent in British commercial activity since the nineteenth century; see Constantine, *Buy and Build*; Mackenzie (ed.), *Propaganda and Empire*.
3. Moore-Gilbert, *Writing India 1757–1990*, 7.
4. This line, perhaps unsurprisingly given his own complicated personal life, is Philip Larkin's, used to describe Scott's *Staying On* during his stint as a judge for the Booker Prize, and is included on the 1978 paperback printing. Scott, *SO*, n.p.

5. Emphasis in original. Rushdie, MARBL, Nonfiction, 'The Haunted House: An essay', n.p.
6. Rachel, *Don't Look Back in Anger*; Arday, *Cool Britannia and Multi-Ethnic Britain*.
7. Saunders, 'Brexit and Empire'.
8. *BBC.co.uk*, 'Theresa May: We Want a Red, White and Blue Brexit'.
9. *Gov.uk*, 'Apply for a UK Global Health Insurance Card'.
10. Cowburn, '"We're a much better country"'. On 31 December, Williamson was again in the news stating categorically that the UK would not enter another lockdown; the UK went into its longest lockdown to date on 5 January 2021. Stone, 'There won't be another national lockdown'.
11. World Health Organisation, 'WHO Coronavirus Disease (COVID-19) Dashboard'.
12. Crerar, 'Sick Man of Europe'.
13. *Black Lives Matter*; *The National Trust*, Colonial Countryside Project; or Fowler, *Green Unpleasant Land*.

Bibliography

Akala, *Natives: Race and Class in the Ruins of Empire* (London: Two Roads, 2018).

Alshammari, Shahd, *Literary Madness in British, Postcolonial, and Bedouin Women's Writing* (Newcastle-upon-Tyne: Cambridge Scholars Publishing, 2016).

Anon., *Forbes's East India and Colonial Guide* (London: Houlston and Stoneman, 1841).

Anon., *Medical Times and Gazette*, vols I and II (London: John Churchill, 1854).

Anon., *Gazetteer of the Simla District*, Punjab District Gazetteers, vol. VIII-A (Punjab: Indus Publishing, 1904).

Anon., *The Imperial Guide to India, Including Kashmir, Burma and Ceylon* (London: John Murray, 1904).

Anon., 'Edited Extracts from Prince Charles's Travel Journal', *Daily Telegraph*, 23 February 2006, <https://www.telegraph.co.uk/news/uknews/1511203/Edited-extracts-from-Prince-Charless-travel-journal.html> (last accessed 19 March 2021).

Arargüç, Mehmet Fikret, 'Imperialist Nostalgia in Masters's To the Coral Strand', *CLCWeb Comparative Literature and Culture*, 14:1 (2012).

Arday, Jason, *Cool Britannia and Multi-Ethnic Britain: Uncorking the Champagne Supernova* (Abingdon: Taylor & Francis, 2019).

Arnold, David, *Science, Technology and Medicine in Colonial India* (Cambridge: Cambridge University Press, 2000).

Arnold-Forster, Agnes and Alison Moulds, 'Medical women in popular fiction', *British Medical Journal* blog, 26 September 2018, <https://blogs.bmj.com/bmj/2018/09/26/agnes-arnold-forster-alison-moulds-medical-women-popular-fiction/> (last accessed 16 September 2020).

Ashbridge, Chloe, '"It aye like London, you know": The Brexit Novel and the Cultural Politics of Devolution', *Open Library of the Humanities*, 6:1 (13 May 2020), 15.

Atia, Nadia and Kate Houlden (eds), *Popular Postcolonialisms: Discourses of Empire and Popular Culture* (London: Routledge, 2019).

Bachelard, Gaston, *The Poetics of Space* (New York: Beacon Press, 1994).

Bailin, Miriam, *The Sickroom in Victorian Fiction* (Cambridge: Cambridge University Press, 1994).

Bala, Poonam (ed.), *Medicine and Colonialism: Historical Perspectives in India and South Africa* (London: Routledge, 2015).

Basinger, Jeanine, *The World War II Combat Film: An Anatomy of a Genre* (Middletown, CT: Wesleyan University Press, 2003).

Baskin, Steven I., *Principles of Cardiac Toxicology* (London: CRC Press, 1990).

Bates, Victoria, Alan Bleakley and Sam Goodman (eds), *Medicine, Health and the Arts: Approaches to the Medical Humanities* (London: Routledge, 2014).

BBC.co.uk, 'Theresa May: We Want a Red, White and Blue Brexit', 6 December 2016, <https://www.bbc.co.uk/news/av/38223990> (last accessed 26 February 2021).

BBC.co.uk, 'Jammu and Kashmir: India formally divides flashpoint state', 31 October 2019, <https://www.bbc.co.uk/news/world-asia-india-50233281> (last accessed 16 September 2020).

BBC.co.uk, 'The Singapore Grip: ITV drama called "harmful" and "deeply upsetting"', 9 September 2020, <https://www.bbc.co.uk/news/entertainment-arts-54085249> (last accessed 14 September 2020).

Bennett, Tony and Janet Woollacott, *Bond and Beyond: The Political Career of a Popular Hero* (London: Macmillan, 1987).

Best, Odette, 'Training the "natives" as Nurses in Australia: So What Went Wrong?', in Helen Sweet and Sue Hawkins (eds), *Colonial Caring: A History of Colonial and Post-Colonial Nursing* (Manchester: Manchester University Press, 2015), 104–26.

Bhabha, Homi K., *The Location of Culture*, 2nd edn (London: Routledge, 2005).

Black, Jeremy, *Imperial Legacies: The British Empire Around the World* (London: Encounter Books, 2019).

Black Lives Matter, <https://blacklivesmatter.com> (last accessed 19 February 2021).

Boccardi, Mariadele, *The Contemporary British Historical Novel: Representation, Nation, Empire* (London: Palgrave Macmillan, 2009).

Boehmer, Elleke, *Colonial and Postcolonial Literature* (Oxford: Oxford University Press, 1995).

Bombay Sapphire, <https://distillery.bombaysapphire.com/venue-hire/the-empire-bar)> (last accessed 19 March 2021).

Bose, Sugata, *A Hundred Horizons: The Indian Ocean in the Age of Global Empire* (Boston: Harvard University Press, 2006).

Boyd, Kenneth M., 'Disease, Illness, Sickness, Health, Healing and Wholeness: Exploring Some Elusive Concepts', *BMJ Medical Humanities*, 26 (2000), 9–17.

British Association for Cemeteries in South Asia, <http://www.bacsa.org.uk> (last accessed 14 August 2020).

British Library, 'Two Centuries of Indian Print', <https://www.bl.uk/projects/two-centuries-of-indian-print> (last accessed 19 March 2021).

Bryden, James L., 'Epidemic Cholera in the Bengal Presidency: A Report on the Cholera of 1866–68' (Calcutta: n.p., 1869).

Buettner, Elizabeth, 'Cemeteries, Public Memory and Raj Nostalgia in Post-colonial Britain and India', *History and Memory*, 18:1 (2006), 5–42.

Byatt, A. S., *On Histories and Stories: Selected Essays* (London: Chatto & Windus, 2000).

Byrne, Eleanor, 'Salman Rushdie and the Rise of Postcolonial Studies: *Grimus*, *Midnight's Children* and *Shame*', in Robert Eaglestone and Martin McQuillan (eds), *Salman Rushdie: Contemporary Critical Perspectives* (London: Bloomsbury, 2013), 22–34.

Carbajal, Alberto Fernández, *Compromise and Resistance in Postcolonial Writing: E. M. Forster's Legacy* (London: Palgrave, 2014).

Carel, Havi, *Illness: The Cry of the Flesh* (Durham: Acumen Press, 2008).

Chakravarty, Gautam, *The Indian Mutiny and the British Imagination* (Cambridge: Cambridge University Press, 2005).

Charon, Rita, *Narrative Medicine: Honoring the Stories of Illness* (Oxford: Oxford University Press, 2008).

Christoyannopoulos, Alexandre, 'Stop calling coronavirus pandemic a war', *The Conversation*, 7 April 2020, <https://theconversation.com/stop-calling-coronavirus-pandemic-a-war-135486> (last accessed 15 September 2020).

Clay, John, *John Masters: A Regimented Life* (London: Michael Joseph, 1992).

Coates, Sam, 'Ministers aim to build "empire 2.0" with African Common-wealth', *The Times*, 6 March 2017, <https://www.thetimes.co.uk/article/ministers-aim-to-build-empire-2-0-with-african-commonwealth-after-brexit-v9bs6f6z9> (last accessed 11 September 2020).

Collingham, E. M., *Imperial Bodies: The Physical Experience of the Raj, 1800–1947* (London: Polity, 2001).

Collinson, S. R., 'Mary Ann Dacomb Scharlieb: A Medical Life from Madras to Harley Street', *Journal of Medical Biography*, 7:1 (1999), 25–31.

Coly, Ayo A., *Postcolonial Hauntologies: African Women's Discourses of the Female Body* (Lincoln: University of Nebraska Press, 2019).

Connor, Steven, *The English Novel in History 1950–1995* (London: Routledge, 1996).

Constantine, Stephen, *Buy and Build: The Advertising Posters of the Empire Marketing Board* (London: HMSO, 1986).

Coverley, Merlin, *Psychogeography* (London: Oldcastle, 2010).

Cowburn, Ashley, '"We're a much better country": Brexit not the reason UK approved vaccine first, Williamson suggests', *Independent*, 3 December 2020, <https://www.independent.co.uk/news/uk/politics/gavin-williamson-brexit-us-france-belgium-covid-vaccine-b1765562.html> (last accessed 8 February 2021).

Crane, Ralph J., *Inventing India: A History of India in English Language Fiction* (London: Palgrave Macmillan, 1992).

Crane, Ralph J., *Ruth Prawer Jhabvala* (New York: Twayne Publishers, 1992).

Crane, Ralph J. and Jennifer Livett, *Troubled Pleasures: The Fiction of J. G. Farrell* (Dublin: Four Courts Press, 1997).

Crerar, Pippa, 'Sick Man of Europe', *The Daily Mirror*, 21 December 2020.

Cresswell, Tim, *Place: A Short Introduction*, 2nd edn (London: Blackwell, 2014).

Cronin, Richard, *Imagining India* (Basingstoke: Macmillan, 1989).

Cundy, Catherine, *Salman Rushdie* (Manchester: Manchester University Press, 1996).

Danticat, Edwidge, *The Art of Death: Writing the Final Story* (Minneapolis: Graywolf Press, 2017).

Davis, Lennard, *Resisting Novels: Ideology and Fiction* (New York: Methuen, 1987).

de Courcy, Ann, *The Fishing Fleet: Husband-Hunting in the Raj* (London: Weidenfeld & Nicolson, 2012).

Dean, Malcolm, 'An Insight Job', *The Guardian*, 1 September 1973, 12.

Dix, Hywel, *Postmodern Fiction and the Break-Up of Britain* (London: Continuum, 2010).

Dovey, Kim, *Framing Places: Mediating Power in Built Form*, 2nd edn (London: Routledge, 1999).

Duke, Joshua, *Queries at a Mess Table: What Shall I Eat? What Shall I Drink?*, 2nd edn (Calcutta and Simla: Thacker, Spink & Co., 1908).

Eaglestone, Robert and Martin McQuillan (eds), *Salman Rushdie: Contemporary Critical Perspectives* (London: Bloomsbury, 2013).

Edwards, Justin D., *Postcolonial Literature: A Reader's Guide to Essential Criticism* (London: Palgrave, 2008).

Farrell, J. G., *The Hill Station* (London: Orion, 1993).

Farrell, J. G., *Troubles* (London: Phoenix, 2001).

Farrell, J. G., *The Siege of Krishnapur* (London: Phoenix, 2007).

Farrell, J. G., *The Singapore Grip* (London: Weidenfeld & Nicholson, 2010).

Fhlathúin, Máire ni, *British India and Victorian Literary Culture* (Edinburgh: Edinburgh University Press, 2015).

Fifield, Peter, *Modernism and Physical Illness: Sick Books* (Oxford: Oxford University Press, 2020).

Fischer-Tiné, Harald, 'The drinking habits of our countrymen: European Alcohol Consumption and Colonial Power in British India', *Journal of Imperial and Commonwealth History*, 40:3 (2012), 383–408.

Fischer-Tiné, Harald and Jana Tschurenev (eds), *A History of Alcohol and Drugs in Modern South Asia: Intoxicating Affairs* (London: Routledge, 2014).

Fleming, N. C., 'Echoes of Britannia: Television History, Empire and the Critical Public Sphere', *Contemporary British History*, 24:1 (2010), 1–22.

Forrest, G. W., *A History of the Indian Mutiny – Reviewed and Illustrated from Original Documents, Vol. I* (London: William Blackwood & Sons, 1904).

Forty, Adrian and Susanne Küchler, *The Art of Forgetting* (London: Berg, 2001).

Foucault, Michel, *The Birth of the Clinic: An Archaeology of Medical Perception* (London: Routledge Classics, 2003).

Fowler, Corinne, *Green Unpleasant Land: Creative Responses to Rural England's Colonial Connections* (Leeds: Peepal Tree Press, 2020).

Francis, C. R., 'On the Best Means of Preserving Health in India: Alcohol' (Bristol: J. W. Arrowsmith, Printer, 1889).

Francis, Gavin, 'John Berger's A Fortunate Man: a masterpiece of witness', *The Guardian*, 7 February 2015, <https://www.theguardian.com/books/2015/feb/07/john-sassall-country-doctor-a-fortunate-man-john-berger-jean-mohr> (last accessed 15 September 2020).

Frank, Arthur W., *The Wounded Storyteller: Body, Illness, Ethics*, 2nd edn (Chicago: University of Chicago Press, 2013).

Fraser, G. M., *Flashman in the Great Game* (London: William Collins, 1981).

Garagazof, Rauf, *Collective Memory: How Collective Representations About the Past Are Created, Preserved and Reproduced* (New York: Nova, 2015).

Gilbert, Pamela K., *Cholera and Nation: Doctoring the Social Body in Victorian England* (New York: State University of New York Press, 2008).

Gill, A. A., 'Brexit: A. A. Gill argues the case for In', *The Times*, 12 June 2016 <https://www.thetimes.co.uk/article/aa-gill-argues-the-case-against-brexit-kmnp83zrt> (last accessed 1 May 2018).

Gilmore, Thomas B., *Equivocal Spirits: Alcoholism and Drinking in Twentieth-Century Literature* (London: Chapel Hill, 1987).

Gilmour, David, *The Ruling Caste: Imperial Lives in the Victorian Raj* (London: John Murray, 2005).

Gilroy, Paul, *After Empire: Melancholia or Convivial Culture* (London: Routledge, 2004).

Goodman, Sam, 'A Great Beneficial Disease: Colonial Medicine and Imperial Authority in J. G. Farrell's *The Siege of Krishnapur*', *Journal of Medical Humanities*, 36 (2015), 141–56.

Goodman, Sam, 'Lady Amateurs and Gentleman Professionals: Emergency Nursing in the Indian Rebellion of 1857', in Helen Sweet and Sue Hawkins (eds), *Colonial Caring: A History of Colonial and Post-Colonial Nursing* (Manchester: Manchester University Press, 2015), 18–40.

Goodman, Sam, *British Spy Fiction and the End of Empire* (London: Routledge, 2016).

Goodman, Sam, 'Literature and Disease: A Novel Contagion', in Mark Jackson (ed.), *The Routledge History of Disease* (London: Routledge, 2016), 547–65.

Goodman, Sam, 'Everything Must Go: Prize Culture, Popularity and the Postcolonial Novel', in Nadia Atia and Kate Houlden (eds), *Popular Postcolonialisms: Discourses of Empire and Popular Culture* (London: Routledge, 2018), 170–92.

Goodman, Sam, 'Spaces of Intemperance and the British Raj 1860–1920', *Journal of Imperial and Commonwealth History*, 48:4 (2020), 591–618.

Goonetilleke, D. C. R. A., 'J. G. Farrell's Indian Works: His Majesty's Subjects?', *Modern Asian Studies*, 37:2 (May 2003), 407–27.

Goonetilleke, D. C. R. A., *Salman Rushdie*, 2nd edn (London: Palgrave Macmillan, 2010).

Gopal, Priyamvada, *Insurgent Empire: Anticolonial Resistance and British Dissent* (London: Verso, 2019).

Gourlay, Jhana, *Florence Nightingale and the Health of the Raj* (Aldershot: Ashgate, 2003).

Gov.uk, 'Apply for a UK Global Health Insurance Card', <https://www.gov.uk/global-health-insurance-card> (last accessed 12 February 2021).

Greacen, Lavinia, *J. G. Farrell: The Making of a Writer* (London: Bloomsbury, 2000).

Greenwood, Anna and Harshad Topiwala, *Indian Doctors in Kenya: The Forgotten Story, 1895–1940* (London: Palgrave Macmillan, 2015).

Gurnah, Abdulrazak (ed.), *Cambridge Companion to Salman Rushdie* (Cambridge: Cambridge University Press, 2007).

Hall, Macer, 'Soft Brexit will be biggest "national humiliation since Suez Crisis" warns Mogg', *Daily Express*, 25 March 2018, <https://www.express.co.uk/news/politics/936844/brexit-news-eu-exit-uk-jacob-rees-mogg-speech> (last accessed 30 September 2020).

Hames, Gina, *Alcohol in World History* (London: Routledge, 2012).

Hamlin, Christopher, *Cholera: The Biography* (Oxford: Oxford University Press, 2009).

Hanne, Michael and S. J. Hawken, 'Metaphors for illness in contemporary media', *BMJ Medical Humanities*, 33 (2007): 93–9.

Hardy, Anne, *Health and Medicine in Britain Since 1860* (Basingstoke: Palgrave Macmillan, 2001).

Harrison, Mark, *Public Health in British India: Anglo-Indian Preventive Medicine 1859–1914* (Cambridge: Cambridge University Press, 1994).

Harrison, Mark, *Climates and Constitutions: Health, Race, Environment and British Imperialism in India 1600–1850* (Oxford: Oxford University Press, 2002).

Hartveit, Lars, 'The Imprint of Recorded Events in the Narrative Form of J. G. Farrell's *The Siege of Krishnapur*', *English Studies*, 75:4 (1993), 451–69.

Healy, Margaret, 'Bodies politic: somatic politics and "meaning making" in medicine and literature', *BMJ Medical Humanities, Journal of Medical Ethics*, 37:1 (June 2011), 13–17.

Heffernan, Teresa, *Post-apocalyptic Culture: Modernism, Postmodernism, and the Twentieth-century Novel* (Toronto: University of Toronto Press, 2008).

Herring, Jonathan, Ciaran Regan, Darin Weinberg and Phil Withington (eds), *Intoxication and Society: Problematic Pleasures of Drugs and Alcohol* (London: Palgrave Macmillan, 2013).

Hervey, H., *The European in India* (London: Stanley Paul & Co, 1913).

Hobbs, Harry, *Indian Dust Devils* (Calcutta: privately printed, 1937).

Hobbs, Harry, *Scraps from My Diaries* (Calcutta: privately printed, 1954).

Howell, Jessica, *Malaria and Victorian Fictions of Empire* (Cambridge: Cambridge University Press, 2019).

Huggan, Graham, *The Postcolonial Exotic: Marketing the Margins* (London: Routledge, 2001).

Hull, Edmund C. P., *The European in India: or Anglo-Indian's Vade-Mecum, with Medical Guide for Anglo-Indians* (London: Henry S. King & Co., 1874).

Hunsaker-Hawkins, Ann, *Reconstructing Illness: Studies in Pathography* (West Lafayette, IN: Purdue University Press, 1999).

Hutcheon, Linda, *The Politics of Postmodernism*, 2nd edn (London: Routledge, 2002).

Hutcheon, Linda, *A Theory of Adaptation* (London: Routledge, 2006).

IMDb, The Far Pavilions (1978), <https://www.imdb.com/title/tt0086711/> (last accessed 3 July 2018).

Ivison, Douglas, 'Travel Writing and the End of Empire; A Pom Named Bruce and the Mad White Giant', *English Studies In Canada*, 29 (December 2003), 3–4.

James, Lawrence, *Raj: The Making and Unmaking of British India* (London: Abacus, 1998).

James, Lawrence, *The Rise and Fall of the British Empire* (London: Abacus, 2001).

Jamison, Leslie, 'Grand Unified Theory of Female Pain', *Virginia Quarterly Review*, 90:2 (Spring 2014), n.p.

Jhabvala, Ruth Prawer, *The Householder* (London: Penguin, 1980).

Jhabvala, Ruth Prawer, *A Stronger Climate* (London: Grafton, 1983).

Jhabvala, Ruth Prawer, *Heat and Dust* (London: John Murray, 2003).

Jhabvala, Ruth Prawer, *A Backwards Place* (London: John Murray, 2005).

Johnson, Alan, 'Ghosts of Irish Famine in J. G. Farrell's *The Siege of Krishnapur*', *Journal of Commonwealth Literature*, 46:2 (2011), 275–92.

Jurecic, Ann, *Illness as Narrative* (Pittsburgh: University of Pittsburgh Press, 2012).

Kenny, Alexander and Shelley Leigh Hunt, *On Duty Under a Tropical Sun* (London: W. H. Allen, 1882).

Kenny, Alexander and Shelley Leigh Hunt, *Tropical Trials: A Handbook for Women in the Tropics* (London: W. H. Allen, 1883).

Kincaid, Dennis, *British Social Life in India 1608–1937* (London: Routledge & Kegan Paul, 1938).

King, Anthony D., *The Bungalow: The Production of a Global Culture* (New York: Oxford University Press, 1995).

Kipling, Rudyard, 'The White Man's Burden', in *Selected Poems* (London: Penguin Classics, 2000), 82–3.

Kipling, Rudyard, *Plain Tales from the Hills* (Oxford: Oxford University Press, 2009).

Klaver, Claudia, 'Domesticity under Siege: British women and Imperial Crisis at the Siege of Lucknow, 1857', *Women's Writing*, 8:1 (2001), 21–58.

Klein, Ira, 'Cholera: Theory and Treatment in Nineteenth-Century India', *Journal of Indian History*, 58 (1980), 35–51.

Koegler, Christine, Pavan Kumar Malreddy and Marlena Tronicke (eds), *Journal of Postcolonial Writing*, 56:5 (2020), Special Issue: 'Writing Brexit: Colonial Remains'.

Kortenaar, Neil Ten, *Self, Nation, Text in Salman Rushdie's Midnight's Children* (Quebec: McGill Queen's University Press, 2004).

L'Estoile, Benoît, 'The Past as It Lives Now: An Anthropology of Colonial Legacies', *Social Anthropology*, 16:3 (2008), 267–79.

Levine, Philippa, *Prostitution, Race and Politics: Policing Venereal Disease in the British Empire* (London: Routledge, 2003).

Levine, Philippa (ed.), *Gender and Empire* (Oxford: Oxford University Press, 2004).

Lycett, Andrew, *Ian Fleming: The Man Who Created James Bond* (London: Phoenix, 1995).

Mackenzie, John M. (ed.), *Propaganda and Empire: The Manipulation of British Public Opinion 1880–1960* (Manchester University Press, 1984).

Magubane, Zine, *Bringing the Empire Home: Race, Class and Gender in Britain and Colonial South Africa* (Chicago: University of Chicago Press, 2004).

Mahone, Sloan and Meghan Vaughan (eds), *Psychiatry and Empire* (Basingstoke: Palgrave Macmillan, 2007).

Mantel, Hilary, *Ink in the Blood: A Hospital Diary* (London: Fourth Estate, 2010).

Martin, A. Lynn, 'Drinking: An Apprentice's Diary, 1663–74', in Mack P. Holt (ed.), *Alcohol: A Social and Cultural History* (King's Lynn: Berg, 2006), 93–107.

Martin, N. A., 'The Madness at Deolali', *BMJ Military Health*, 152 (2006), 94–5.

Masters, John, *To the Coral Strand* (London: Four Square, 1965).

Masters, John, *Bhowani Junction* (London: Penguin, 1971).

Masters, John, *The Nightrunners of Bengal* (London: Sphere Publishing, 1985).

Mathieson, Charlotte (ed.), *Sea Narratives: Cultural Responses to the Sea, 1600–Present* (London: Palgrave Macmillan, 2016).

Maude, Ulrika, *Samuel Beckett and Medicine* (Cambridge: Cambridge University Press, 2020).

McDonald Centre, 'Ethics and Empire', <https://www.mcdonaldcentre.org.uk/ethics-and-empire> (last accessed 19 March 2021).

McGonagle, Pauline, 'A Transnational History of a Writer in Four Packages From Ruth Prawer Jhabvala's literary archive', *Wasafiri*, 34:3 (21 August 2019), 28–33.

McLeod, John, *J. G. Farrell* (Horndon: Northcote House Publishers, 2007).

Menkel, H. C., *Healthful Diet for India* (Lahore: Civil and Military Gazette Press, 1927).

Meyers, Jeffrey, *Disease and the Novel 1880–1960* (Hong Kong: Macmillan, 1985).

Middlebrow: An Interdisciplinary Transatlantic Research Network, <https://www.middlebrow-network.com> (last accessed 21 March 2021).

Mills, James, 'The History of Modern Psychiatry in India, 1858–1947', *Journal of the History of Psychiatry*, 12:48 (2001), 431–58.

Mills, Sarah, 'Gender and Colonial Space', *Gender, Place and Culture*, 3:2 (1996), 125–48.

Mishra, Vijay, *Annotating Salman Rushdie: Reading the Postcolonial* (London: Routledge, 2018).

Moore-Gilbert, Bart, *Cultural Closure: The Arts in the 70s* (London: Routledge, 1994).

Moore-Gilbert, Bart, *Writing India 1757–1990: The Literature of British India* (Manchester: Manchester University Press, 1996).

Moretti, Franco, *Atlas of the European Novel 1800–1900* (London: Verso, 1998).

Morey, Peter, *Fictions of India: Narrative and Power* (Edinburgh: Edinburgh University Press, 2000).

Morris, David B. and Simon van Rysewyk (eds), *Meanings of Pain* (Cham: Springer International, 2016).

Moulds, Alison, 'The "Medical-Women Question" and the Multivocality of the Victorian Medical Press, 1869–1900', in *Journal of Media History*, 25:1 (2019), Special Issue: 'Reading the Nineteenth Century Medical Journal', 6–22.

Nairn, Tom, *The Break-up of Britain: Crisis and Neo-nationalism, 1965–75* (London: NRB, 1979).

Noor, Poppy, 'Beecham House is a "flipping radical thing"', *The Guardian*, 18 June 2019, <https://www.theguardian.com/film/2019/jun/18/gurinder-chadha-beecham-house-is-a-flipping-radical-thing> (last accessed 8 October 2019).

Nora, Pierre, *Realms of Memory: Rethinking the French Past, vol 1 – Conflicts and Divisions* (New York: Columbia University Press, 1996).

Novillo-Corvalán, Patricia, 'Reinterpreting the wound of Philoctetes: Literature and Medicine', in Victoria Bates, Alan Bleakley and Sam Goodman (eds), *Medicine, Health and the Arts: Approaches to the Medical Humanities* (London: Routledge, 2014), 128–45.

Open University, 'Beyond the Frame: Indian British Connections' (2007–12), <https://www.open.ac.uk/arts/research/asianbritain/> (last accessed 19 March 2021).

O'Toole, Fintan, *Heroic Failure: Brexit and the Politics of Pain* (London: Apollo, 2018).

Pandya, Sunil, *Medical Education in Western India: Grant Medical College and Sir Jamsetjee Jejeebhoy's Hospital* (Newcastle-upon-Tyne: Cambridge Scholars Press, 2019).

Paris, Alderson, Babington, Tweedie and Bagshaw-Ward, 'On the Treatment of the Epidemic of Cholera' (London: Royal College of Surgeons, 1855).

Pati, Biswamoy and Mark Harrison, *The Social History of Health and Medicine in Colonial India* (Oxford: Routledge, 2009).

Phillips, Roderick, *Alcohol: A History* (Chapel Hill: University of North Carolina Press, 2014).

Piette, Adam, *The Literary Cold War: 1945–Vietnam* (Edinburgh: Edinburgh University Press, 2009).

Plock, Vike Martina, *Joyce, Medicine and Modernity* (Miami: University of Florida Press, 2010).

Porter, Bernard, *The Absent-Minded Imperialists: Empire, Society, and Culture in Britain* (Oxford: Oxford University Press, 2004).

Porter, Roy, 'Drinking Man's Disease: the "Pre-History" of Alcoholism in Georgian Britain', *British Journal of Addiction*, 80 (1985), 385–96.

Potts, M., M. Graff and J. Taing, 'Thousand-year-old depictions of massage abortion', *BMJ Sexual and Reproductive Health*, 33 (2007), 233–4.

Pratt, Mary Louise, *Imperial Eyes: Travel Writing and Transculturation* (London: Routledge, 1992).

Rachel, Daniel, *Don't Look Back in Anger: The Rise and Fall of Cool Britannia, Told by Those who Were There* (London: Orion, 2019).

Raghuram, Parvati, 'Thinking UK's medical labour market transnationally', in John Connell (ed.), *The International Migration of Health Workers* (London: Routledge, 2008), 182–98.

Rajan, V. G. Julie: 'Indian Writing in the West: Imperialism, Exoticism and Visibility', in Om Prakesh Dwivedi and Lisa Lau (eds), *Indian Writing in English and the Global Literary Market* (London: Palgrave, 2014), 81–98.

Ramaswarmy, Chita, 'A Suitable Boy review – a very British, Indian period drama', *The Guardian*, 26 July 2020, <https://www.theguardian.com/tv-and-radio/2020/jul/26/a-suitable-boy-review-a-very-british-indian-period-drama> (last accessed 14 September 2020).

Rasch, Astrid, '"Keep the balance": The Politics of Remembering Empire in Post-Colonial Britain', *Journal of Commonwealth and Postcolonial Studies*, 7:2 (2019), 212–30.

Rediker, Marcus, *Outlaws of the Atlantic: Sailors, Pirates, and Motley Crews in the Age of Sail* (London: Verso, 2014).

Reed, James, 'A medical perspective on the adventures of Sherlock Holmes', *BMJ Medical Humanities*, 27:2 (2001), 76–81.

Roberts, Emma, *The East India Voyager, or Ten Minutes' Advice* (London: J. Madden, 1839).

Robinson, Jane, *Angels of Albion: Women of the Indian Mutiny* (London: Viking, 1996).

Rosaldo, Renato, 'Imperialist Nostalgia', in *Representations*, 26 (Spring 1989), Special Issue: 'Memory and Counter-Memory', 107–22.

Rose, Arthur, Stefanie Heine, Naya Tsentourou, Corinne Saunders and Peter Garratt, *Reading Breath in Literature* (London: Palgrave Macmillan, 2018).

Rushdie, Salman, *Midnight's Children* (London: Picador, 1982).

Rushdie, Salman, *Shame* (London: Jonathan Cape, 1983).

Rushdie, Salman, 'Outside the Whale', *Granta*, 1 March 1984, <https://granta.com/outside-the-whale/> (last accessed 16 September 2020).

Rushdie, Salman, *Imaginary Homelands: Essays and Criticism 1981–1991* (London: Vintage, 2010).

Russell, William Howard, *The Indian Mutiny: A Diary of the Sepoy Rebellion* (London: George Routledge and Sons, 1860).

Sakr, Rita, *Monumental Space in the Post-Imperial Novel: An Interdisciplinary Study* (London: Bloomsbury, 2012).

Samuel, Raphael, *Theatres of Memory: Past and Present in Contemporary Culture* (London: Verso, 1994).

Sar, Vedat and Erdinc Ozturk, 'What Is Trauma and Dissociation?, *Journal of Trauma Practice*, 4:1–2 (2006), 7–20.

Saunders, Robert, 'Brexit and Empire: "Global Britain" and the Myth of Imperial Nostalgia', *Journal of Imperial and Commonwealth History*, 48:6 (2020), 1140–74.

Scarry, Elaine, *The Body in Pain: The Making and Unmaking of the World* (Oxford: Oxford University Press, 1985).

Schivelbusch, Wolfgang, *The Railway Journey: The Industrialization of Time and Space in the Nineteenth Century* (Berkeley: University of California Press, 1986).

Scott, Paul, *The Day of the Scorpion* (London: Granada, 1973).

Scott, Paul, *The Jewel in the Crown* (London: Granada, 1973).

Scott, Paul, *The Towers of Silence* (London: Granada, 1973).

Scott, Paul, *A Division of the Spoils* (London: Granada, 1977).

Scott, Paul, *Staying On* (London: Granada, 1978).

Servitje, Lorenzo, *Medicine is War: The Martial Metaphor in Victorian Literature and Culture* (New York: SUNY Press, 2021).

Sharma, H. K., B. M. Tripathi and P. J. Pelto, 'The Evolution of Alcohol Use in India', *AIDS and Behaviour*, 14, supplement 1 (August 2010), 8–17.

Shaw, Katy, *Hauntology: The Presence of the Past in Twenty-First-Century English Literature* (London: Palgrave, 2018).

Simpson, Julian, *Migrant Architects of the NHS: South Asian Doctors and the Reinvention of General Practice 1940s–1980s* (Manchester: Manchester University Press, 2018).

Singh, Francis B., 'Progress and History in J. G. Farrell's *The Siege of Krishnapur*', *Chandrabhaga*, 2 (1979), 23–9.

Smith, Matthew, 'How Unique Are British Attitudes to Empire?', 11 March 2020, <https://yougov.co.uk/topics/international/articles-reports/2020/03/11/how-unique-are-british-attitudes-empire?utm_source=twitter&utm_medium=website_article&utm_campaign=British_Empire_attitudes> (last accessed 11 September 2020).

Smith, Sidonie and Julia Watson, *Reading Autobiography: A Guide For Interpreting Life Narratives* (Minneapolis: University of Minnesota Press, 2010).

Sontag, Susan, *Illness as Metaphor and AIDS and its Metaphors* (London: Penguin, 1991).

Spurling, Hilary, *Paul Scott: A Life* (London: Pimlico, 1991).

Stacey, Jackie, *Teratologies: A Cultural Study of Cancer* (London: Routledge, 1997).

Steadman-Jones, Richard, 'Colonial Fiction for Liberal Readers: John Masters and The Savage Family Saga', in Rachael Gilmour and Bill Schwarz (eds), *End of Empire and the English Novel since 1945* (Manchester: Manchester University Press, 2011).

Stephen, Daniel, *The Empire of Progress: West Africans, Indians, and Britons at the British Empire Exhibition 1924–25* (London: Palgrave Macmillan, 2013).

Stone, John, 'There won't be another national lockdown, Cabinet minister Gavin Williamson says', *Independent*, 31 December 2020, <https://www.independent.co.uk/news/uk/politics/lockdown-uk-coronavirus-schools-gavin-williamson-b1780727.html> (last accessed 19 February 2021).

Strongman, Luke, *The Booker Prize and the Legacy of Empire* (Amsterdam: Rodopi, 2002).

Surawicz, Borys and Beverly Jacobson, *Doctors in Fiction: Lessons from Literature* (Oxford: Radcliffe Publishing, 2009).

Sweet, Helen and Sue Hawkins (eds), *Colonial Caring: A History of Colonial and Post-Colonial Nursing* (Manchester: Manchester University Press, 2015).

Swenson, Kristine, *Medical Women and Victorian Fiction* (Columbia: University of Missouri Press, 2005).

Teverson, Andrew, *Contemporary World Writers: Salman Rushdie* (Manchester: Manchester University Press, 2007).

The National Trust, Colonial Countryside Project, <https://www.nation-altrust.org.uk/features/colonial-countryside-project> (last accessed 19 February 2021).

Thompson, Andrew (ed.), *Britain's Experience of Empire in the Twentieth Century* (Oxford: Oxford University Press, 2012).

Turner, Alwyn W., *Crisis? What Crisis? Britain in the 1970s* (London: Aurum Press, 2009).

Upstone, Sara, *Spatial Politics in the Postcolonial Novel* (London: Ashgate, 2009).

Valverde, Mariana, *Diseases of the Will: Alcohol and the Dilemmas of Freedom* (Cambridge: Cambridge University Press, 1998).

Van Der Kolk, Bessel, *The Body Keeps the Score: Brain, Mind, and Body in the Healing of Trauma* (London: Penguin, 2015).

Verma, Rahul, 'Colonial Countryside: Facing up to Britain's murky past', *BBC*, 28 July 2020, <https://www.bbc.com/culture/article/20200724-colonial-countryside-facing-up-to-britains-murky-past> (last accessed 11 September 2020).

Vlitos, Paul, *Eating and Identity in Postcolonial Fiction: Consuming Passions, Unpalatable Truths* (London: Palgrave, 2018).

Wald, Erica, *Vice in the Barracks: Medicine, the Military and the Making of Colonial India, 1780–1868* (London: Palgrave Macmillan, 2014).

Walton, Samantha, *Guilty But Insane: Mind and Law in Golden Age Detective Fiction* (Oxford: Oxford University Press, 2015).

Wasson, Sara, 'Before narrative: episodic reading and representations of chronic pain', *BMJ Medical Humanities*, 44 (2018), 106–12.

Waugh, Patricia, *Harvest of the Sixties: English Literature and Its Background, 1960–90* (Oxford: OPUS, 1995).

Whitehead, Anne and Angela Woods (eds), *The Edinburgh Companion to the Critical Medical Humanities* (Edinburgh: Edinburgh University Press, 2016).

Woods, Angela, 'The limits of narrative: provocations for the medical humanities', *BMJ Medical Humanities*, 37 (2011), 73–8.

Woolf, Virginia, *Mrs Dalloway* (London: Penguin, [1925] 1994).

Woolf, Virginia, *On Being Ill* (Ashfield, MA: Paris Press, [1926] 2012).

World Health Organisation, 'WHO Coronavirus Disease (COVID-19) Dashboard', <https://covid19.who.int/table> (last accessed 19 February 2021).

YouGov, <https://yougov.co.uk/news/2014/07/26/britain-proud-its-empire/>; <https://d25d2506sfb94s.cloudfront.net/cumulus_uploads/document/95euxfgway/InternalResults_160118_BritishEmpire_Website.pdf> (last accessed 11 September 2020).

Younge, Gary, 'Ambalavaner Sivanandan obituary', *The Guardian*, 7 February 2018, <https://www.theguardian.com/world/2018/feb/07/ambala-vaner-sivanandan> (last accessed 17 May 2019).

Ziegler, Rebecca, *J. G. Farrell's Empire Novels: The Decline and Fall of the Human Condition* (Dublin: Four Courts Press, 2018).

Archival sources

British Library, India Office Archive

Amies, Basil, Indian Army 1915–47, Mss Eur E418: 1914–1947.

Barnes, Mrs M. O., wife of Maj. Humphrey Aston Barnes (1900–40), IPS 1927, Political Agent, Zhob 1939–40, Mss Eur F226/1: 1929–1940.

Bowman, Archibald Ian, Mss Eur F180/73.

Collection 233/2 Beer supply, Madras and lower Burma: questionable economy of accepting tender of Nilgiri and Muree Brewery Co. IOR/L/MIL/7/9936: 1884–1886.

'Compulsory retirement of G. A. Weston', Superintendent of Police, Punjab: L/PJ/6/3571/19, 1919.

Downing, Henry Julian, Mss Eur F180/50.

Dunlop, Sidney William Cecil, Mss Eur F180/51.

Faruqui, Nasir Ahmad, Mss Eur F180/27.

Hall, Margery, 'And the Nights Were More Terrible Than the Days', Memoir of Margery Hall, Mss Eur F226/11 (1938–47).

Le Bailly, William Francis Grahame, Mss Eur F180/65.

Orr, John Ward, Mss Eur F180/22.

Paterson, Noel Kennedy, Mss Eur F180/46.

Rahmatullah, Shahabuddin, 'Unpublished Memoir', Mss Eur F180/14.

Redpath, Alexander William, 'Recollections of a Political Officer in India', Mss Eur F226/24: 1929–1947 (1982).

Symons, Ronald Stuart, Memoir, Mss Eur F180/82.

Thompson, Sir (Joseph) Herbert (1898–1984), Indian Civil Service, Madras 1923–26, IPS 26, Resident, Punjab States 1945–47, 'Icarus went East': memoirs of his career in the Royal Naval Air Service, Mss Eur F226/29: 1916–1947.

J. G. Farrell, personal papers and manuscripts, Trinity College Library, Dublin

Box 9139: *The Siege of Krishnapur*, agent's copy (edited).

Box 9141: *The Siege of Krishnapur*, 'Early fragments'.

Box 9142: Index cards, notes and photocopies of materials.

Box 9152: Manuscript (typed) of *The Hill Station*.

Box 9153: *The Hill Station*, 'Notes and Index Cards'.

Box 9155: 'Unpublished diary' (1965).

Box 9159–60: 'Miscellaneous papers'.

Salman Rushdie papers, Stuart A. Rose Manuscript, Archives, and Rare Book Library (MARBL), Emory University

Series 2, Nonfiction, 'The Haunted House: An essay on the relationship of Britain and India', typescript [fragment], 49/8.

Series 2, Nonfiction, 'The New Empire: Notes written for Channel 4 programme "Opinions"', typescript [fragment], 49/45.

Subseries 2.1, Fiction, *Midnight's Children*, MSS/1000 Box 15/10, *Midnight's Children*, 'First Draught' [*sic*].

Subseries 2.1, Fiction, MSS/1000 Box 17/8, 'Midnight's Children Notes'.

Subseries 2.1, Fiction, 20/6: *Shame*, 'Notes, Manuscript and Typescript'.

Index

narrative structure, 194
in 1970s Britain, 3–4, 123, 190, 205
post-imperial nostalgia, 4, 6, 7, 10, 190, 191–2
role of the Booker Prize, 9–11
television and cinema productions, 2–3, 4–7
term, 2, 4
see also Anglo-Indian fiction
Redpath, Alexander, 75–6
Rushdie, Salman
within Anglo-Indian fiction, 17–18
as a Booker Prize winner, 10
on British nostalgia, 190
criticism of Paul Scott, 158
Grimus, 12
Indian identity, 11–12, 17, 118
'The New Empire', 204
notion of the journey, 117–18
within postcolonial studies, 11–12
The Satanic Verses, 11
Shame, 11, 12
spatiality in the works of, 115–16
temporal legacies of Empire, 20
term 'Raj Revival', 2, 4
thematic treatments of Ayurvedic medicine, 22
themes of illness, health and medicine, 22, 23–4, 206–7
see also *Midnight's Children* (Rushdie)

Samuel, Raphael, 190
Sassall, John, 38, 83
Saunders, Robert, 209
Scarry, Elaine, 60
Schama, Simon, 4
Scott, Paul
alcoholism, 146–7, 192
as a Booker Prize winner, 10
boundaries between physical and mental health, 61, 62
career and life of, 15–16, 17
colonial prejudice in the works of, 128–9
embodiment in the novels of, 47, 57
examination of the British in India, 16
examination of the imperial body, 47–8

gendered divisions in medical practice, 92–3
health of the British body, 119
hill stations in the works of, 121–2
historical record and literary narrative in, 36
lack of scholarly focus on, 15
memorialisation tropes, 192
military service in India, 15, 118, 147
notion of the journey, 117–18
political and metaphorical significance of bodies, 47, 48
poor health, 39, 51, 52, 53, 192
as a postmodernist author, 102
Rushdie's criticism of, 158
spatiality in the works of, 115–16
temporal legacies of Empire, 20
themes of illness, health and medicine, 22, 24, 206–7
see also *Raj Quartet, The* (Scott); *Staying On* (Scott)
Shaw, Katy, 191
Siege of Krishnapur, The (Farrell)
adventure narrative as critique, 40–1
as both postmodernist and postcolonial, 41–2, 46
British and Indian characters, 41, 60
causes of contemporary British decline, 42
doctors in, 45–6, 78, 79–81
within the 'Empire Trilogy', 12, 13
historical record and literary narrative in, 36, 42, 45–6
Indian Rebellion setting, 36, 41, 42
links between individual and social health, 79–81
medical source texts, 42–3, 44, 45–6, 79
medicine and the British presence in India, 43–4, 45
medicine as satire of British colonialism, 46–7
phrenology, 79–80
representation of cholera, 44–7, 79–80
Simla hill station, 120–2
Sivanandan, Ambalavaner, 20–1, 28 n.26

EU representative:
Easy Access System Europe
Mustamäe tee 50, 10621 Tallinn, Estonia
Gpsr.requests@easproject.com

www.ingramcontent.com/pod-product-compliance
Lightning Source LLC
Chambersburg PA
CBHW050127030726
47505CB00007B/2065